Confucianism Reconsidered

A volume in the SUNY series in Asian Studies Development

Roger T. Ames and Peter D. Hershock, editors

Confucianism Reconsidered

Insights for American and Chinese Education in the Twenty-first Century

Edited by

XIUFENG LIU AND WEN MA

Cover calligraphy / "scholar" or "Confucianism" / iStock by Getty Images

Published by State University of New York Press, Albany

© 2018 State University of New York

All rights reserved

No part of this book may be used or reproduced in any manner whatsoever without written permission. No part of this book may be stored in a retrieval system or transmitted in any form or by any means including electronic, electrostatic, magnetic tape, mechanical, photocopying, recording, or otherwise without the prior permission in writing of the publisher.

For information, contact State University of New York Press, Albany, NY
www.sunypress.edu

Library of Congress Cataloging-in-Publication Data

Names: Liu, Xiufeng, 1962– editor. | Ma, Wen, editor.
Title: Confucianism reconsidered : insights for American and Chinese education in the twenty-first century / edited by Xiufeng Liu and Wen Ma.
Description: Albany, NY : State University of New York Press, Albany, [2018] | Series: SUNY series in Asian Studies Development | Includes bibliographical references and index.
Identifiers: LCCN 2017032628 | ISBN 9781438470016 (hardcover) | ISBN 9781438470023 (pbk.) | ISBN 9781438470030 (ebook)
Subjects: LCSH: Education—Philosophy. | Education—Aims and objectives—United States. | Education—Aims and objectives—China. | Confucianism and education. | Philosophy, Confucian.
Classification: LCC LB14.7 .C65248 2018 | DDC 370.1—dc23
LC record available at https://lccn.loc.gov/2017032628

10 9 8 7 6 5 4 3 2 1

Contents

Foreword   ix
    Guofang Li

Acknowledgments   xiii

Introduction
Why Is Confucianism Still Relevant in the Globalized
Twenty-First Century?   1
    Xiufeng Liu and Wen Ma

Part 1
Relevance of Confucianism to American and Chinese Education

Chapter 1
Becoming Confucian in America Today   17
    Pamela G. Herron

Chapter 2
Teaching Deliberation: Abandoning Aristotelian Persuasion and
Embracing Confucian Remonstration   33
    Arabella Lyon

Chapter 3
Confucian Educational Thought: Enlightenment and Value
for Contemporary Education in China   47
    Fangping Cheng

Chapter 4
Confucian Rituals and Science in Modern Chinese Education   65
    Xiaoqing Diana Lin

Part 2
Confucian Insights on Teaching and Learning

CHAPTER 5
Neo-Confucianism as a Guide for Contemporary Confucian
Education   87
   Yair Lior

CHAPTER 6
Learning as Public Reasoning (*gongyi*): A Paradigmatic Shift
of the Late-Imperial Confucian Educational Tradition in
17th-Century China   111
   Yang Wei

CHAPTER 7
The Confucian Philosophy of Education in Hexagram Meng
(Shrouded) of the *Yijing*   131
   Bin Song

CHAPTER 8
Facilitating Critical Thinking of Chinese Students: A Confucian
Perspective   151
   Yin Wu

Part 3
Confucianism and the Social and Moral Functions of Education

CHAPTER 9
From Self-Cultivation to Social Transformation: The Confucian
Embodied Pathway and Educational Implications   169
   Jing Lin

CHAPTER 10
Confucian Selfhood and the Idea of Multicultural Education   183
   Chenyu Wang

CHAPTER 11
Confucian Philosophical Foundations for Moral Education
in an Era of Advanced Technology   203
   Vincent Shen

Chapter 12
Rethinking Confucian Values in a Global Age 221
  Huey-Li Li

List of Contributors 237

Index 239

Foreword

The American presidential election in 2016 has exposed the direst state of social division in the United States and around the world, particularly along racial, class, and gender lines. These climaxes of social divisiveness are not a one-time occurrence but are the culminating effects of a long-term failure of institutional, civic, and cultural building that cultivates social, economic, and political cohesion and justice-oriented mind-sets. The social division has had important impact on education. Look at the following statistics on the condition of American education in 2016:

- The immediate college enrollment rate for high school completers in 2014 for those from high-income families (81%) was nearly 29 percentage points higher than the rate for those from low-income families (52%). The 2014 gap between those from high- and low-income families did not measurably differ from the corresponding gap in 1990.

- In 2015, the percentage of young adults aged 18 to 19 neither enrolled in school nor working was higher for those from poor families (26%) than for their peers from nonpoor families (10%).

- In 2015, the percentage of White 25- to 29-year-olds who had attained a bachelor's or higher degree increased from 1995 to 2015, as the size of the White-Black gap widened from 13 to 22 percentage points and the size of the White-Hispanic gap widened from 20 to 27 percentage points.

- Differences in employment outcomes of all young adults aged 25 to 34 with a bachelor's or higher degree were observed by sex and race/ethnicity. For example, female full-time, year-round workers earned less than their male colleagues in nearly all of the occupation groups examined and for every employment sector (e.g., private for-profit, private nonprofit, government). Black young adults who worked full time, year round also earned less than their White peers in a majority of the occupations analyzed. (NECS, 2016)

Similarly, in China, there is a growing education gap between rural and city/urban schools, between the rich and the poor, and between the ethnic majority and minorities. More than 60 million students in rural schools are "left-behind" children, cared for by their grandparents as their parents seek work in faraway cities, and taught by underqualified teachers in underresourced schools (Gao, 2014). It is, therefore, not surprising that fewer than 5% of China's rural students make it to college while more than 84% of their peers in the major cities such as Shanghai go to university (Stout, 2013). A recent study reveals that from 2007 to 2013, almost half the students in poor areas (also ethnic minority–concentrated areas) in the central and western parts of the country in China had left school by grade nine, and by grade 12, nearly two-thirds dropped out (Sheng, 2016).

In addition to the persistent class gap in Chinese education, gender and ethnic inequality in educational attainment also persists, especially in rural areas. While nearly no significant gender inequality was found in urban/city areas, rural girls, especially when they reach high school, still face inequality in educational access and achievement (Zeng, Pang, Zhang, Medina, & Rozelle, 2014). There is also growing disparity in educational attainment between ethnic minorities and Han Chinese created by China's transformation to the market economy; and the gap has extended from that in basic education before 2000 to that in higher education after 2000 (Chen, 2016).

While the two countries differ in their policies and contexts, similar core social values, such as those of profit-driven competition and self-interest (over public good) that govern these policies and processes, are believed to lead to these parallel educational inequalities. In the United States, an example of such workings is the recent confirmation of Elizabeth DeVos, a billionaire philanthropist who does not believe in public education, as secretary of Education in February 2017. In China, the recent "growth at all cost" market-driven economic policies have engendered the sole focus on "money acquisition" and public "moral decay" (He,

2015) that has contributed to the high dropout rates among poor rural students and the inequalities described above. In both societies, such self-interest and profit-driven ideologies on the part of the rich, the powerful, and the dominant racial groups dominate our political, economic, and social discourse and have bred "a culture of extreme individualism and profit-seeking, which is undermining our social relationships and moral values" (Y. Kim & J. Kim, 2013, p. 13).

There is an urgent need for both societies to restore both public and individual morality, reverse the moral decline, and awaken ethical consciousness to achieve an equal, harmonious society where persistent achievement gaps across class, race, and gender lines can be eliminated. For both countries, reconstructing such a justice-oriented moral order means that each can leverage its own strengths and supplement with those powerful lessons and teachings from other cultures and societies. Confucianism, a system of social and ethical philosophy that promotes governing and living by the dao of "ren/仁" (humaneness, love, and kindness) and "li/礼" (respect) with the goal of achieving "da tong/大同" (the great equal society), is an ideal tool for both societies to achieve the urgently needed social restoration and transformation for the public good.

Xiufeng Liu and Wen Ma's volume on the application of Confucianism in K–12 and higher education in both U.S. and Chinese contexts is a timely response to this urgent need to reverse the trend. The thoughtful collection of high-quality, interdisciplinary, multimethod articles powerfully demonstrates that Confucianism is not only relevant to the 21st-century educational aspirations and demands globally, but also a compelling alternative to the current ideologies that fail to provide equal education for the disadvantaged. I urge readers to read on and learn about the various ways that Confucianism can be reconsidered in various educational contexts in both the West and the East and join the movement of restoration through your own scholarship, practice, and everyday life.

Guofang Li, Ph.D.
Professor and Tier 1 Canada Research Chair
University of British Columbia, Canada
April 4, 2017

References

Chen, Y. (2016). Ethnic inequality in education. In X. Zhang (Ed.), *Handbook of ethnic minorities in China* (pp. 316–340). Northampton, MA: Edward Elgar Publishing Limited.

He, H. (2015). *Social ethics in a changing China: Moral decay or ethical awakening?* Washington, DC: Brookings Institution.

Gao, H. (2014, Sept. 4). *China's education gap*. Retrieved from https://www.nytimes.com/2014/09/05/opinion/sunday/chinas-education-gap.html

Kim, Y., & Kim, J. (2013). *The great equal society: Confucianism, China and the 21st century*. Singapore: World Scientific Publishing Company.

NECS (2016). *The condition of education in 2016*. Washington, DC: U.S. Department of Education.

Sheng, M. (2016, March 24). China's rural youngsters drop out of school at alarming rate, researchers find. *Caixin Media*, Retrieved from http://reap.fsi.stanford.edu/news/caixin-media-chinas-rural-youngsters-drop-out-school-alarming-rate-researchers-find

Stout, K. L. (2013, December 17). *Mind the gap: China's great education divide*. Retrieved from http://www.cnn.com/2013/12/17/world/asia/china-education-gap-stout/

Zeng, J., Pang, X., Zhang, L., Medina, A., & Rozelle, S. (2014). Gender inequality in education in China: A meta-regression analysis. *Contemporary Economic Policy, 32*(2), 474–491.

Acknowledgments

There are many individuals to whom we are indebted as we complete this edited volume. First of all, we would like to thank the chapter authors who have shared their scholarly insights on the values and applications of Confucian ideas and practices in the American and Chinese classrooms. We are grateful to our editor, Christopher Ahn, for his guidance in the lengthy publication process; to the anonymous reviewers for their invaluable comments and suggestions; and to Guofang Li for writing an eloquent foreword. We sincerely thank the Confucius Institute at the University at Buffalo (UB), State University of New York, for sponsoring the *International Symposium on Confucianism and Education*, held on October 17–19, 2014; the seed for this volume germinated from that symposium. Finally, our special gratitude goes to Prof. Jiyuan Yu, who was the director of UB's Confucius Institute at the time of the symposium but passed away unexpectedly in late 2016. A renowned scholar of ancient Greek, classical Chinese philosophy, and comparative philosophy, Professor Yu's passion for Chinese classical philosophy was a driving force for the symposium and will continue to inspire scholarship on Confucianism and education both inside and outside China. We respectfully dedicate this volume to his memory.

Roger T. Ames and the late Henry Rosemont gave permission for Pamela Herron (chapter 1) to use the following quotes from the book titled "The analects of Confucius: A philosophical translation" (1998, New York: Ballantine Books): pages 71, 117, 128, 166–167, 189, 206, and 254; and Roger T. Ames and D. L. Hall gave permission to use following quotes in the book titled *"Dao de jing—"Making this life significant": A philosophical translation* (2003, New York: Ballantine Books): pages 77, 143, and 205.

PART (Practice and Research Together), a Canadian membership-based research utilization initiative, has given permission for Yin Wu to reproduce Figure 8.1 to be included in the chapter titled "Facilitating Critical Thinking of Chinese Students: A Confucian Perspective." Harvard Education Press gave permission for Huey-Li Li (chapter 12) to adapt some materials in her chapter as follows: Li, H. (1998). Some thoughts on Confucianism and ecofeminism. In J. Berthrong & M. E. Tucker (Eds.), *Confucianism and ecology: The interrelation of heaven, earth, and humans* (pp. 293–311). Cambridge: Harvard University Press.

Introduction

Why Is Confucianism Still Relevant in the Globalized Twenty-First Century?

XIUFENG LIU AND WEN MA

Since 2004, China's Hanban (Office of Chinese Language Council International) has established hundreds of Confucius Institutes at universities around the world to teach Chinese language and culture rooted in Confucianism. While attitudes toward these institutes have generally been positive, there are concerns that they are cultural tools of the Chinese government to spread political influence to foreign countries. Amid this milieu, students from Chinese and other Confucian-heritage cultures (Watkins & Biggs, 1996) experience extraordinary academic achievement (especially in STEM fields) across the educational spectrum, further perpetuating the so-called "model minority" discourse. Although the model minority myth has been increasingly debunked by researchers (e.g., Lee, 1996; Liu & Li, 2008; Ma & Li, 2016; Zhao & Qiu, 2009), there remains a common perception that Chinese students and families maintain a special set of Confucian values about education that positively contributes to their academic and career success. The "tiger mother" (Chua, 2011) publicity and the triple package claim, that is, the combination of superiority complex, insecurity, and impulse control (Chua & Rubenfeld, 2014), have piqued curiosity in the West about core Chinese cultural values, particularly educational beliefs. More recently, Confucius's impact has even been felt in U.S. judicial circles. For instance, the majority opinion written by Justice Anthony Kennedy for the landmark *Obergefell v. Hodges* case that makes same-sex marriage a right nationwide includes the statement "Confucius taught that marriage lies at the foundation of government."

Inarguably, Confucianism is widely viewed as the foundation of Chinese education. Many commonplace Chinese pedagogical viewpoints and practices—for example, *teaching in accordance with the student's aptitude*; *studying extensively, inquiring prudently, thinking carefully, distinguishing clearly, and practicing earnestly*; and *learning without thinking leads to confusion, thinking without learning ends in danger*—are rooted in classic Confucian texts such as the *Analects of Confucius* (论语) and the *Doctrine of the Mean* (中庸). As Lee (2000) puts it, Chinese educational tradition is "formulated and shaped almost entirely by Confucian ideology. The staying power and pervasiveness of the influence of Confucianism on Chinese education can scarcely be exaggerated" (p. 29).

However, Confucianism's pervasive influence on Chinese society has been controversial, particularly in its recent history. For instance, after the Chinese Communist Party took control of Mainland China in 1949, Confucianism was considered a feudal legacy and the cause of all troubles in China's past. Yet the situation has changed since China opened its door and deepened its economic reforms in the late 1970s; China has since emerged as the second-largest economy in the world. The so-called Chinese "economic miracle," combined with earlier economic success in such Asian countries and economies as Singapore, South Korea, Taiwan, and Hong Kong, as well as the growing exposure of socioeconomic problems in Western societies (e.g., corporate greed, shaky family structure, racial tension), has prompted scholars inside China to reevaluate the strengths and weaknesses of Confucianism. There is newfound confidence for Chinese officials and intellectuals, as well as ordinary citizens, to reembrace Confucianism as a core value of Chinese culture, education, and society.

Why are the ideas of Confucius, who lived more than 2,500 years ago, still relevant and important in the 21st century? According to Rainey (2010), we face many of the same problems Confucius faced, such as distrust in governments; great social, economic, and technological changes; a tendency to resort to military intervention; and moral decay in society, to name but a few. Confucianism may offer many solutions and insights to solving these problems both inside and outside China. Concerning education, in response to the unprecedented sociocultural changes brought by digital technologies and global trade, countries around the world are reforming their education systems not only by raising curriculum standards but also by exploring how to make upcoming generations globally competitive, socially responsible, and morally sound citizens. As educators, policy makers, and the public all search for new conceptual lenses and effective practices, the ancient wisdom of Confucianism could provide a unique perspective for solving current problems in education, too. Indeed, as a bold educational experiment, the BBC even invited a group of Chinese teachers to British schools for four weeks and made a documentary about their practices (Clark, 2015; The Open University, 2015). But what does Confucianism offer to Chinese teachers and, through them, to the rest of the world?

Confucianism: Its Ideas and Practices

Let us take a closer look at some core Confucian ideas and practices. While Confucianism has been claimed to be at once a religion and a philosophy, neither category completely captures the comprehensiveness of Confucianism. This is because Confucianism pertains to both, and throughout Chinese history it has been constantly interpreted and reinterpreted, indeed reconstructed. On the one hand, Confucianism is a religion because it has strong moral expectations of individuals and governments, follows strict rituals (e.g., wedding and funeral procedures), and even has temples for people to worship the legendary sage Confucius. However, unlike other religions, there are no priests; no supreme leaders such as the Roman Catholic pope; no primary sacred texts such as the Christian Bible or Islamic Qur'an; nor does Confucianism promote belief in God or an afterlife. On the other hand, Confucianism obviously shares many of the characteristics of a philosophy. It lays out a worldview of how society, government, and even the universe operate. Confucianism also explains how things in the universe change, and how various changes follow the same principle and are thus highly predictable. Although Confucianism also promotes the idea of Heaven, unlike in Western religions, Heaven is both the source of virtue or moral authority and nature or Dao. Thus, there are many insights from Confucianism about ontology, ethics, and epistemology.

Even though Confucianism is attributed to Kong Fuzi, commonly known as Confucius, who lived during the Spring and Autumn Warring States era of Chinese history (475–221 BCE), Confucian ideas originated much earlier than Confucius's time, predating the Xia dynasty (2100–1600 BCE), Shang dynasty (1600–1100 BCE), and Zhou dynasty (1100–256 BCE). Confucius was credited for having systematically studied histories and records from previous dynasties and developing a coherent and comprehensive system of ideas applicable to individuals, families, societies, and governments. Even more important, his ideas were widely disseminated through his teaching of thousands of disciples, who in turn taught their students Confucian ideas. Generation upon generation of Confucian believers interpreted and reinterpreted Confucian ideas over thousands of years, and the process continues today. Thus, Confucianism is not a static system of ideas; it is alive and continuously evolving.

There are some key ideas in original Confucian teachings. One of them is filial piety—respect and reverence for one's parents and ancestors. Filial piety extends to other family relationships, such as those between husband and wife and older brother and younger brother. Filial piety is also practiced in relationships beyond the family, such as teacher and student, young and old, master and apprentice, and so on. Filial piety may further be extended to government and society at large. For example, loyalty is expected of officials who hold different positions within government hierarchy. Lower-ranked officials should be loyal to higher-ranked officials, and, ultimately, all people should be loyal to the emperor. Other key ideas include honesty, uprightness, courage, wisdom, sympathy, and compassion. Possessing these values or virtues leads to humanity (*ren* 仁) or benevolence. Rituals also assume an important place in Confucianism. Rituals are customs and conventions to observe, governing both public events, such as the installation of an emperor and opening of a court hearing, weddings and funerals, dress codes, and even classroom behavior. Persons who possess these virtues are called gentlemen (*junzi* 君子). A gentleman is one with high ethical and ritual standards, the result of many years' education and practice. Government officials should be gentlemen who can lead by example. The preceding key ideas are derived from the Confucian classics, namely, the Four Books (*Analects* 论语, *Mencius* 孟子, *Great Learning* 大学, and *Doctrine of the Mean* 中庸) and the Five Classics (*Classic of Poetry* 诗经, *Classic of History* 史记, *Classic of Rites* 礼记, *Book of Changes* 易经, and *Spring and Autumn Annals* 春秋).

It should be emphasized that Confucianism is not only the philosophy of becoming a gentleman, but it is also a guide for good governance. Because of its direct implications for governance, Confucianism has been fully integrated into Chinese civil service as a state ideology for more than one thousand years. This integration began in the Sui dynasty (581–618) when the imperial examination system was created. The purpose of the imperial examination was to select people for different levels of civil service. The content of the examination was knowledge and understanding of Confucian classical texts. The examination was multitiered; those who passed different levels were assigned to different civil posts of importance. For 1,300 years after the Sui dynasty, the imperial examination system continued until 1905, when the call for reform was adopted by the late Qing dynasty.

Despite the longevity of Confucianism as a state ideology, there have been brief times during Chinese history when Confucianism was criticized, condemned, and even forbidden. The first emperor, Qin Shihuang, of unified China during the Qin dynasty (221–207 BCE) adopted a Legalist ideology for governance and ordered all Confucian texts burned and Confucian scholars buried alive. During the late Qing dynasty, the last dynasty before the establishment of the Republic of China in 1911, with rising technological power in the West and repeated defeat and humiliation of the Chinese imperial army, reform-minded Confucian scholars such as Kang Youwei (1858–1927) called for reform of Confucian ideology and Chinese society by embracing Western science and technology. They proposed that Confucianism be viewed as providing moral direction, while Western science and technology were practically applied. Reformers also succeeded in ending the thousand-plus-year-old imperial examination system. After the establishment of the Republic of China, founders of the Chinese Communist Party Chen Duxiu and Li Dazhao, as well as other reform-minded Confucian intellectuals such as Lu Xun, called for replacing Confucianism with Western science and democracy. Around 1915, the May Fourth Movement perceived Confucianism as the cause of the decline of Chinese military and economic power and the decay of Chinese society in recent history. After the founding of the People's Republic of China by the Communist Party of China in 1949, Confucianism continued to be the target of criticism, which peaked during the Cultural Revolution in the 1960s and 1970s when thousands of intellectuals were sent to labor camps for reeducation.

Although Confucius contributed foundational ideas for Confucianism, major reconstruction and enrichment of those ideas took place throughout Chinese history, particularly during the Han and Song dynasties. During Han dynasty (206 BC–220 AD), Dong Zhongshu advanced the theories of *yin-yang* (阴阳) and the five elements to explain meanings of Confucian classics. It was believed that there existed two opposing but complementary identities, *yin* (i.e., earth, cold, wife) and *yang* (i.e., sun, hot, husband), in the universe, and the symbiotic relation between them gives meaning to all things. Connecting *yin* and *yang* is the movement of *qi* (or energy). The five-element theory was based on the assumption that there are five basic elements—metal, wood, water, fire, and earth—that move in a fixed cycle, that is, earth is overtaken by wood, wood by metal, metal by fire, fire by water, and water by earth. Thus, by aligning all things in the universe with the five elements, such as the five directions (east, west, south, north, and center) and five human organs (liver, heart, spleen, kidney, and lungs), we can understand all changes in the universe. During the Song dynasty (960–1279), Neo-Confucian thinkers such as Zhu Xi (1130–1200) and Lu Jiuyuan (1139–1193) advanced the theory of Principle. According to this theory, there exists a Supreme Ultimate (*Tai Ji* 太极) that transcends time and space; *Tai Ji* is an abstract entity that underlies the movement of *qi* and thus the foundation of *yin-yang*.

It must be pointed out that even when Confucianism was under attack in China during the 1950s through the 1970s, Confucian scholars in Singapore, South Korea, Taiwan, Britain, and the United States continued to advance Confucian ideas in modern contexts, resulting in New Confucianism. More recently, scholars inside China are joining this growing movement, arguing that Confucianism as practiced in ancient China was not authentic and was manipulated by rulers. While Western science, technology, and democracy have advantages, the serious problems or ills commonly identified with Western societies and governments, such as corporate greed, dysfunctional families, and lack of compassion, could be tackled by a Confucian approach. Therefore, for New Confucian scholars, Confucianism should remain at the core of any harmonious society and government.

Objectives

Books in English on Confucian history, religion, philosophy, politics, and Chinese culture, as well as comparisons between Chinese education and American education, are many (e.g., Chang & Kalmanson, 2010; Gardner, 2014; Rainey, 2010; Richey, 2008; Schuman, 2015; Zhao, 2009), but few of them focus explicitly on the necessity of a quality 21st-century education from a Confucian perspective. Because of the growing common interest both in the East (including the Greater China region) and the West to critically examine Confucian educational thought, 39 scholars in education, philosophy, culture, history, and East Asian studies from China, Canada, and the United States gathered in Amherst, New York, for the International Symposium on Confucianism and Education, October 17–19, 2014. Inspired by the rich interdisciplinary dialogue at the conference, twelve papers were carefully selected and significantly revised to form the core of this volume on Confucianism and contemporary education.

This book not only fills a gap in research, but it also has unique value in a number of ways. First of all, wrestling with the relationship between Confucianism and education and its relevance to today's education in China and the United States, the book explores the Confucian perspective on education as its singular focus, and it does so interdisciplinarily. As its chapters demonstrate, the book addresses several thematic strands, including how and why Confucianism is relevant to American and Chinese education, what Confucian pedagogical principles may be used across various sociocultural settings, and what social and moral functions Confucianism plays. Each of the chapters, while situated within its own theoretical and methodological framework, represents a critical piece in a larger multidimensional puzzle. Together, these chapters form a thought-provoking text, with both conceptual lenses and concrete examples of why and how the Confucian perspective still matters across the educational scene in China, the United States, and beyond. As such, this book will be informative to faculty, researchers, policy makers, school administrators, and parents, as well as students in Chinese and East Asian studies.

Organization

In addition to the foreword and this introduction, there are twelve chapters divided into three sections. Section 1 begins with the central question of why and how Confucianism is relevant in diverse American and Chinese classrooms today. Chapter 1 studies teaching Confucian ideas to American undergraduate students. Using translations of the *Daodejing* (道德经) and the *Analects of Confucius*, Pamela Herron guides students to read, examine, and critically analyze these ancient texts, while prompting them to make meaningful connections with current events. Based on this teaching experience, she recognizes the educative value for U.S.-born students to study important Confucian concepts such as *ren* (仁) or compassion, *yi* (义) or righteousness, *junzi* (君子) or exemplary person, and *shu* (恕) or forgiveness. She notes that the "shift to understand and appreciate cyclical rather linear thinking is complex but most critical for students to accept." Chapter 2 takes on the writing mandate in the U.S. Common Core Standards for K–12 students. Arguing that these standards promote a linear deliberation or decision making in the Western tradition of argumentation and persuasion, Lyon maintains that the Chinese rhetorical tradition of remonstration (*jiàn* 谏) may serve as a useful conceptual lens for writing. Viewing it as a means to respect the audience, build trusting relationships, and engage the social order in ways that exceed legal, political, or partisan boundaries, the author proposes that such Confucian rhetorical practice may supplement, even enrich, the rigid analytical mode of written discourse in English. Chapter 3 describes China's ongoing movement to revive Confucianism as the core of Chinese traditional culture. Presenting a list of important Confucian viewpoints relevant to today's Chinese education, the author explains why and how these ideas may provide viable solutions to some of the pressing problems confronting China and Chinese education. Chapter 4 looks at the role and mechanism of ritual in education. Citing multiple Confucian texts on rituals, the chapter portrays a vibrant continuation of rituals in Chinese education today despite repeated attacks on Confucianism in China. Combined, these chapters showcase concrete applications of different Confucian educational principles and practices, elucidating why and how Confucianism is relevant in classroom settings across both China and the United States.

Section 2 contextualizes how various Confucian teaching and learning practices come into being and in what ways such time-honored insights may be reinterpreted to better serve the present needs. Chapter 5 addresses the development of Neo-Confucianism in the Song dynasty and its implications for current Chinese education and society. Drawing from Kuhn's (1996) seminal work on scientific paradigm, Yair Lior predicts a paradigmatic shift in contemporary Confucianism because geopolitical changes require the construction of an alternative cultural paradigm to satisfy the needs of an increasingly sophisticated population excluded from the traditional center of authority. Though China is in the process of revitalizing its traditional culture and education, Lior suggests both presentation and structural changes are needed to aid in the paradigmatic shift. Chapter 6 centers on redefining the notion of learning as public reasoning in 17th-century China. With this redefinition seriously challenging the Song-era orthodox Confucian view about how to access the Heavenly Principle (*tianli* 天理) and Way (*dao* 道), the chapter calls for approaching learning through open-ended, dynamic, inclusive, and collective processes. Chapter 7 is a textual analysis of the notions of learning in the *Book of Changes* (*Yijing* 易经). Based on the *Yijing*, "elementary learning" (小学) differs from "great learning" (大学)—the former emphasizes text-oriented public education, and the latter facilitates individuals' personal development and creative contribution to build a more vibrant and harmonious society. Therefore, the author maintains that contemporary Chinese education needs to be rebalanced by following an integrated approach, in which strengths from both approaches may complement each other. Chapter 8 deals with the topic of critical thinking. Contrary to popular views, critical thinking is highly emphasized in classic Confucian writings as well as in Confucian pedagogical practices. These chapters not only underscore the relevance of Confucianism for improving teaching and learning outcomes, but they also help to dispel some common stereotypes and misconceptions related to Confucian conceptions of learning.

Finally, section 3 turns to the social and moral functions and the intellectual values of education. Chapter 9 holds that the embodied Confucian approach not only involves acquiring knowledge and information about the world, but it also invokes inner change through cultivation of virtue to elevate one's heart-mind. Only then can the learner become a transformative force to improve the world. Therefore, Confucianism offers a method to integrate the personal with the social, the outer with the inner, and the learning of knowledge with transformative action. Chapter 10 connects Confucianism with multicultural education. Based on the Confucian notion of selfhood, which is defined as a relation, an expanding process, and the realization of Heaven-Endowed Humanity, Wang argues that Confucianism can help refine the current multicultural education framework, while multiculturalism can also give new ground for Confucian thought to evolve. Chapter 11 discusses moral and ethical education in light of ever-accelerating technological advancement and globalization. Because an individual goes through formation of moral character, commitment and critique, and reflection and action as ways of life, the chapter insists that moral education should carefully consider both the founding process and manifesting process of moral life. Finally, chapter 12 concludes with a critical inquiry into the intricate and complicated conceptual connections among Confucianism, democracy, and the global education movement. While Confucian values compatible with modern cosmopolitan democracy can render critical support for community-based sustainable economic development, Li cautions us against romanticizing Confucianism because the Confucian ideal of a cohesive polity is simultaneously conducive to the modern nation-state that promotes economic growth at the cost of ecological decline. In summary, these chapters inform us of the social and moral missions and functions that education plays. Extending our thinking way beyond a specific set of disciplinary rules and job skills, this section highlights the centrality of social and moral functions within a Confucian educational framework. The implications of these chapters follow.

Implications

As editors of this volume, we are impressed by the level of diversity that penetrates the pages, both in terms of wide-ranging research areas (e.g., K–12 and college teaching, Chinese and American education, and various historical periods) and different approaches (e.g., case study, conceptual comparison, discourse analysis, pedagogical reflection, and theory-driven inquiry). This, we believe, reflects the incredible depth and breadth of Confucian ideas; it is also a reflection of the complex and diverse educational situations in which Confucian principles and practices may be applied. As editors, we view this as a strength of the book and a demonstration of the potential for more systematic scholarly inquiry.

As manifested across different chapters, Confucianism is an invaluable mine of wisdom beneficial to Chinese and American students alike. In addition to broad educational principles, there are numerous time-honored Confucian practices, ranging from well-known adages to core Confucian pedagogical guidelines, that are compatible with the latest research-based pedagogical practices (e.g., *education for all without discrimination, connecting theory with practice, knowledge and action go hand in hand, lifelong learning*, etc.). As elaborated by Fangping Cheng (chapter 3, this volume), many of the core Confucian values are being preserved, adapted, and revived in China's current educational and sociocultural fabric, including reverence to teachers and the elderly, balancing the acquisition of professional knowledge and skills, and the cultivation of personhood and moral values.

Because many Confucian ideas have universal value, we believe that they can benefit Chinese and American students alike. For instance, drawing on her actual teaching experience with American college students, Herron argues in chapter 1, "If all the world followed the precepts taught by Confucius and Mencius, the world would surely be a more peaceful, better governed, and more harmonious place. The best we can strive for in education is to share the teachings of Kong Fuzi with our students and hope that instilling those values and principles will guide them to make their world and the world of our future children a better place to live." At the K–12 level, Lyon (chapter 2) recognizes that the goal of the Western argument through persuasion is "to formulate a position more than to engage an audience," whereas the Confucian model of remonstration (*jiàn* 谏) adds the benefit of engaging the audience and considering its response, thus making remonstration a useful supplement in the Common Core Standards for writing. Furthermore, because the Confucian notion of the Great Harmony embraces differences while adhering to harmony, Wang (in chapter 10) sees the Confucian notion of selfhood as a useful conceptual lens to expand the current multicultural educational framework beyond the confinement of the prevailing cultural mainstream. All these implications convey one key message: The Confucian perspective has much to offer to the field of education in China and the United States.

We recognize that "anti-Confucianism" arguments exist in the literature. One such argument is related to the sensitive topic of China's "soft power." Undeterred by concerns that teaching Confucianism adds to China's efforts to promote its "soft power," Herron queries why people seldom question the traditions and teachings of Judaism and the Torah, Christianity and the Bible, or Islam and the Qur'an but are concerned about teaching the Confucian perspective. While it is prudent to keep in mind Li's (chapter 12) remarks about not "romanticizing" Confucianism in the 21st century's global context, it will be wise to carefully consider how to make the past serve the present. This is the real "soft power" that lies beneath both teaching and learning Confucius's ideas.

We also acknowledge the arguments that some of Confucius's ideas promote rigidity, hierarchy, and conformity, which may have contributed to today's Chinese education system being both the best and worst in the world (Zhao, 2014). We do not imply that Confucianism is sufficient for any education system; thus, Confucianism must be followed entirely or blindly. We propose that Confucianism is not a "dead" school of thought that belonged only to the past. Nor is Confucianism static; it is constantly evolving. As demonstrated by chapters of this book, Confucianism is a complex system of diverse ideas. In fact, New Confucianism scholars in China have already started to critically reexamine its cultural legacy, to inherit its useful elements, and then to apply them in accordance to today's specific sociocultural conditions and circumstances. What is real Confucianism remains a topic of scholarly debate. For example, Wu (2011) argues that the authentic pedagogy of Confucianism is not what the classic texts literally convey in terms of modern language lexicon; instead, the indigenous identity of Confucian pedagogy is to use language to "name the unspeakable and strives to withdraw itself to complete forgetfulness. What remains in terms of emptiness of symbolic meaning is the essence of pedagogic intelligibility" (Wu, 2011, p. 569). In other words, Confucianism is a heuristic; it creates a space for situational understanding, action, and interaction in order to approach the Way (Tao). As Tao De Jing states, "The way that can be spoken of is not the constant Way; the name that can be named is not the constant Name" (Lao-tzu). Only time can tell whether all above efforts will amount to the paradigm shift or historical transformation that Lior predicts in chapter 5. Nevertheless, Confucianism can, and should, advance with the times to keep pace with teaching and learning in current globalized classrooms, just as any other educational perspective does.

Ma (2014) encourages educational communities in the United States and China to learn about and from one another. It is certainly beyond the scope of this volume to take on that task, and some volumes already address this topic (e.g., Huang, 2014). However, "meeting on the middle ground" (i.e., following the Confucian "golden mean"), such as co-core synergy education practiced by Chinese-Americans for their children to become "hybrid tigers" (Huang, 2014), may help to bring out the best from both sides. Given the prevalence of Western theories and practices, the global community would benefit from exploring the Confucian ideal of harmonious society through dialogue with this non-Western cultural tradition.

In conclusion, the chapters of this volume not only enrich the literature on Confucianism from an interdisciplinary perspective, but they also offer valuable insights on why and how Confucianism is both relevant and important for teaching and learning in the 21st century.

Confucius's vision of education as empowerment is that one acquire wisdom and achieve self-fulfillment for social transformation, for peace, and for justice for all. This book is a small step on that thousand-mile-long journey.

References

Chang, W., & Kalmanson, L. (Eds.). (2010). *Confucianism in context: Classic philosophy and contemporary issues, East Asia and beyond*. Albany: State University of New York Press.
Chua, A. (2011). *Battle hymn of the tiger mother*. New York: Penguin.
Chua, A., & Rubenfeld, J. (2014). *The triple package: How three unlikely traits explain the rise and fall of cultural groups in America*. New York: Penguin.
Clark, R. (2015, August 4). Chinese teachers are RIGHT about British education. Retrieved from http://www.express.co.uk/comment/expresscomment/595826/Chinese-teachers-right-about-British-education-Ross-Clark
Gardner, D. K. (2014). *Confucianism: A very short history*. Oxford: Oxford University Press.
Huang, Q. (2014). *The hybrid tiger: Secrets of the extraordinary success of Asian-American kids*. Amherst: Prometheus Books.
Kuhn, S. T. (1996). *The structure of scientific revolution* (3rd ed.). Chicago: University of Chicago Press.
Lee, S. J. (1996). *Unraveling the "model minority" stereotype: Listening to Asian American youth*. New York: Teachers College Press.
Lee, T. H. (2000). *Education in traditional China: A history*. Boston: Brill.
Liu, X., & Li, G. (2008). Diversity and equity in science education for Asians in North America: Unpacking the model minority myth. In M-W. Roth & K. Tobin (Eds.), *World of science education: Handbook of research in North America* (pp. 369–388). Rotterdam: Sense.
Liu, X., & Zhang, B. (2014). Editorial of special issue: International conference on science education. *Journal of Science and Education Technology, 23*, 207–210.
Ma, W. (Ed.). (2014). *East meets West in teacher preparation: Crossing Chinese and American borders*. New York: Teachers College Press.
Ma, W., & Li, G. (Eds.). (2016). *Chinese-heritage students in North American schools: Understanding hearts and minds beyond test scores*. London: Routledge.
The Open University. (2015). Debate: What can British schools learn from the Chinese education system? Retrieved from http://www.open.edu/openlearn/education/debate-what-can-british-schools-learn-the-chinese-education-system
Rainey, L. D. (2010). *Confucius and Confucianism: The essentials*. West Sussex: Wiley.

Richey, J. L. (2008). *Teaching Confucianism*. New York: Oxford University Press.
Schuman, M. (2015). *Confucius: And the world he created*. New York, NY: Basic Books.
Watkins, D. A., & J. B. Biggs (Eds.). (1996). *The Chinese learner: Cultural, psychological, and contextual influences*. Hong Kong: University of Hong Kong Press.
Wu, Z. (2011). Interpretation, autonomy, and transformation: Chinese pedagogic discourse in a cross-cultural perspective. *Journal of Curriculum Studies*, 43(5), 569–590.
Zhao, Y. (2009). *Catching up or leading the way: American education in the age of globalization*. Alexandria: ASCD.
Zhao, Y. (2014). *Who's afraid of big bad dragon? Why China has the best (and worst) education system in the world*. San Francisco: Jossey-Bass.
Zhao, Y., & Qiu, W. (2009). How good are the Asians? Refuting myths about Asian-American academic achievement. *Phi Delta Kappan*, 90(5), 338–334.

PART I

RELEVANCE OF CONFUCIANISM TO
AMERICAN AND CHINESE EDUCATION

1

Becoming Confucian in America Today

Pamela G. Herron

Analect 1.1 The Master said, "Having studied, to then repeatedly apply what you have learned—is this not a source of pleasure? To have friends come from distant quarters—is this not a source of enjoyment? To go unacknowledged by others without harboring frustration—is this not the mark of an exemplary person (*junzi*)."

—Ames & Rosemont, 1998, p. 71

This first of the analects or teachings of Confucius is probably one of the most often-quoted passages and the beginning of any class or course on Confucianism. It speaks of the importance of education, friendship, and appropriate behavior, surely the foundation of a Confucian person. But what is a Confucian person? What does it really mean to follow the teachings of a man who lived 2,500 years ago? Do the teachings of Confucius still hold any meaning or relevance to contemporary society in either China or the rest of the world?

Confucius 孔子 is also known as K'ung fu tzu, Kong Fuzi, Master Kong, or Kongzi. This philosopher and teacher lived from 551 to 479 BCE. Often in Western academia, Confucianism is classified as a religion in a religious studies program or as a philosophy. Indeed, over time in China, Confucianism accumulated sufficient ritual and dogma to be considered a religion, or at least a spiritual practice. Daoism, Buddhism, and Confucianism are often referred to as the three-legged pot, *ding* 鼎, of Chinese spiritual thought and philosophy. The primary purpose of

Confucius's teachings was to prepare young men for civil service. His students would go on to become advisors to rulers and overlords. Many would make a living continuing his tradition of training new generations of civil servants and advisors.

For today's purposes, Confucianism is better considered as a philosophy or guide to harmonious living that is deeply ingrained in Chinese and Asian culture. A statue of Confucius greets visitors at the entrance of the Confucius Temple in Beijing, and this is repeated in most major cities in China and at many universities. Confucius Institutes now number nearly 500 worldwide with more than 70 in the United States alone.

Recently, there has been much in the news regarding the "soft power" of the Confucius Institutes and their relationship with academic freedom in both the United States and Europe. Confucius Institutes have made it possible for elementary and secondary schools, along with communities, colleges, and universities all over the world, to be able to offer Chinese-language instruction to students who otherwise would have no access to such instruction. The real "soft power," though, lies in the teachings of Confucius himself.

It is interesting that no one questions those who follow the traditions and teachings of Judaism and the Torah, Christianity and the Bible, or Islam and the Qur'an, but the classic teachings of China and Confucius seem too often to be ignored or dismissed as something only of historic significance, or only important to scholars studying Asia or China. Is Confucianism relevant to students in America in the 21st century? Does a 2,500-year-old philosophy have anything to offer contemporary society? This chapter endeavors to detail the pedagogy and development of a successful approach to teaching Confucianism and Daoism to undergraduate students from a variety of disciplines, the majority of whom have not previously been exposed to Chinese history, culture, or philosophy.

In 2012, the director of the Religious Studies Program at the University of Texas at El Paso asked me to consider developing a course on Confucianism. The class was enthusiastically received and quite successful. Originally a "Special Topics" course, Confucianism and Daoism now has its own assigned course number designation and is offered annually in the spring semester. My university has a long-standing relationship with Confucius. The main interest of the late David L. Hall (1937–2001) of our Department of Philosophy was Chinese philosophy, specifically Confucianism and Daoism. It is the translation of the *Dao De Jing* by Roger T. Ames and David L. Hall that is the foundation text for my

Confucianism and Daoism course and my newly developed Daoism and the Environment course.

My approach to teaching Confucianism is to not teach it as a religion, although the classes are offered through the Religious Studies Program. Instead, my students read and analyze translations of these classic texts and then attempt to apply what they've learned to contemporary society and culture. As the Confucian analect says, "Having studied, to then repeatedly apply what you have learned—is this not a source of pleasure?" Although certain passages in the *Analects of Confucius* are devoted to rituals, such as what type of hat was appropriate or how many times to bow, that may no longer seem relevant to us today, culture evolves and society develops new rituals that are as significant to us today as the rituals of the time of Kongzi. In this course, students are asked to examine and analyze these ancient texts with the intention of determining their relevance to today's people and circumstances. Many of the techniques used in this course were developed from the teachings of Roger Ames (Peking University and the University of Hawaii at Manoa), the late Henry Rosemont Jr. (Brown University), and Tian Chenshan (Beijing Foreign Studies University) demonstrated at the first Nishan Confucius Summer Institute in Nishan, Shandong, China, in 2011. I was honored to have been selected as a participant in this first international endeavor that paired Western scholars with Chinese scholars to explore and achieve a deeper understanding of the teachings of Confucius.

One of the most difficult concepts to explain to students is a fundamental difference in Eastern and Western thinking. Most students in American universities are used to individualistic thinking, whereas many Asian students will focus on the community and their place and relationship to those within communities. Roger Ames uses the lesson that we are not human beings; rather, we are "human becomings" who are constantly changing and evolving. Who we are and who we become is based on our progression of relationships with others. Each of us is someone's son or daughter, parent, friend, sister or brother, colleague, professor or student—and the list continues. Each of those relationships helps to define who we are and determine our appropriate behavior in any given situation.

American students are also trained to look for absolutes; they expect answers to be black or white. If something is true, isn't it always true? They are not prepared for the nuances in Chinese relationships where one must always evaluate what is the most appropriate response in this particular situation or these particular circumstances. The answer one time may not be the correct answer considering a different set of variables. Most American students are also most familiar with concepts from Judeo-Christian belief systems where there is always a focus or search for the transcendent. Westerners tend to think in a more linear fashion, while the roots of Daoism and Confucianism are cyclical and more in tune with a seasonal agrarian-based culture where the only constant is change. Western belief systems are based on the quest for perfection and the search for a reward either in the present or in the afterlife. Chinese philosophy is rooted in constant self-evaluation and self-cultivation. There is no search for perfection; rather, what is most auspicious or appropriate in any given circumstances is sought. This shift to understand and appreciate cyclical rather than linear thinking is complex but most critical for students to accept. This is the first step in helping our students become more open-minded and aware of the possibility of misinterpretation if they read these texts only through only a Western lens.

In my Confucianism and Daoism course I arrange my texts chronologically, which means students read the *Daodejing* first. Many might consider the *Daodejing* to be rather esoteric and perhaps beyond the understanding of many of our students in the United States. The *Daodejing* precedes the time of Confucius; indeed, Confucius references the *Dao* many times in the *Analects*, so it is important that students understand that Confucius himself was attempting to determine and follow the *Dao*. Ames and Hall have an excellent introduction that sets up what to expect while reading and studying this text, including a glossary of terms and references to choices made in translation. Most of the students in my region will have had little to no exposure to Chinese history, culture, or language, so it is of paramount importance to spend some time talking about what is often lost in translation. One of the first exercises is to expose them to multiple translations of a sample of chapters from the *Daodejing*. They listen to several translations for chapter 1 of the *Daodejing*:

> Tao can be talked about but not the Eternal Tao. Names can be named, but not the Eternal Name.
> As the origin of heaven-and-earth, it is nameless: As "the Mother" of all things, it is nameable. (Wu, 1961, p. 3)

The Tao (Way) that can be told of is not the eternal Tao;
The name that can be named is not the eternal name.
The Nameless is the origin of Heaven and Earth;
The Named is the mother of all things. (Chan, 1963, p. 139)

The Tao that can be told is not the universal Tao.
The name that can be named is not the universal name.
In the infancy of the universe, there were no names.
Naming fragments the mysteries of life into ten thousand
   things and their manifestations. (Dale, 2002, p. 3)

And, finally, the Ames and Hall translation chooses to include significant Chinese terms that are not readily translatable word-for-word into English, their reasoning being that students of Chinese philosophy and spiritual thought must accept that some Chinese words are greater concepts that must be internalized without processing through a Western filter.

Way-making (*dao*) that can be put into words is not really
   way-making,
And naming (*ming*) that can assign fixed reference to
   things is not really naming.
The nameless (*wuming*) is the fetal beginnings of everything that is happening (*wanwu*),
While that which is named is their mother. (Ames & Hall,
   2003, p. 77)

Ames and Hall go on to provide footnotes with even one more alternative translation, which is:

The indeterminate (*wu*) is the beginning of everything that
   is happening;
While the determinate (*you*) is the mother of everything
   that is happening. (Ames & Hall, 2003, p. 205)

Which translation is the best? Which is the most correct and true to the original Chinese? All are valid. Each translation makes an honest effort to bring its interpretation of the original text into an understandable form for English speakers. Each brings its own background, beliefs, fluency in classical Chinese, and, perhaps most importantly, comprehension of the original text. The *Daodejing* reads more like poetry, and, much like poetry, the *Daodejing* is subject to infinite interpretations. This is reflected in the variances of translations over time.

After reading the *Daodejing*, students are asked to choose three passages that particularly resonate with them. They share these with their classmates in an open class discussion. Often one student explaining what a passage meant to him or her can greatly improve or illuminate the meaning to classmates in a way that a professor's lecture never could. Their second assignment is to then choose three passages they had not chosen before based on the passages shared by their peers in the classroom. Students may then decide to discuss a passage they previously rejected because they did not understand it, or perhaps because of a lack of appeal. After participating in roundtable discussions with their classmates, they find new meaning in passages they had overlooked or dismissed. Particularly lively discussions can occur when students have differing interpretations of the same passage, but that only enhances their understanding by helping them see the multiple possible meanings for a few simple words.

After struggling to understand the *Daodejing*, many students find that the straightforward text of the *Lunyu* comes as quite a relief. In the *Analects of Confucius*, there is less use of ambiguity and repetition. Before reading the *Analects*, certain concepts of Confucianism are essential for students to understand and make connections with in the text. Ames and Rosemont spend pages in their introduction providing extensive explanations and examples of these fundamental concepts. These terms are freighted with meaning in the classic texts and cannot be readily translated into English with one or two words. They are interconnected and require critical study before the text is read; otherwise comprehension of the text is compromised. Some of these basic concepts include the following:

    rén (仁, humaneness or compassion)
    yì (義, righteousness or justice)
    lǐ (禮, proper rites or ritual)
    zhì (智, knowledge or wisdom)
    xìn (信, integrity or keeping one's word)
    zhōng (忠, doing one's utmost or loyalty)
    xiao (孝, filial piety)

yì (義, righteousness)
tian (天, heaven)
jūnzǐ (君子, exemplary person)

One of best exercises to get students to start thinking is the famous Confucian story of the sheep, which I use in class to illustrate the concept of *xiao* (孝) or filial piety.

> Analect 13.18 says: The Governor of She in conversation with Confucius said, "In our village there is someone called 'True Person.' When his father took a sheep on the sly . . ."
> (Ames & Rosemont, 2003, pp. 166–167)

At this point, students are asked to determine what the son should do. Should he report his father to the authorities? Should he remonstrate with his father? Should he accuse his father or return the sheep himself? The possibilities are endless, but what is the most appropriate action for the son? Our students today are so hesitant, or perhaps unable, to use critical thinking skills, most likely the result of years of rote standardized tests in elementary and secondary education. The discussion often begins with students trying to discern what answer the professor wants to hear. Sometimes the discussion ends up evenly divided into those who believe the son should report his father to the authorities and those who think the son should stand behind his father, even if he has committed a crime. They often want to know why the father has stolen the sheep, but that information is not provided. Most of my students are Hispanic or Mexican American, so they have strong feelings about loyalty to family.

This exercise graphically demonstrates the Confucian concept of *xiao* (孝), filial piety. In the individualistic society of America, the concept of *xiao* sometimes seems to be lost or at least unacceptable to some students. The answer is that in Confucian principles, filial piety trumps all else, which often generates extensive discussion.

> Analect 13.18 continued: ". . . he reported him to the authorities." Confucius replied, "Those who are true in my village conduct themselves differently. A father covers for his son, and a son covers for his father. And being true lies in this."
> (Ames & Rosemont, 2003, pp. 166–167)

Ames and Rosemont go on to explain further in their footnotes, citing other sources of this anecdote that clarify: "In the tension between family and the Governor's law, Confucius is saying the law does not trump the family. Order begins at home" (Ames & Rosemont, 2003, p. 254n213).

The first major assignment for the students with the *Analects of Confucius* is to study all the references to these significant terms or Confucian concepts that appear in the text, such as *xiao* (孝), *rén* (仁), *yì* (義), *lǐ* (禮), *zhōng* (忠), *xìn* (信), and the others listed earlier. There are several indices or concordances available. Edward Slingerland has excellent material in his appendices in the back of his translation of *Confucius Analects: With Selections from Traditional Commentaries*. Kurtis Hagen of SUNY Plattsburgh identifies some Confucian key terms with their locations in the classic texts on his university website. The late Henry Rosemont of Brown University provides an extensive "*Lunyu* Finding List of Key Philosophical Terms" to his students. This Confucian concept assignment is most productive when students work together in pairs. Having a partner ensures that students discuss and thoroughly understand the concept being examined. Then the partners present their concept, and their understanding and explanation of it, to their classmates. Often their first reading of the *Analects* is cursory, but having to seek out and understand these individual references on important concepts enhances their total comprehension and engagement with the text.

The second major assignment is to use a concordance to study the disciples, the men learning from Confucius. With close critical reading of the text, students can readily identify that the Master, Confucius, does not always give the same answer to the same question from different disciples. The major disciples differ greatly, ranging from greatly beloved disciples whom Confucius sets up as exemplars to overachievers who just cannot quite seem to get the point of some of the teachings. These men have different personalities and vary in their learning, their experience, their age, and their commitment to study. By analyzing the various responses and comments from Confucius to these students, our own students gain a deeper, less superficial reading and understanding of the text. If the question remains the same, why does Confucius respond in a different manner? As students become aware of the differences, the strengths, and the weaknesses of the Confucian disciples, they often become more discerning of their own approaches to learning, and even more sensitive to the differences among themselves and their classmates.

The inspiration and process for these two assignments came directly from the late Henry Rosemont Jr. of Brown University. In studying Confucianism under the late Dr. Rosemont, I developed a greater understanding of the *Analects* and a deeper appreciation for the classic texts. The results with my undergraduate students have been very satisfying and sometimes astounding. Students often retain and refer to these exercises in their other courses on China and Asia. Clearly this method of studying the *Analects* is highly effective and results in an impressive retention of the material along with an ability to apply it to other circumstances and new learning situations.

One of the most important concepts to teach is that of what it means to be *jūnzǐ* (君子), an exemplary person. Being *jūnzǐ*, or striving to become *jūnzǐ*, encompasses all the other aspects of being Confucian. Becoming an exemplary person is compared to being a North Star that others can look to for guidance and a living example of the way to live one's life and treat others. Throughout China's history there are Confucian exemplars, both men and women, who are held up as examples on which to model our own behavior. Often it is helpful to show the progression from a person who is *rén* (仁), working on self-cultivation in hopes of becoming *jūnzǐ* (君子).

Students often find the writing of Mencius or *Mèng Zǐ* (孟子) even easier to understand. They enjoy his belief that people are inherently good but that they need to work on constantly evaluating themselves through self-cultivation and improvement. Mencius reinforces concepts in the *Analects* and restates them in such a straightforward manner that students find him a pleasure to read. Students also respond well to Zhuangzi (莊子), but it is best to save Zhuangzi until after they have acquired some basic understanding of the *Daodejing* and the *Lunyu*. These texts are quite accessible for students who have little to no prior knowledge of Chinese culture or history. For an excellent overview and introduction, my class uses Bryan Van Norden's *Introduction to Classical Chinese Philosophy* and his *The Essential Mengzi: Selected Passages with Traditional Commentary*. Although these are not bilingual texts, they provide good introductory material, glossaries, and additional resources.

Because Confucianism has been a profound influence throughout Chinese history, examining the *Analects* can lead to a better understanding of Chinese people and culture. One significant aspect found in the *Analects* is that it seems apparent that Confucius considered himself an observer of both humanity and the practices that seemed to be successful and positive contributions to society over time. There is no evidence that Confucius wrote the *Analects*; China provides a wealth of opportunities to study the significance and tradition of oral transmission. It is believed that his students wrote down his teachings after his death. Although Confucius has been regarded as a sage for generations, he did not see himself as a sage. Throughout the *Analects* and the writings and commentaries of his students and the students of his students, he resists being called a sage, but he had great respect for those who continued an attitude of lifelong learning. According to the *Analects*, a person's character should be fixed, beyond reproach, and serve as an exemplar for others, but this does not mean that one's intellect is fixed or unchangeable. Confucius abhorred inflexibility of the mind. Being a sage would imply that no one could teach him anything, but repeatedly he refers to continued learning, learning from his students, and using learning "for making distinctions in the world around you" (Analect 17.9, Ames & Rosemont, 2003, p. 206).

Confucius came from a time when oral tradition was extremely important and part of the fabric of society. Many beliefs and practices were carried down through generations and reinforced by oral tradition. Confucius expressed modesty about his learning and wisdom throughout the *Analects* and gave credit for what he had learned to those who came before him.

> Analect 7.1 The Master said, "Following the proper way, I do not forge new paths; with confidence I cherish the ancients." (Ames & Rosemont, 2003, p. 111)

> Analect 7.28 The Master said, "There are probably those who can initiate new paths while still not understanding them, but I am not one of them. I learn much, select out of it what works well. And then follow it. I observe much, and remember it. This is a lower level of wisdom." (Ames & Rosemont, 2003, p. 117)

More than anything, Confucius provides a model for learning and encouragement for education. Education and continued learning were most important to him, no matter a person's class or social status.

Analect 9.8 The Master said, "Do I possess wisdom (*zhi* 知)? No, I do not. But if a simple peasant puts a question to me, and I come up empty, I attack the question from both ends until I have gotten to the bottom of it." (Ames & Rosemont, 2003, p. 128)

My classes open with and reinforce that we are all students of Confucianism together. A teacher of Confucianism must always be open to new interpretations and views. As leaders in the discussion and exploration of Chinese philosophy, we have an opportunity to learn from our students and enhance our own depth of understanding.

One of the most repeated and significant teachings of Confucius is what is known as the Silver Rule or the Rule of Reciprocity. This Confucian concept predates the teaching of Jesus Christ in Matthew 7:12 and could serve as a constant guideline for all peoples.

Analect 15.24 Zigong asked, "Is there one expression that can be acted upon until the end of one's days?" The Master replied, "There is *shu* 恕: do not impose on others what you yourself do not want." (Ames & Rosemont, 2003, p. 189)

The word *shu* 恕 also translates to forgiveness, pardon, or excuse. This Rule of Reciprocity could also serve as a standard for relations between men and women, within families, and even between governments. Throughout the tapestry that is China's history, there have been golden periods in which women were educated, literate, and produced significant works of art, poetry, and literature. The Tang dynasty is only one example of a period in which evidence of significant women's work has survived. On the other hand, women writers in the more recent history of the West felt the need to use their initials, or a pen name, to conceal their gender. Some scholars believe that despite the excesses and destruction that accompanied the Cultural Revolution of the 1960s and 1970s, it heralded a new period of equality for women. This is evident even in recent events in China with the new "tiger" businesswomen, some of whom have climbed from poverty to great wealth and power.

An interesting note on both the Daoist text and the *Analects of Confucius* is that, overall, they are not gender specific, and when they do specify gender, it is with an effort to achieve harmony and balance.

Although China, like the United States and the rest of the world, has gone through periods in which women were certainly not equal to men and, in fact, have been considered subservient to men, this is not reflected in its classic texts. Considering the status of women at present, China still has far to go, as do we in the United States, but China also has a unique harmonious and balanced legacy from the past. The ancient classic texts recognize the importance of women and their place in the world. From the ancient Chinese creation legends of Fu Xi and his wife, Nu Wa, who mended the sky to protect the fragile humans she created from the earth, to the *Daodejing*, Chinese myths, legends, and texts celebrate the inseparable blend of male and female, *yin* and *yang*, that are forever interrelated and interdependent on each other. Chapter 42 of the *Daodejing* says:

> The Dao gives rise to continuity,
> Continuity gives rise to difference,
> Difference gives rise to plurality,
> And plurality gives rise to the manifold of everything that is happening (*wanwu*).
> Everything carries *yin* on its shoulders and *yang* in its arms
> And blends these vital energies (*qi*) together to make them harmonious (*he*). (Ames & Hall, 2003, p. 143)

More so than those of any Western culture, the ancient Chinese texts provide a refreshing view of the harmonious relations of men and women. Class consciousness is evident in the *Analects*, but in actual practice the Chinese civil service system was open to anyone who could pass the civil service examination, which was based solely on knowledge and understanding of the classic texts. Unlike enforced master-slave states such as ancient Rome or caste systems as in India, a man from a poor family had as much right to rise to a governing position as a nobleman's son, as long as he had access to study the Classics. Women, too, from ancient times advocated education in the Classics. Ban Zhao (ca. 45–120 AD) of the Han dynasty wrote of the importance of educating women. As the first female Chinese historian, she had received a classical education herself and believed that to raise intelligent, educated children, women must be educated as well. She supported the education of women in her "Lessons for Women" for the good of the entire nation. Long before England's Mary Wollstonecraft of the 18th century or the later European and American suffragists and feminists of the 19th and 20th centuries, Ban Zhao was an advocate for her sex. Many of her ideas were quite forward thinking centuries in advance of any women's rights movements. A noted scholar and historian, throughout 2,000 years of Chinese history Ban Zhao is held up as a Confucian exemplar. She applied her learning of the Classics to defend her ideas and beliefs.

The final project for my students in their Confucianism and Daoism class is to take what they have learned about Daoist and Confucian principles and apply it to some aspect of today's society or current event. This information on the final project is in the course syllabus and is explained in detail before students begin reading either the *Daodejing* or the *Analects*. Every semester the results are astounding. Students have taken what they have learned and applied these concepts to such diverse topics as environmental degradation, sustainability, the failure of the American education system, human trafficking, consumerism, mining disasters, political scandals, sporting events, vegetarianism and veganism, treatment of Native Americans, LGBTQIA issues, and much more. Recently, a student chose to apply Confucian principles to a local scandal in El Paso regarding standardized tests and the discriminatory treatment of English Language Learners. One young woman informed the class of a project of the El Paso Sheriff's Department that provided education, health care, and opportunities for self-improvement for women arrested for prostitution rather than the usual bailout and return to the streets that happens in many communities. Another student, a history major and an Asian studies minor, is achieving admirable fluency in his second year of studying the Chinese language. He has a continued interest in the focus and scope of the Confucius Institutes because they have provided the opportunity for him to study Chinese. He chose to present on the purpose and mission of the Confucius Institutes and is closely following current news stories in the United States, Europe, and China on the future of the Confucius Institutes.

Students who choose to take Confucianism and Daoism are not primarily students of Asian studies. They come from varied disciplines throughout the university. In any given class, there might be students from creative writing, criminal justice, communication or journalism, history, engineering, business, sociology, psychology, metallurgy, computer engineering, and even more. Every semester, students who are either active-duty military members or reservists in the armed forces register for the course. All are hungry to learn more about a culture and country that is increasingly in the news. Their backgrounds and areas of study are different and so are their interests. We all learn from each other in the presentation of final projects because of this diversity. Many students choose topics that are within their body of knowledge because of their areas of study or perhaps their jobs or chosen career paths.

The goal of studying Confucianism and Daoism is for students to develop the ability to comprehend and apply Confucian and Daoist principles and work toward identifying and exploring the relevance within their own daily lives and their goals for the future. In addition, they see that the scope and relevance of Confucian thought could be of benefit to all peoples of the world.

Students in the course draw conclusions and make connections showing how Confucian or Daoist principles might advance their own study, and they learn to see the value of the ethics and interconnectedness taught through these ancient texts. There is good reason for the fact that Confucianism and Daoism have influenced Chinese culture for millennia. In these readings of translations of classic Chinese teachings, students have an opportunity to contrast the model of individualistic linear Western thinking with the more cyclical focus on community and interrelation of Chinese thinking, with the recognition that these principles have guided and influenced Chinese society and culture for 2,500 years.

Will my students be influenced by soft power? Maybe. Are Confucian Institutes detrimental to American students and others? I don't think so. Is Confucianism still relevant in the 21st century? I believe Confucius had many of the right answers 2,500 years ago. I teach Confucianism in the hope that my students will indeed become more Confucian. If everyone followed the precepts taught by Confucius and Mencius, the world would surely be a more peaceful, better governed, and more harmonious place. The best we can strive for in education is to share the teachings of Confucius with our students and hope that instilling those values and principles will guide them to make their world and the world of our children a better place to live.

Acknowledgments

Dedicated to my Confucian teachers, who set my feet on the path of becoming Confucian: Roger T. Ames of the University of Hawaii at

Manoa, the late Henry Rosemont Jr. of Brown University, and Tian Chenshan of Beijing Foreign Studies University.

References

Ames, R. T., & Hall, D. L. (2003). *Dao de jing—"Making this life significant"*: A philosophical translation. New York: Ballantine Books.
Ames, R. T., & Rosemont Jr., H. (1998). *The Analects of Confucius: A philosophical translation*. New York: Ballantine Books.
Ban Zhao. (n.d.). Lessons for a woman. In *Pan Chao: Foremost Woman Scholar of China* (N. L. Swann, Trans.). New York: Century Co., 1932. Retrieved from http://acc6.its.brooklyn.cuny.edu/~phalsall/texts/banzhao.html
Chan, W. (1963). *A source book in Chinese philosophy*. Princeton: Princeton University Press.
Dale, R. (2002). *Tao te ching: A new translation and commentary*. New York: Fall River Press.
Hagen, K. (n.d.). Confucian key terms: Dao, tian, li, yi, liyi, ren, zhi, junzi. Retrieved from http://faculty.plattsburgh.edu/kurtis.hagen/index.html
Slingerland, E. (2003). *Confucius Analects: With selections from traditional commentaries* (E. Slingerland, Trans.). Indianapolis: Hackett.
Van Norden, B. (2009). *The essential Mengzi: Selected passages with traditional commentary* (Abridged ed.). Indianapolis: Hackett.
Van Norden, B. (2011). *Introduction to classical Chinese philosophy*. Indianapolis: Hackett.
Yuen Ting Lee. (n.d.) Ban Zhao: Scholar of Han dynasty China. Retrieved from http://worldhistoryconnected.press.illinois.edu/9.1/lee.html
Wu, J. (1961). *Tao te ching: Lao Tzu*. New York: St. John's University Press.

2

Teaching Deliberation

Abandoning Aristotelian Persuasion and Embracing Confucian Remonstration

Arabella Lyon

After spending much of the 20th century on what Stephen Angle (2012) calls "life support," new philosophical and public movements in Asia are reviving Confucianism (p. 2). New Confucianism (*xīn rújiā* 新儒家) has evolved and grown over the last 30 years, first as academic analysis, then as political discourse (Angle 2012; Bell 2008; Chan 2014). In no small part, its rapid recovery is facilitated by the breadth and intensity with which the Confucian tradition informs East Asian cultures. During its 2,500-year history, Confucianism has had many manifestations and implications in endeavors, including the ethical, educational, philosophical, social, rhetorical, and political, which remain evident and relevant. Rather than focus on its contemporary practices, compelling as they are, in this chapter, Confucianism is seen as an ideal set of standards serving as a critical lens for analyzing contemporary practices in U.S. education; this approach is in keeping with that of Joseph Chan (2014), who argues that his scholarship is dependent on a critical reconstruction of Confucian ideas and who uses Confucian ideals as a standard for assessing existing practices. My reconstruction of a Confucian theory of deliberation or decision making can be seen (1) as an interpretive guide to political and rhetorical engagement, one significant for understanding and participating in decision making in a globalized world, and (2) as a critical approach or speculative instrument for examining the assumptions of the Common Core State Standards (CCSS, the Common Core).

In offering a Confucian approach to decision making, this chapter contributes to an understanding of political and rhetorical thought; however, more relevant to the purposes of *Confucianism Reconsidered: Insights for American and Chinese Education in the 21st Century*, Confucianism offers a contrastive approach to Western theories of communication as they appear in contemporary U.S. secondary education. Through understanding the significance of the Confucian tradition of communication in relationship to the focus of the CCSS, educators might use Confucianism as a critical lens to assess the Common Core's commitment to increasing the capacity of students "to understand other perspectives and cultures through reading and listening" and "to communicate effectively with people of varied backgrounds" (2010, p. 7). Although the commitment to cross-cultural engagement is admirable, cross-cultural communication is complex, easier to list as a learning outcome than to achieve. In developing the differences between Western traditions of argumentation through persuasion and Confucian remonstration, this chapter attends to key limitations of the CCSS: its focus on one culture's theory of communication, one that emphasizes decision making based in reason and structure, not relationship.

Common Core State Standards

As arguably the most encompassing educational reform in U.S. history, CCSS intends to prepare students for college, work, and critical citizenry in the 21st century, and it proposes to do this in no small part by increasing emphasis on writing and textual production (Applebee, 2013; Calkins, Ehrenworth, & Lehman, 2012). In English Language Arts, through requiring *speaking* and *writing* in full partnership with listening and reading, CCSS stresses the teaching of textual production and increases the requirement of student writing: "The standards' focus on evidence-based argument along with the ability to inform and persuade is a significant shift from current practice" (http://www.corestandards.org/other-resources/key-shifts-in-english-language-arts). To achieve the shift in pedagogical practices, CCSS emphasizes the development of three particular forms of writing: narrative, informational or explanatory writing, and argumentation. In Appendix A, which has an entire section devoted to "The Special Place of Argument in the Standards," it is made clear that argumentation is the principle form of writing:

> While all three text types are important, the Standards put particular emphasis on the students' ability to write sound arguments on substantive topics and issues as this ability is critical to college and career readiness. (CCSS, 2010, p. 24)

Argumentation is defined as "a reasoned, logical way of demonstrating that the writer's position, belief, or conclusion is valid" (23). In its emphasis on argumentation, the Common Core recognizes the place of persuasion (Hackney & Newman, 2013). Persuasive argument, basic to democratic practices since Aristotle's *Rhetoric*, traditionally comprises emotion and the speaker's character as well as logic. Although the Common Core stresses the logical aspects of argument, it recognizes that persuasion underlies language. Even informational writing requires the foregrounding of key concepts, in effect creating a worldview through organization and so engaging and moving others to share that view of information.

Given the scope of its proposed changes, the Common Core has been copiously praised and criticized. Among the most prevalent criticisms are concerns about the variation in teachers' beliefs about writing and writing instruction, their inadequate preparation to teach new forms of writing, an inadequate developmental theory of writing, and the lack of availability of clear, research-based materials to support increased writing instruction (Applebee, 2013; Troia & Olinghouse, 2013; Whitney & Shannon, 2014). As well, the focus on argumentation as preparation for career and college readiness has frustrated some K–12 educators who value either more personal forms or writing to learn projects (Calkins, Ehrenworth, & Lehman, 2012). The sudden expectation of evidence-based, reasoned argumentation produces a sudden increase in the complexity of many high school curricula. On the other hand, many university faculty are pleased by an argument-based preparation of high school students, imagining that it will provide a common platform of knowledge from which first-year writing syllabi can build (Conley et al., 2011; Jones & King, 2012). If freshmen arrive at the university able to write evidence-based arguments, then writing in the university might proceed quickly to engage the methods, discourses, and genres appropriate to students' disciplines.

This chapter examines the limitations of the Common Core's emphasis on formulating reasoned arguments, advocating, in fact, for more complexity at this critical juncture. Reasoned, evidence-based argumentation does not sufficiently represent a sophisticated understanding of communication, decision making, and civic engagement. At best, in CCSS discussions, argumentation is imagined in a constrained, Enlightenment-era focus on reason, but, at the worst, argumentation is presented as a universal pattern, a prescribed organization or genre, or a continuation of the inert, five-paragraph structure (Monte-Sano, de La Paz, & Felton, 2014; Wolpert-Gawron, 2014). Although there may be pedagogical reasons for the limited definition of argumentation—that is, the teaching of writing may require a sequencing of assignments, a layering of skills, or a developmental approach—the argumentative focus of the Common Core does not teach decision making as negotiation between respectful parties. In its emphasis on an individual's reason and the persuasive force of evidence, the Common Core locates deliberation or decision making in the Western tradition of argumentation and persuasion. Consequently, the Common Core emphasizes persuasion and the power of the author to create an argument that convinces any reader, and, in so doing, it emphasizes consensus and community as individually driven.

Despite great progress in emphasizing textual production and the value of contemporary writing pedagogy, the Writing Standards are formulaic in ways that are of limited use for citizens negotiating the complexities of contemporary multiculturalism. Reason, persuasion, and argumentation, which so dominate the Western rhetorical tradition, have been regularly critiqued as potential tools of oppression (Foss & Griffin, 1995; Katz, 1992; Lyon, 2013); they are only one set of lenses for understanding deliberation. Other traditions of deliberation do not focus formalistically on strategy and textual structure, but rather imagine different types of relationships among interlocutors. Even in classical Athens, deliberation can be imagined differently, as evidenced in the relational, audience-driven dialogues of Plato and Sophocles. Instead of rehearsing competing strands of Western rhetoric, this chapter examines the concept of remonstration (*jiàn* 谏) in the Confucian tradition, arguing that it has the advantage of respecting the audience, building trusting relationships, and engaging the social order in ways that are not driven by individual desires. It is safe to say that the CCSS will not turn to Confucians for a theory of communication, but the Confucian concept of remonstration provides a telling critique of the formulaic, argumentative, audience-bare model of writing that it offers.

Confucian Remonstration

Centuries before the Greeks, Chinese scholars considered civic questions about communication: How does one communicate within a good state? By what discursive means are a people led? They did not answer these questions in solitude, but responded to earlier thought and competing theorists, soliciting the support of particular rulers in a variety of ways (Goldin, 2005; Lyon, 2010; Mao, 2010). Despite the diversity of answers within Chinese classics, without overly generalizing, one can argue that early Chinese political and rhetorical thinking was characterized by the demands of an authoritarian state and communitarian values. These characteristics worked to orient political communication away from fantasies of persuasive powerful speakers and the control of reason. With rare exception, such as the *Hanfeizi* and the *Guiguzi*, classical Chinese thinking eschews persuasion and argument as dangerous and inappropriate to human relationships.[1] Persuasion and success-driven argumentation were often regarded as inept discursive strategies (Lyon, 2004). Instead, a good advisor speaks to others with respect for their mutual positions and the needs of the community.

To constrain the inquiry into the Confucian tradition of communication, the chapter focuses on the *Lunyu* (论语) or the *Analects*, a set of dialogues and assertions presented in small excerpts, composed and layered between 479 and 249 BCE. Written three centuries after the death of Confucius (Kongzi), it advocates remonstrating, as oppose to persuading, within a relationship of trust (3.21, 4.18, 18.1, 18.5, 19.10). Though persuasion and political change may be an effect of remonstration, they should not be seen as necessary or even positive effects, as they may disrupt stability. In the Confucian tradition, the audience, often a superior, is recognized as powerful as well as logical and perceptive. The rhetor (writer or speaker) does not, in fact cannot, assume control of the situation or outcome. Confucian communication begins with recognizing the other's position and commitment to the validity of his or her worldview. In recognition of the power of the other, Confucian communicators seek the appropriate level of responsiveness between interlocutors. Rather than actively pursuing means, ends, or futures strategically, rather than rushing to a persuasive precipice, Confucian rhetors imagine communitarian agency contained and restrained by cultural authorities, rites, and traditions. This worldview is not irrelevant to contemporary writing situations. Many situations value community building and are hierarchical, for example, the workplace, which so prominently informs the Common Core's purposes. Unlike argumentative, evidence-driven writers in the Common Core, in the *Analects*, communicators should be both slow to speak and relenting in attempts to engage or convince another (see 4.24, 4.26, 12.23, 12.3). The communicative act is an opening of the undecided and uncontrolled future to mutual consideration by interlocutors.

The denotations and connotations of the words "persuasion" (*shuì* 說) and "remonstration" (*jiàn* 谏) construct very different rhetorical situations and relationships between interlocutors. Examination of the linguistic roots of persuasion and remonstration reveals their core difference. *Per* and *suadere* together imply a bringing *through by speech*. *Monstrare*, however, emphasizes the act of showing or demonstrating. Persuasion may be an effect of demonstration, but it need not be, and consequently the audience's interpretative skills and power of resistance are more prominently figured. An audience sees or hears the act or demonstration, and, based on their assessment, they respond. Remonstration evades defining explicit power differences between the speaker and the listener in the service of developing communitarian values.

One can push this difference of linguistic roots further with some basic tools of ordinary language philosophy. Building on insights in Aristotle's *Metaphysics*, Gilbert Ryle (1954, pp. 102–109) discusses the difference between verbs of terminus and process verbs. Process verbs, like "seek," describe ongoing action. On the other hand, terminus verbs, like "find," declare an end. "Remonstrate" is a process verb, lacking a telos. "Persuade" is a terminus verb. If I say, "I persuaded them that . . . ," there has been an end. The act of persuasion rarely occurs in the present tense as an ongoing process. It is unusual to say "I am persuading them"; one can imagine the context for this, but it is unusual. Almost always when one speaks of persuading, there has been a change in him, and the act of persuading is ended. In fact, if we think of this in temporal terms, the future and the past are the realms of persuasion: "I will persuade you" or "I persuaded you." This is all less true of remonstrate, which even lacks the grammatical object, a person to be moved. If I say, "I remonstrate that . . . ," it is less clear that there has been an end, what would constitute an end, who would judge an end. Simply, the rhetor stopped. Hence, the ending of an act of remonstration is very different from the ending of an act of persuasion. In remonstrating, one can run out of time, energy, or materials, but otherwise one can continue the performance, always in the present. In persuading, one has a temporal progression, a narrative from a strategic beginning to an end marked by a change in the audience, reflecting a change in the human realm. The rhetor may do most of the action, but the end is changing an audience. With remonstration, the effect is less clear and unnecessary for judging the speech act: The speaker will do all the identified action. The end is when the demonstration finishes, the moment the show stops, rather than when an audience changes, jointly decides, or enacts an event. Although an audience is implied in remonstration, there is neither defined manipulation nor argument. The remonstrator simply shows something. Those who observe the performance are free to interpret it, heed it, repeat it, ignore it, or refute it.

One can see how respect and the desire for relationship are evident in the *Analects*. Using the family as a model of healthy interaction and decision making as well as a model for relationships in a healthy city-state, Confucius advises his followers, "In serving your father and mother, remonstrate with them gently. On seeing that they do not heed your suggestions, remain respectful and do not act contrary. Although concerned, voice no resentment" (4.18).[2] In this passage, there is no sense of the Common Core's definition of argument as reason, evidence, with a nod to the counterargument. Yes, it is possible that the remonstrator uses evidence and reason, but the primary desire of remonstration is not persuasion and conversion. More important than effect or outcome is the continuation of a respectful relationship. The child who remonstrates with the parent offers the errant parent a chance to find his or her potential while preserving the relationship between parent and child. Not only are both parties spared acts of aggression and disrespect, but the possibility of inappropriate action is curtailed by the gentility of the engagement. Furthermore, if the child cannot move the parents, at least his or her own integrity and moral worth are preserved. Successful communication is assessed not by moving an audience or in compiling evidence, but in ethical values and preserved relationships.

Passages 18.1 and 19.10 more clearly demonstrate the political nature of remonstration, which is sometimes hard to see in the interpersonal dialogues of the *Analects*. Passage 18.1 notes the execution of Bi Gan for remonstrating with the evil Shang ruler Zhou, a useful note for understanding that remonstration, like persuasion, can be a dangerous act; the consequences of overstepping political boundaries are fully acknowledged. A rhetor may be killed by the values espoused. In contrast to the dire warning of failure, in 19.10, Zixia, one of Confucius's more scholarly disciples, addresses the role of an exemplary minister, defining the nature of relationships with people above and below him in a political hierarchy:

> Only once exemplary persons (*junzi* 君子) have won the confidence (*xin* 信) of the common people do they work them hard; otherwise, the people would think themselves exploited. Only once they have won the confidence of their lord do they remonstrate with him; otherwise, their lord would think himself maligned.

In this passage, leadership is closely tied to an ongoing, respectful relationship. In a Confucian approach to decision making, an exemplary person's character proven over time supersedes the requirement of evidence or reason. In contrast to evidence, reason, or winning an argument, the role of confidence or trust is the primary concern. Of particular note in this passage, it is equally important to have the confidence of the common people and the lord. Although Confucianism is often criticized as rigidly hierarchical, the nature of the hierarchy is complex in its interdependence. Hence, inherent in 19.10's parallel structure is a paradoxical sense of equality within the hierarchy of the state. The minister, balanced between the lord and commoners, owes each a consistent commitment, one worthy of confidence.

The Confucian rhetor respects audiences. In the *Analects*, one should be slow to speak and be relenting in attempts to engage or convince another (see 4.24, 4.26, 12.23, 12.3). With such a diminished place for speaking and persuasion, Confucian rhetoric has a very different speaker-audience relationship than Aristotelian rhetoric or the Core's insistence on argument. Despite the intimacy and importance of harmony implied in self-in-relationship, there is little sense that one *must* reach a consensus; Confucius observes, "people who have chosen different ways cannot make plans together" (15.40). While one's consciousness and subject-position are defined in relationship, one follows one's own path without direct responsibility for or control over the actions of others. One does not fashion the way, but follows the Way, perhaps enlarges the Way. Unlike the Common Core's model, order is aesthetic and relational rather than reasoned, and so social order is modeled on an interrelationship of human and nature (*tian*), not on autonomous human construction. More significantly, remonstration recognizes the place of disagreement and protest in a frame other than division, argument, and counterclaim. It presents remonstration as a part of self-cultivation; one must preserve values and care enough for others that they can cultivate their own way, that they can "realize it" (8.9).

Diminishing persuasion and argument, Confucian communication expands the significance of human recognition within deliberation, considering its hierarchies, difficulties, and ethical implications more robustly than Aristotle's focus on the speaker and audience, and certainly more robustly than the Common Core's emphasis on evidence and prescriptions of argumentative form. In part because the Confucian tradition values engagement over argumentation and persuasion, the nature of political utterance is more tied to relationships and community (Lyon, 2004). In remonstration, in the demonstrating or performing of the best course of action, every speech act entails the speaker's offer to make good on its meaning, and every true understanding implies an interlocutor's acceptance of the offer of meaning. Understanding does not mean that the decision is made through the power of the rhetor, but that interlocutors share sufficient meaning that a decision is possible. The emphasis is not on the decision, but on the potential for ongoing understanding and meaning making, what philosophers might call a shared lifeworld. Evidence-based remonstration that results in a decision or an action is certainly a possibility, but the engagement is more important than the evidence or the outcome; the process is more formative of decisions and actions than the product.

It is important to note three potential criticisms of remonstration as a model of deliberation and a genre of writing. The act of remonstration itself might seem as bare of the requirement of dialogue, as is the Common Core with its emphasis on an individual's compilation of reason and evidence. Therefore, one might imagine remonstration as solipsistic, isolating, and bare of recognition, too. Remonstration, however, does not serve the individual. Instead, remonstration aims to keep a community engaged in ongoing communication. If argumentation with its claim and counterclaim seemingly promises engagement with the Other, the sense of winning inherent in argument and persuasion diminishes the engagement. Winning an argument presumes a zero-sum game and an end point. In the broader frame of Confucian political theory and communitarian agency, individuation is not the purpose of action. The purpose of an act of remonstration is cultivating good character and good relationships in ways that are communitarian and communicative (13.18).

Another critique of remonstration: Confucian concern with family and state hierarchies initially may be seen as inappropriate for democratic, civic engagements. Clearly, the acceptance of power differentials is at odds with modernist theories of politics, and, given our democratic history, U.S. students have developed a healthy appreciation of the concept of equality among citizens. The critique of Confucian hierarchy, however, ignores Confucian respect for all humans, both as lord and commoner. In addition to demanding that exemplary people have the confidence of all, the critique ignores the uncomfortable points that communication is rarely egalitarian or simply reciprocal and that hierarchy and inequality require acknowledgment in rhetorical situations. In acknowledging the hierarchy and thus the power of other people, including common people, remonstration values a hierarchy no more extreme than the family. The metaphor of the family underscores ongoing relationships and shared outcomes and imagines politics in a healthy state as intimate engagement, not adversarial wrangling. When the Common Core emphasizes evidence and reason as textual features, it omits the complexity of communicating with other people within the workplace, certainly a hierarchical place.

As well, remonstration may seem inappropriate for hostile or antagonistic engagements in that its valuing of both gentle words and respect is not appropriate to all rhetorical situations. If one does not have power and is politically oppressed, the desire for community and relationship in remonstration may require pathological self-sacrifice and ultimately be too conservative and even dangerous. In certain rhetorical and political situations, a rhetor may need alternative means, such as persuasion or even manipulation, to achieve justice. In turn, however, remonstration also demonstrates how persuasion, reason, and evidenced-based argumentation are not appropriate to all rhetorical situations. In the end, respectful, ongoing relationships may be the most important tool for change. Finally, in refusing persuasion's clear ending point, remonstration instead may offer a realistic timeline to resolution of complex issues. Injustice rarely resolves quickly. In a globalized era, a wise rhetor needs more than one strategy for addressing others and recognizing alternative cultures of communication. Real-life deliberation is more nuanced than the "Gun Control: Yes or No" arguments that many students write.

In closing, I must note that it is *possible* to affiliate aspects of the Common Core's model of argumentation with aspects of remonstration.

This does not mean that they are the same or have similar trajectories, but it does suggest that, with some tweaking, a smart educator could use the concept of remonstration to critique argumentation, the limitations of reason, and the overdependence on any single strategy of decision making. That is, culturally and conceptually different theories of communication can be and should be placed in productive dialogue. Together they can be used to develop an approach to decision making that is not based in argumentation, counterargument, and evidence.[2]

Conclusion

In her essay "Rhetoric, Deliberation, and Democracy in an Era of Standards," Amy J. Wan (2015) observes that "the CCSS, with their advocacy of 'critical thinking' and 'cogent reasoning skills,' seem to support intellectual struggle, deliberation, even democratic practices, as a goal" (p. 493). She laments the Common Core Standards' assessment by large-scale testing, but hopes that educators will find a way to support democratic and deliberative practices in their implementation. I share her hopes but worry that the Common Core fails to consider adequately the significance of an ongoing relationship with the audience, the demands of communication in a multicultural and globalized America, and the need for developing writers to understand argumentation as more than formulas of evidence and reason. In overly depending on the Enlightenment values of evidence and reason, the Common Core offers a writing pedagogy in which the writer crafts an argument without adequate concern for engaging another. Rather than imagine argumentation as a form of communication, the writer demonstrates her viewpoint as an exercise in valuing certain frames of evidence and reason. Generously, one might consider the framing of authorial knowledge as the first draft of an argument, but a robust consideration of the writing process would require student writers to consider their purposes in relationship to others.

Despite valuing students' need to formulate a position more than to engage an audience, the Common Core is not fatally flawed. Wise use of its process approach would allow a moment of revision in which a smart teacher might address the ethics of persuasion, deep respect for difference, the possibility that consensus is not possible or desirable, and the need to preserve relationships so that the discussion can begin or continue. That is, before an audience is imagined or addressed, once a reasonable position is formulated, student writers would benefit from a discussion of community, dialogue, and harmonious relationship. Before the audience is engaged, student writers might analyze the place of recognition, responsiveness, and responsibility in communication and revise their writing appropriately.

An ideal of Confucian communication, remonstration provides a critique of argumentation driven by end points and winning. Remonstration, as the alternative that both emphasizes engagement and values difference, demonstrates the limitations of how U.S. students are taught to deliberate and reflect on their ideas and commitments. In the new bounty of textual production, educators must continue to consider what kinds of texts are produced and for what purposes. A new emphasis on writing will require teachers to develop complex theories and models of writing. The Common Core is a shift in thinking about the nature of English Language Arts, and that shift has significant, ongoing implications that will lead to extensions. Although the Common Core develops an appropriate trajectory of writing instruction in K–12 (from opinion toward claim and evidence), the progression ends too soon, leaving students without either education in audience awareness or an adequate understanding of response and responsibility within deliberative acts. Ideally, high school instruction would supplement these omissions in ways that prepare students for writing in college and career.

Notes

1. *Hanfeizi* addresses persuasion explicitly, though as a very dangerous undertaking. See Lyon (2008). *Guiguzi* was less influential; see Michael Robert Broschat (1985) for a translation and discussion.

2. Direct quotations of the *Analects* in this chapter are from Ames & Rosemont, 1999.

3. Discussing individual pieces of U.S. and Chinese writing is beyond the scope of this chapter. Xiaoye You (2008) provides discussions of the complexity of teaching English writing to Chinese speakers.

References

Ames, R., & Rosemont, H., Jr. (1999). *The Analects of Confucius: A philosophical translation.* New York: Ballantine Books.

Angle, S. C. (2012). *Contemporary Confucian political philosophy*. Boston: Polity.
Applebee, A. N. (2013). Common Core State Standards: The promise and the peril in a national palimpsest. *English Journal*, 103(1), 25–33.
Bell, D. A. (2008). *China's new Confucianism: Politics and everyday life in a changing society*. Princeton: Princeton University Press.
Broschat, M. R. (1985). "Guiguzi": A textual study and translation (Doctoral dissertation). University of Washington. Retrieved from https://digital.lib.washington.edu/researchworks/handle/1773/15506
Calkins, L., Ehrenworth, M., & Lehman, C. (2012). *Pathways to the Common Core: Accelerating achievement*. Portsmouth, NH: Heinemann.
Chan, J. (2014). *Confucian perfectionism: A political philosophy for modern times*. Princeton: Princeton University Press.
Common Core State Standards. (2010). http://www.corestandards.org
Conley, D. T., Drummond, K., de Gonzalez, A., Rooseboom, J., & Stout, O. (2011). Reaching the goal: The applicability and importance of the Common Core State Standards to college and career readiness. Eugene: Educational Policy Improvement Center. Retrieved from http://www.epiconline.org/publications/documents/ReachingtheGoal-FullReport.pdf
Foss, S. K., & Griffin, C. L. (1995). Beyond persuasion: A proposal for an invitational rhetoric. *Communication Monographs*, 62, 2–18.
Goldin, P. R. (2005). *After Confucius: Studies in early Chinese philosophy*. Honolulu: University of Hawaii Press.
Hackney, S., & Newman, B. (2013). Using the rhetorical situation to inform literacy instruction and assessment across the disciplines. *English Journal*, 103(1), 60–65.
Han Fei. (1963). *Basic writing of Han Fei Tzu* (B. Watson, Trans.). New York: Columbia University Press.
Jones, A. G., & King, J. E. (2012). The Common Core State Standards: A vital tool for higher education. *Change: The Magazine of Higher Learning*, 44(6), 37–43.
Katz, S. (1992). The ethics of expediency: classical rhetoric, technology, and the holocaust. *College English*, 54(3), 255–275.
Lyon, A. (2004). Confucian silence and remonstration: A basis for deliberation. In C. S. Lipson & R. A. Binkley (Eds.), *Rhetoric before and beyond the Greeks* (pp. 131–145). Albany: State University of New York Press.
Lyon, A. (2008). Rhetorical authority in Athenian democracy and the Chinese legalism of Han Fei. *Philosophy and Rhetoric*, 41(1), 51–71.
Lyon, A. (2010). Writing an empire: Cross-talk on authority, act, and relationships with the other in the *Analects*, *Daodejing*, and *Hanfeizi*. *College English*, 72(4), 350–366.
Lyon, A. (2013). *Deliberative acts: Democracy, rhetoric, and rights*. University Park: Pennsylvania University Press.

Mao, L. (2010). Searching for the Way: Between the what's and the where's of Chinese rhetoric. *College English, 72*(4), 329–349.

Monte-Sano, C., de La Paz, S., & Felton, M. (2014). *Reading, thinking, and writing about history: Teaching argument writing to diverse learners in the Common Core, grades 6–12.* New York: Teachers College Press.

Ryle, G. (1954). *Dilemmas.* New York: Cambridge University Press.

Troia, G. A., & Olinghouse, N. G. (2013). The Common Core State Standards and evidence-based educational practices: The case of writing. *School Psychology Review, 42*(3), 343–357.

Wan, A. J. (2015). Rhetoric, deliberation, and democracy in an era of standards. *College English, 77*(5), 480–494.

Whitney, A., & Shannon, P. (2014). Metaphors, frames, and fact (checks) about the Common Core. *English Journal, 104*(2), 61–71.

Wolpert-Gawron, H. (2014). *Writing behind every door: Teaching Common Core writing in the content areas.* Hoboken: Taylor and Francis.

You, X. (2008). Rhetorical strategies, electronic media, and China English. *World Englishes, 27*(2), 233–249.

3

Confucian Educational Thought

*Enlightenment and Value for
Contemporary Education in China*

FANGPING CHENG

Over the past century and a half, China has been learning a lot about developing modern education from Western countries, which has resulted in comprehensive progress in educational ideology, systems, methods, techniques, and content in China. Meanwhile, China's contemporary educational practices have proven that duplication of the modern Western models cannot meet all its specific needs across the educational spectrum. In contrast with the limitations and problems associated with Western models in dealing with cultural conflict, social development, and educational reforms, Oriental traditions, especially Chinese traditions in education, show increasing value inside China. This chapter first reviews the process of reviving Confucian ideas in China, then presents a list of important Confucian ideas highly relevant to today's Chinese education, and finally discusses how Confucian ideas may provide solutions to some major problems facing today's Chinese educators.

Revival of Confucian Traditions in China

Ever since the mid-19th century, when the Western powers gained footholds in China, Chinese culture and education began to change in content, form, and system toward greater westernization. Even while seeking national independence and liberation, many Chinese fetishistically worshiped Western culture and education while irrationally denying or rejecting even the best Chinese cultural and educational traditions. At the end of the Great Cultural Revolution, Chinese scholars and researchers lagged far behind their foreign counterparts in Chinese studies in research of Chinese traditions.

It was not until the end of the 1980s that Chinese scholars began to rethink these issues, and their reflections were prompted by a few sociocultural conditions. First, after the Great Cultural Revolution ended, the country's orientation toward development became the focus of public concern, and how to make traditional heritage relevant to the present during a wave of learning from foreign experience also drew the widespread attention of academic circles and society at large. Second, China's neighboring countries, such as Singapore, Japan, and Korea, which historically belonged to the Confucian Cultural Circles of East Asia, did not abandon their cultural traditions on the road to modernization, but carried forward the excellent traditions to realize harmonious and stable social development. Third, according to some independent-minded Chinese scholars, China had many special cultural and social features, and the inheritance of excellent traditions could contribute to a better understanding and adaptation of these unique features, which in turn could facilitate China's modernization while maintaining Chinese characteristics and advantages.

In its course of ideological emancipation and economic reforms, there are many events that represent practical breakthroughs. For example, Xing Bensi (1978) published an article titled "Practice: Criterion for Testing Truth," which broke the rigid mode of thinking after the Great Cultural Revolution. In his article "Shed some light on 'the Doctrine of the Mean' (Zhongyong)," Pang Pu (1981) provided a thorough and in-depth introduction to and analysis of dialectical thought in Confucian traditions. With the joint efforts of Liang Shuming, Feng Youlan, and other famous Chinese and foreign scholars, Tang Yijie established the Academy of Chinese Culture at Peking University to give lectures on integrating Chinese traditional culture with the influx of foreign ideas. This has had far-reaching influence within cultural and educational circles in China. Meanwhile, universities and colleges also offered relevant specialties and courses on Chinese cultural traditions, involving the histories of Chinese education, culture, science and technology, philosophy, legislation, management, psychology, religion, ethnic issues, examinations, character, cultural exchange, and so on, and corresponding studies in these fields yielded fruitful results.

However, the policy of openness to the outside world and a lopsided understanding of Chinese traditions made China's cultural and educational reforms focus on foreign models after 1978. For example, of the 220,000 published books, including 130,000 new books, a considerable proportion were introduced from abroad or written about foreign countries. More than half of the 112,000 papers and articles published by universities, colleges, and research institutions in 2008 were about foreign problems or based on foreign theories. Obviously, the loss of research on China was very serious at that time.

After China joined the World Trade Organization (WTO) in 2000, other countries' practice of preserving their cultural traditions during internationalization made China further realize that the preservation of a country's cultural and educational traditions is a crucial principle in the drive to reform and develop. In an integrated world, if a nation has no cultural and educational traditions of its own, it simply means that that nation has lost its cultural value. Hence, bottom-up efforts to strengthen concern about traditional culture were started in China by some civil groups, followed by schools and government organizations. After 2000, one-third of schools reinforced their study of Chinese traditional culture. Renmin University of China and other institutions of higher learning set up academies of Chinese studies and integrated the specialties, courses, and research related to Chinese traditional culture. Even in the development of emerging cultural industries, the promotion of Chinese elements was emphasized. In 2006, the government of Jining City, Shandong Province, made an application to and was offered a fund by UNESCO for setting up a Confucius Education Award to recognize those institutions, organizations, and individuals for their contributions to literacy education, education for all, and teacher training throughout the world. In April 2014, the Ministry of Education of China issued the Guiding Outline for Improving Education of Excellent Chinese Traditional Culture, cultivating Chinese characteristics in education and supporting educational advances nourished specifically by traditional Chinese culture.

During my last 41 years of study on education theories and practices in China, I have not only acquired general knowledge of educational traditions and philosophies in the West, but I have also closely examined the history and real problems related to education in China during the Sui and Tang dynasties; the Five Dynasties period; and the Liao, Jin, and

Yuan dynasties, which made me appreciate the everlasting importance of Chinese traditional culture.[1] Moreover, my past experience in establishing private schools and education institutes reveals the limitations of one system and one set of values, and thus the necessity of an open mind in thinking, self-reliant consciousness in research, and independence in decision making.

Main Contents and Contemporary Value of Confucian Educational Thought

For more than 2,000 years, Confucian thought occupied a dominant and leading position in the history of China. Because of the continuous integration of advanced cultures from abroad, the connotation and methods of Confucian culture were enriched, and the content was expanded and developed as time progressed. For example, the well-known book *Answers to Questions about Bibliography*, written by the famous educational reformer Zhang Zhidong in the late Qing dynasty, involved not only the traditional classics of Confucian doctrine, but also other theories of the Taoist, Legalist, Mohist, and Yin-Yang schools; military strategies and agricultural science; the religions of Buddhism, Islam, Christianity, and folk religions; and knowledge concerning mathematics, calligraphy, astronomy, astrology, medicine, construction, smelting, casting, agriculture, forestry, transportation, and geographical science. In those academies of Chinese studies at that time, students could learn about Western science and technology and attend the lectures given by both Chinese and foreign teachers. Such a spirit of inclusivity, which reflects the key connotations of the Confucian educational tradition and ideology, was later adopted by President Cai Yuanpei of Peking University as the basic principle and aim of Chinese cultural education.

Many scholars in the West and quite a few in the East and in China hold the view that Confucianism is an outdated school of thought that serves dictators, butchers individualism, smothers democracy, and upholds hierarchy because Confucianism has been used as the predominate ruling philosophy by monarchs since the Han dynasty. However, Confucianism is in fact a school of thought that balances dictatorship and democracy. For example, the principle of "loyalty to the sovereign" does not advocate an absolute obedience to the monarch. In fact, it justifies the legitimacy of the people's rebellion against the monarch and the establishment of a new dynasty if the monarch does not love or respect people.[2] That explains why the *Mencius* and other Confucian classics dotted with democratic advocacy were held as disrespectful of the monarchy and were excluded from the orthodox education system. The importance of hierarchy is also upheld by Confucianism. Confucianism believes that hierarchy serves as a necessary motivation for a man to rise rather than a standard to diminish or deny one's value. Wang Tong, a Confucian scholar in the Sui dynasty, once said that a man's worthiness does not grow with his seniority, nor does the truth come with his social rank.[3] The essence of many Confucian classics, such as the *Book of Changes, Analects of Confucius, Mencius, Doctrine of the Mean,* and *The Great Learning,* among others, can be traced back to his philosophy.

Throughout China's long history, enlightened emperors, virtuous ministers, and upright scholars, such as Emperor Tangtaizong, Tao Yuanming, Wei Zheng, Li Bai, Su Shi, and Bao Zheng, are respected and loved; on the other hand, tyrants, corrupted ministers, and spineless intellectuals, such as King Zhouwang of Shang, first emperor of Qin; Emperor Yang of Sui; and He Shen are despised and abandoned. Confucianism has consistently served as the standard for morality. China's traditional ruling system and code of ethics rely not only on strict discipline, but also on the coordination of law, protocol, and morality. Thus, a society that encourages fairness and creativity is forged, promoting both the progress of China's history as well as the cultivation of social talents.

Love, peace, development, and common prosperity are the core of Confucian educational thought. As the founder of Confucianism, not only was Confucius a famous politician, thinker, and philosopher, but he also was a world-renowned educational theorist. He keenly understood that the task of realizing human beings' good wishes must be based on cultivating and educating younger generations to become talented people with lofty ideals, a sense of responsibility, morality, capability, and wisdom. On this basis, Confucius himself, Confucian scholars, and educational theorists in later dynasties worked to develop the basic objective laws of teaching and educating people, and they accumulated rich and forward-looking results in such fields as the theory of learning, pedagogy, educational diversification, informal education, lifelong education, development of teaching materials, training of thinking, development of a learning-based society, and social education.

A review of the current most representative educational thought with the most universal value indicates that we find important references for all of them from the traditional thought and practice of Confucius and Confucian education:

1. Education for all, compulsory education, popularization of education, education equality (全民教育、义务教育、普及教育和人人平等)
   Provide education for all people without discrimination (*Analects of Confucius*); everyone can become Yao and Shun (*The Works of Mencius*)
   有教无类《论语》
   人人可以为尧舜《孟子》

2. Multiple intelligence and personalized education (多元智能和个性化教育)
   Teach students in accordance with their aptitude (*Analects of Confucius*); everyone has shortcomings and merits; a prodigal who returns is more precious than gold
   因材施教《论语》
   尺有所短寸有所长、浪子回头金不换 (俗语)

3. Cooperative learning, group learning, learning community (合作学习、小组学习、学习共同体)
   There is always someone to learn from; studying alone without friends makes one ill-informed and ignorant (*Analects of Confucius*).
   三人行必有我师；独学无友孤陋寡闻《论语》
   三个臭皮匠赛过诸葛亮 (俗语)

4. Learning to learn, teaching method (学会学习、教授方法).
   Tao, the truth, imitates Nature; give a man a fish and you feed him for a day, but teach a man to fish and you feed him for a lifetime (Lao Tzu).
   There are no fixed methods (Diamond Sutra); teachers are those who could propagate the doctrine, impart professional knowledge, and resolve doubts (*On Teaching*).
   道法自然，授人以鱼不如授人以渔《老子》
   法无定法《金刚经》；师者，传道、授业、解惑《师说》

5. Teacher development and relative teacher-student relationship (教师发展与相对的师生关系).
   To teach is to learn. Those who learn know their own deficiencies; those who teach know the difficulties of learning (*The Subject of Education*).
   Where there is the truth, there is a teacher. A teacher is not necessarily more virtuous and talented than his or her students, nor is a student necessarily inferior to his or her teacher (*On the Teacher*).
   教学相长,学然后知不足教然后知困《学记》
   道之所存、师之所存,师不必贤于弟,弟子不必不如师《师说》

6. Broaden horizons, enhance thinking, and integrate theory with practice (开阔视野、善于思考、理论联系实际).
   Study extensively, inquire prudently, think carefully, distinguish clearly, and practice earnestly (*Doctrine of the Mean*).
   Knowledge and action should go hand in hand (*Instructions for Practical Living*).
   博学之、审问之、慎思之、明辨之、笃行之《中庸》
   知行合一《传习录》

7. Comprehensive talent evaluation (综合全面的人才评价).
   Appoint people according to their merits (*Book of History*).
   Serve as a model (*Analects of Confucius*).
   Have both integrity and talent; in every trade, a master appears.
   任人唯贤《尚书》
   以身作则《论语》
   德才兼备、360 行行行出状元 (俗语)

8. Lifelong learning, informal education, and building a learning-based society. (终身学习、非正规教育与建设学习型社会)
   Life is short; learning is limitless (*Zhuangzi*).
   One is never too old to learn; cultivate knowledge to bequeath to the family.
   生也有涯,知也无涯《庄子》
   过到老学到老; 耕读传家 (俗语)

9. Social and environmental influences upon education (社会和环境影响教育).
   Human attributes are like silk. What is dyed in blue becomes blue, what is dyed in yellow becomes yellow (*Mozi*). Mencius's mother moved three times, an idiom that refers to the importance of finding the proper environment for raising children. Mencius's mother moved the household three times before finding a location that she felt was suitable for the child's upbringing (*The Works of Mencius*).
   When one is surrounded by the virtuous, one will become upright (*Xunzi*); use methods in line with local circumstances.
   人性如素丝, 染于苍则苍, 染于黄则黄《墨子》
   孟母三迁《孟子》
   蓬生麻间不扶自直《荀子》

10. Strengthening will and in-depth study (锻炼意志与深入钻研).
    The knight must be strong and bold; my way is that of an all-pervading unity (*Analects of Confucius*).
    His wisdom will not be far-reaching whose purpose is not firm (*Mozi*).
    Devote oneself heart and soul (*The Works of Mencius*).
    Patience wears out stones (*Xunzi*).
    士不可以不弘毅、吾道一以贯之《论语》
    志不强者智不达《墨子》
    专心致志《孟子》
    锲而不舍金石可镂《荀子》

11. Understanding and tolerance (理解与宽容).
    Do not do to others what you would not have them do to you (*Analects of Confucius*).
    Universal Love and Condemnation of War (*Mozi*).
    Combine Confucianism, Buddhism, and Taoism into one (*Wen Zhongzi*).
    The first concern is affairs of state, while enjoying pleasure comes later (*On Yueyang Tower*).

Be strict with oneself, but be lenient with others (*The Wisdom of Ancient Aphorisms*).
己所不欲勿施于人《论语》
兼爱非攻《墨子》
三教合一《文中子》
先天下之忧而忧，后天下之乐而乐《岳阳楼记》
严以律己宽以待人《增广贤文》

12. Advocating science-based spirit of exploration and independent thinking (崇尚探究和独立思考的科学精神).
    Do not decline to shoulder a responsibility; learning without thinking leads to confusion; thinking without learning ends in danger (*Analects of Confucius*).
    Believing everything in books is worse than having no books; all things under heaven are being prepared for me (*Works of Mencius*).
    Seeking the truth is based on modesty and deliberate thinking (*Zhuzi Yulei*).
    The space is my heart, and my heart is the space (*Lu Jiuyuan set*).
    Heart/mind is the ultimate source that encompasses the principle (*Instructions for Practical Living*).
    当仁不让、学而不思则罔思而不学则殆《论语》
    尽信书不如无书、万物皆备于我《孟子》
    穷理以虚心静虑为本《朱子语类》
    宇宙便是吾心，吾心便是宇宙《陆九渊集》
    心即理《传习录》

13. Multilevel learning activities can complement each other and help learners reach a free state (多层次的学习可相辅相成，最重要的是达到自由境地).
    Stick strictly to the Way, align with virtue and abide by benevolence in handing matters, and immerse in the arts (*Analects of Confucius*).
    The Dao is inaction. A man empties himself during his time in the world (*Zhuangzi*).
    志于道、据于德、依于仁、游于艺《论语》
    天道无为，虚己以游世《庄子》

14. Emphasizing cultivation of citizens' moral sense and involvement in social development (注重"公民"道德意识的培养,参与社会发展).
    The world is for all (*Liji*). The rise and fall of the nation is the concern of every citizen.
    天下为公《礼记》
    天下兴亡匹夫有责 (俗语)

15. Emphasizing the harmonious development of economy and society (强调经济和社会的和谐发展).
    A noble man makes his wealth in ethical means (*The Works of Mencius*).
    君子爱财取之以道《孟子》

16. Attaching importance to contracts, sincerity and dignity of laws (重视契约、诚信和法律的尊严).
    Goals will never be accomplished without honesty and faithfulness (*Mozi*).
    With fully actualized sincerity, you are like a god (*The Doctrine of the Mean*).
    The prince who breaks the law will be punished the same as the common people.
    言不信者行不果《墨子》
    至诚如神《中庸》
    王子犯法与民同罪 (俗语)

17. Emphasize self-discipline, consciousness, and self-improvement (强调自律、自觉、自强).
    Knowing shame is akin to courage, examining oneself daily leads to correction of faults and respect by others. (*Analects of Confucius*).
    Be cautious and self-disciplined (*Great Learning*).
    知耻近乎勇,吾日三省吾身,若能改过人皆仰之《论语》
    慎独《大学》

18. Lofty ideal and joint development (立志高远与共同发展).
    To completely overcome selfishness and maintain propriety is the essence of humanity. The noble man is in harmony but does not follow the crowd. Flexibility is important (*Analects of Confucius*).

Investigation of things, extension of knowledge, sincerity of the will, rectification of the mind, cultivation of the personal life, regulation of the family, national order, world peace (*Great Learning*).
克己复礼为仁，和而不同，和为贵《论语》
格物、致知、正义、诚心、修身、齐家、治国、平天下
《大学》

Please note that the English translations of the preceding Confucian thoughts are given here as approximations; they may not truly reflect their original Chinese meanings. Those phrases without sources are widespread ideas and concepts among the Chinese for thousands of years, and they reflect the basic ideas of Confucianism.

Whenever Chinese educators imported ideas and experience from abroad, traditional Confucian ideas and rich cases of their application in educational practice always served as localized references and inspiration for Chinese educators to pay due attention to the local characteristics of Chinese education and avoid the error of blind imitation and mechanical application of others' experience.[4] For example, China enjoys a very rich heritage of mathematical research and abundant experience in popularizing and teaching mathematics. In ancient Chinese private schools, a student could master basic math skills within three years and benefit for his or her whole life. Even today, Chinese math and methods can help learners deepen their understanding of the development of Chinese philosophical schools, such as the *Book of Changes, Yin-Yang Five Element Theory, Doctrine of the Mean*, Confucian theory, and Neo-Confucianism; and of Chinese science, technology, and medicine as well (Needham, 1965–1975). But, over the past 50 years, the traditional content and method of Chinese mathematics are overlooked in textbooks of mathematics for primary and secondary schools in China in favor of Western math education theories and approaches. A readjustment of math education appeared on the agenda only a few years ago as a result of the strong appeal made by Wu Wenjun, a renowned Chinese mathematician, and other scholars.[5]

Here lies another example. Howard Gardner from Harvard University pointed out repeatedly on several occasions that, to a considerable extent, he was inspired and influenced by the Confucian idea of teaching according to each student's aptitude when he developed his theory of multiple intelligences, which has provided important theoretical support for teachers and schools throughout the world to overcome the persistent problem of fossilized teaching. Moreover, Hu Shi, a famous scholar and educator in contemporary China, also attempted to determine a modified model of school education integrating the advanced points of the Western school education system with ancient Chinese private schools' tradition of teaching according to each student's aptitude. Obviously, the realization of the aforementioned ideas must be based on the joint efforts of education circles throughout the world when taking for reference the ideas and practical experience of Confucian theories of teaching according to each student's aptitude (Liu, 1982).

Compared with the typical and scaled education mode in modern Western countries, Chinese Confucian educational thought attends to students' independent learning instead of passive acceptance of the teacher's imparting of knowledge. Such a concept was fully reflected in the title of the first article of *Analects* 论语, "Learning First of the Analects of Confucius" (which implies that learning breeds many possibilities of personal development). The traditional Chinese teaching method of adapting to each student's aptitude also emphasizes that the teacher only guides the student to learn, but each student's aptitude will lead to certain development. Especially since 2000, the individual-oriented concept has been acknowledged in China, and one important aspect of education and teaching reforms in China over the past 20 years has been an emphasis on the student's autonomous learning. It was not the case before that; that is, the Chinese schools' overemphasis or limitation to teaching materials 20 years ago left almost no space for students' autonomous learning, expanded reading, and social practice.

As a nation that holds the code of ethics dear, China is famous for the principle of "equal stress on intelligence and virtue" when it comes to talent selection. Western scholars like Voltaire and Gottfried Wilhelm Leibniz all spoke very highly of this feature of the Chinese culture and education system, which indicates that Confucianism contributes a great deal to the establishment of universal human values (Cheng, 1984; Leibniz, 1697; Voltaire, 1963). But, ever since the 1980s, the shock of fast development in the market economy and the weak construction of the legal system have brought about many problems in the social and moral construction in China. Typically, moral education became knowledge-imparting and simple preaching. It could not play an active role in cultivating citizens' moral value and even resulted in serious negative impact. In this regard, it is of great necessity to start the reconstruction of moral education in China. Based on the study of Confucian moral education, Chinese scholars and educators found that such principles as keeping one's behavior exemplary, inferiors imitating their superiors, matching word to deed, taking responsibility, fulfilling commitments, making students completely convinced, and so on can serve as important guidance for overcoming the bad state of moral education in China. Traditional Confucian scholars believe that the cultivation of one's lofty ethics should begin with those small things of daily life and then link to people's perception and experience of life. Empty preaching and beautiful words without substantial content are harmful to the development of individual and social moral ethics. According to Confucian educational theory and experience, the role of moral ethics is truly important for society, but it alone is likely to lead to certain deviations, so moral education must be integrated with the legal system, improvement of the social system, and optimization of the social environment. At present, moral education in schools and social civilization construction in China are being reformed in many ways toward this orientation.

Since the 1980s, along with the ideological emancipation and economic reforms in China, most of the primary and secondary schools, and even universities, have restored and set their school mottoes to demonstrate their own features and goals. Confucian educational ideology constitutes the most important part of these school mottoes. For example, Tsinghua University's school motto of self-discipline and social commitment comes from the *Book of Changes*, joining and reflecting the philosophical spirit of ancient China and Chinese scholars' sense of social responsibility. This is also the case with school mottoes of many primary and secondary schools. Such Confucian ideas as the pursuit of truth, being pragmatic, advocating morality, a sense of responsibility, lofty ideals, harmony, and honesty, among others, are reflected in the school mottoes, which essentially express human beings' best wishes and expectations for students as future builders of the world. China's public and educational communities have realized that a nation with no respect for its traditions or reflections of its own culture can never achieve national self-consciousness and self-esteem in the world.

In the process of reemphasizing the value of Chinese traditional culture in China, problems with teaching materials, teachers' capacity, and talent structure have emerged; that is, there is a great shortage of teachers who are familiar with traditional Chinese culture and are capable of imparting such knowledge, and normal schools and teacher-training institutions do not offer special courses in this regard. In recent years, however, some social institutions and learned societies have undertaken efforts to change the situation. For example, Beijing Sichahai Academy began to offer special training courses on traditional Chinese culture for teachers, principals, and cultural scholars. Not only are famous scholars at home and abroad invited to give lectures, but printed and audiovisual teaching materials also are compiled. The Educational Research Institute of Beijing Haidian District also created an academy-style base for training teachers in traditional Chinese culture, an active exploration of the regression of traditional Chinese culture to school education. Meanwhile, many television stations also broadcast feature programs to introduce knowledge of traditional Chinese culture concerning the Classics, history, characters, literature, calligraphy, drama, poetry, medicine, food, clothing, architecture, military, laws, folk customs, religion, agriculture, mathematics, astronomy calendar, and traditional crafts, indicating that the value of traditional Chinese culture is being reemphasized by more and more Chinese people.

The task of restoring and adding traditional Chinese culture to the overwhelmed Chinese school curriculums is not merely a readjustment of teaching content and method, but rather a problem of idea change, cognition change, and improvement in educational thinking. The blind imitation of Western education models into the current Chinese education system seems an inappropriate solution to the problem. But it is obvious that the inheritance of the good elements of Confucian educational thought will broaden the vision of educational reform and development in China. In China, school education relies on teaching materials excessively, class activities follow the teaching syllabus too strictly, and examination-based evaluation overemphasizes memory ability. Under such circumstances, even the appropriate learning method and the application of new technology in education cannot improve the efficiency of school education, which makes it difficult to cultivate talent with moral ethics and professional capacity. If the traditional Confucian thought of open learning is adopted in education, teachers' improvement and students' autonomous learning can be given more space for free development.

Resembling the way that Westerners acknowledge Greek philosophers such as Socrates and Plato, Chinese scholars have not ignored the limitations of Confucianism while carrying forward its valuable tradition. As a matter of fact, the way forward is through renaissance, to draw benefits from the traditional culture to boost further culture development, so that the value of traditional Chinese culture can be brought to all Chinese and people around the world and the Chinese Method can shed a light on world education reform. During the past two centuries, Western scholars have solved many problems, such as modern diseases and social conflicts, through the efforts of "returning to tradition" and reflection on educational Perennialism in the face of Scientism, Data-ism, and the development of new technology with its impact on society (Lu, 2012). In so doing, they have also broadened the landscape of education reform. Likewise, today's education reform with reflection on tradition in China makes sense.

In recent years, some secondary schools in China have conducted extremely useful explorations of inheriting traditional culture. No. 2 Secondary School Affiliated to Beijing Normal University has opened experimental classes in traditional Chinese culture, in which teaching methods are modified and students are encouraged to have autonomous and cooperative learning. As a result, the graduates' knowledge of Chinese traditional culture has been greatly improved. For another example, Jimeijianzan (吉美坚赞), a Tibetan school in Yushu, Qinghai province, adopted the braid method of Tibetan Buddhism, such as arguing and explaining to each other, to help students have an overall improvement of their knowledge of Tibetan, Han (Mandarin), and English and successfully introduced such content as Tibetan medicine, Tibetan architecture, and Tibetan traditional painting into the school, which greatly heightened students' learning interest and efficiency.[6]

In the process of carrying forward tradition and enhancing local culture by the Chinese educational community, it becomes clear that, instead of blind imitation of others, educational advances in one region, one nation, and one country must respect the characteristics of its own language, tradition, and mind-set. Education reform must start from the objectives of education to identify the traditions that need to be adhered to, carried forward, and amended. Experiments based on real situations are needed to better serve the interests of the people. With vast regional differences and cultural diversity in China, Confucianism, as a school of thought emphasizing humanity, inclusiveness, systematization, and balance, can help the educational community break away from an outdated mindset and thus promote social advances and the process of education reform.

For example, since its full engagement with the world in 2000, China has started reflecting on its own traditional culture. Support for educational reform, such as delegation of power to lower levels, local legislation, diversified textbooks, and independent entrance examinations, has been enhanced under the guidance of a centralized administration. Best solutions in education, self-study, cooperation, and open-sourced reviews for specific regions and groups have been explored through regional experiments. In the future efforts of education reform, nongovernmental explorations are encouraged to strengthen the participation of civil society and industry so as to better understand learners' needs and thus establish a lifelong learning system. During China's recent education exchanges with the United States, United Kingdom, France, Germany, and Japan, China's methods and experiences in setting education standards; improving teachers' quality (mentor and workshop system); teaching mathematics, arts, family morality, and Chinese traditional techniques; building the Chinese way of thinking; and eliminating illiteracy in rural areas have increasingly attracted attention from around the world.

It can thus be seen that Confucian educational thought with great inclusiveness and openness can supplement and enrich the content of educational and teaching reforms in China, and the variety of practical methods of Confucian educational thought can also play a more direct and effective role in education. Therefore, Confucian educational thought not only has demonstrated high value in academic research, but also will play an increasingly important role in educational practice.

Notes

1. See the following works by Fangping Chen: Confucianism in Sui, Tang and Five dynasties; Education History in Liao, Jin and Yuan dynasties; The Evolution of Chinese Calligraphy; Evolution of China Education Reform; Teachers System in China and Other Countries, etc. (Eds.) Selected Translation of Western Works on Education; Western Works on Education in 1990s, etc.

2. See Mencius's *Study and Correction on Ten Doubtful Points about the Time of Zhen Guan Zheng Yao* (Wu, Jin, and Tang dynasties).

3. See Wang Tong, *Zhong Shuo* (On the Doctrine of the Mean) (Sui dynasty).

4. Seventy percent of modern Chinese characters are Western concepts introduced from Japan in recent Chinese history. The language-teaching methods introduced from Western society are better suited to the teaching of Latinized alphabetic writing. China's current education has not yet explored the advantages and inherent features of Chinese language and characters.

5. Experiments in calculating ability are conducted in tens of thousands of schools in China today. The employment of the abacus, figures, and mental

arithmetic have effectively drawn students' interest and reduced the fear and burden of learning. Similar attempts are faring well in some regions of Japan.
6. See www.chinanews.com (1 September 2014).

References

Cheng, F. P. (1984). Voltaire and Confucius, on the influence of Confucianism in West. *Journal of Shanxi Normal University* (2), 12–15.
Cheng, F. P. (Ed.). (2002). *Report on education issues in China*. Beijing: China Social and Science Press.
Cheng, F. P. (Ed.). (2014). *Zhang Zhidong "Quanxue (persuaded to learn)" Explained*. Beijing: Beijing Normal University Publishing Group.
Gu, S. S. (Ed.). (1983). *Quotations compilation of Chinese ancient educators*. Shanghai: Shanghai Education Press.
Leibniz, G. W. (1697). *Novissima Sinica* (Recent edition: Köln: Deutsche China-Gesellschaft VI, 1979).
Liu, F. (1982). *Hu Shi's philosophy on education*. Beijing: Kaiming Press.
Lu, Y. (2012). *Educational philosophy of modern Western society*. Beijing: Peking University Press.
Mao, L. R., & Shen, G. G. (Eds.). (2005). *General history of Chinese education*. Ji'nan: Shandong Education Press.
Needham, J. T. M. (1965–1975). *History of science and technology of China*. Cambridge: Cambridge University Press.
Pang, P. (1981). Shed some light on "the Doctrine of the Mean (Zhongyong)." *Chinese Social Sciences*, No. 1, pp. 1–3.
Tang, Y. J. (Ed.). (2002). *Outlines of ancient Chinese literature*. Wuhan: Hubei Education Press.
Tang, Y. J. (Ed.). (2013). *Confucianism, Buddhism, and Taoism and Chinese traditional culture*. Beijing: China Encyclopedia Press.
Voltaire. "Dictionnaire Philosophique." In *Œuvres complètes de Voltaire* (Vol. 8).
Voltaire. (1963). *Essai sur les moeurs*. Garnier.
Xing, B. (1978, April). Practice: Criterion for testing truth. *Chinese Social Sciences* (*The Philosophy and Religion* edition), No. 1, pp. 1–2.
Ye Shengtao Research Association. (2014). *Research and review of Chinese traditional culture*. Beijing: People's Education Press.

4

Confucian Rituals and Science in Modern Chinese Education

XIAOQING DIANA LIN

This chapter argues that the influence of Confucian teachings on modern Chinese education is as much in the importance attached to learning as in maintaining a social context that values learning, supported by ritualized practices, such as respect for parents and teacher and a reification of knowledge. Such a social context enabled China to switch from traditional education to modern education and successfully implement science education on a massive scale. I begin with a discussion of a synthesis of education as content and education as social milieu in Confucian learning, often implemented in ritualized practices. I then move on to a study of contemporary education and how Chinese education, including science education, continues to emphasize ritualized human relationships and treatment of knowledge that create a social context conducive to the large-scale transmission of science. I conclude with a comparison between Chinese and American educational approaches and discuss the possibility of intercultural exchanges of teaching styles.

Rituals, Social Context, and Confucian Education

Many cultures in the world value the passage of tradition through rituals. Geir Sigurðsson argues that li/rituals in Chinese history constituted "a wide range of interhuman or ethical behavior, gestures, and responses informed and partially prescribed by the cultural tradition" (Sigurðsson,

2015, p. 94). As noted by Roger Ames (2011, p. 109, in Sigurðsson, 2015, p. 96), such rituals would allow individual interpretation and elaboration, emphasizing embodied experience, as shown in the Chinese characters of *ti* 体 (body) and *li* 礼 (rituals), which are cognates, referencing "a living body" and "embodied living," respectively.

Confucius has many passages on rituals (e.g., *Analects* 10.1–10.21). Rituals, as previously mentioned, are not just principles or prescriptions of behavior, but participation and personalization (Ames, 2002, p. 145). *Analects* 10.4 is one of the many examples that depict rituals as a combination of personal behavior and external context:

> When he entered the duke's gate, he would draw his body in, as though the gateway would not accommodate his height. He never stood in the middle of a gateway; he never trod on the threshold. When he walked past his lord's position, his expression would be serious and he would step rapidly. He would speak as if it were difficult for him. (Eno, 2015, p. 46)

This passage captures Confucius's reverence for his superiors in his body language, which, through a combination of facial expression and physiological strain, well reflected the efforts exerted to achieve that state of reverence. Similar passages permeate the *Analects*, which, through myriad contexts, not only showed the expected external behavior, but also enabled the reader to sense the internal exertions in order to achieve the expected outcome. Here is another example from *Analects* 10.22:

> When he [Confucius] saw a person wearing clothes of mourning, though it was someone with whom he was very familiar, he would alter his facial expression. When he saw someone wearing a court cap or a blind person, though it was someone he encountered repeatedly, he would adopt a solemn bearing.
>
> When riding in his carriage, encountering a person in mourning he would bow against the carriage bar, and he would bow also to those carrying documents of state. (Eno, 2015, p. 50)

To Confucius, rituals were the interaction between the proper self-exertions of an individual against myriad contexts to create a perfect mesh between individuals and society. Therefore, the mastery of rituals for an individual was not just the practice of certain values but also how to properly exercise those values in the right social contexts. Rituals became a process, as Ames points out, in which a person gradually revealed both to oneself and to others his or her personhood through "navigating the complexity and range of human interdependencies" (Ames, 2002, p. 147). Learning, on the other hand, was a gradual mastery of rituals and the values behind them. For instance, the student Confucius appreciated most was Yan Hui. When Duke Ai asked which of the disciples loved learning, Confucius said, "There was Yan Hui who loved learning. He never shifted his anger, never repeated his errors" (*Analects* 6.3, Eno, 2015, p. 24). Zixia, another student of Confucius's, said, "A man who daily assesses what he has yet to understand and who, month by month, does not forget what he has mastered may be said to love learning" (*Analects* 19.5, Eno, 2015, p. 104). Here learning refers to the cultivation and mastery of skills to achieve a certain way of behaving.

Rituals, on the other hand, provided not only the behavior expected in a certain context, but also, through a common acknowledgment of these behaviors in the given contexts, created an interactive network where certain practices in given contexts would elicit resonance, allowing reassurance and anticipating corresponding behavior from the environment:

> The Master said: if one is reverent but without *li* one is burdened; if one is vigilant but without *li* one is fearful; if one is valorous but without *li* one causes chaos; if one is straightforward but without *li* one causes affronts. (*Analects* 8.2, Eno, 2015, p. 36)

In other words, the qualities of reverence, vigilance, valor, and straightforwardness would all be properly exercised in a ritualized setting when the social milieu would enable and respond to such exercises. Because of the importance of a responsive context for rituals to take effect, even though Confucius emphasized ritual observance, saying to his most favorite disciple, Yan Hui, "Don't look in a way which is not *li*, don't listen in a way that is not *li*, don't speak in a way that is not *li*, don't move in a way that is not *li*" (*Analects* 12.1), a coordination between ritual practices and the context was crucial, and if necessary, rituals needed to adapt to the context to be more effective. Xun Zi (ca. 310–235 BC), the Confucian disciple who provided a systematic rendition of Confucian teachings in terms of *li*, showed that *li* were "pragmatic devices that gesture at ideals—but not fixed or determinate ones" (Hagen,

2003, p. 373). Patricia Ebrey also recognizes the adaptability of Confucian rites: "although Confucius spoke of conformity to *li*, he expected it to be tempered by reason and custom. Not every detail had to be exactly as in the prescriptions" (Ebrey, 1991, p. 17) In other words, while proper behavior according to standards was important, an interaction between such behavior and a responsive context was central to the fruitful exercise of such behavior. One can say that ritualized behavior would work only when such dynamic interactions were carried out.

There have been extensive writings on the need for adaptation of rituals for them to achieve the desired outcome. Herbert Fingarette (1972) depicts rituals as "a configuration of relations within the social reality, and any notion of a discrete and independent "self" is an abstraction from and in fact a distortion of this same reality. Thick and robust relations are a source of growth in the world, enriching the family, the community, and the cosmos" (quoted in Ames, 2011, p. 126). The structured, almost ritualized social interactions with a community might have much flexibility, comparable to jazz at times: a collective work with individual improvisation (Wilson, 1995), and its rituals are subject to fine-tuning for moral sensitivity (Ivanhoe, 1990). For Confucius, learning was associated with the experience of inducting oneself into this lifelong process of becoming aware of the individual and the social and the creative development of the individual in the social. Thus, learning was often associated with *jue* (觉, becoming aware) (Ames, 2002, p. 148), an experiential process in a social context, with one developing greater awareness of one's own potential and relationship to the social.

In this context, learning is also ritualized behavior, a process in which one develops greater self-awareness of oneself and one's social environment. In Confucius's praise of his favorite student, Yan Hui, for instance, Confucius said Yan was good at learning in the form of personal refinement accomplished through ritualized living (Ames, 2002, p. 148). For Ames, rituals and learning were closely associated for Confucius, because *xue*/learning is "the living character of the community: the on-going aggregating of interpersonal transactions as they unfold to both author and be authored by persisting social life-forms. It is these life-forms, these *li*, that make communal living meaningful by constantly disposing persons in appropriate relations one to another" (148). And *li*/rituals "foster the like-mindedness necessary for a flourishing community" (151). "*Li* defined relationally and processionally with the focus on the familiar is a strategy for orchestrating the 'communicating community' into its fullest resonance, with appropriately disposed members resonating productively in their societal transactions. To the extent that the community is symphonic with minimal dissonance, it is not only therapeutic, but productive of enjoyment for all who reside within its parameters" (155). The essence of Confucianism, to Ames, consists of a "self-understanding that assumes that personal identity is constituted by full participation in communal life forms" (156). To Sigurðsson, ritual serves a pedagogical function comparable to art that induces people to repeatedly perform certain acts that they only later find to be meaningful: "[T]he pedagogical function of ritual is comparable to that of an artistic masterpiece as they both seduce us into repeated and prolonged interaction with them. This will eventually bring our attention to meaningful realms of our experience, and gradually convey a normative approach to our social living, a kind of message, which, however, we ourselves must largely interpret or even create" (Sigurðsson, 2012, p. 233).

In this context, education is not always a direct transmission of knowledge. Z. Wu and M. Hu, in their article "Ritual Hermeneutics as the Source of Meaning," noted: "The participants do not necessarily have a conscious knowledge of their developing social roles, rather they encounter through ritual practice a deeply personal, experiential and transformative form of hermeneutical experience. As a result, they embodied [sic] a situated action-oriented understanding without knowing it consciously" (quoted in Sigurðsson, 2012, p. 233n20). Furthermore, "[b]y immersing the individual in his or her inherited natural and cultural legacy, ritual turns out to be profoundly edifying by cultivating a 'communal sense' in Hans-Georg Gadamer's understanding" (Sigurðsson, 2012, p. 234).

Despite the attacks on Confucian learning in Communist China and the retreat of many Confucian principles, such as reverence to the teacher and to elders, a ritualized approach to education has persisted. Confucian learning, freed from a political center, is much more flexibly interpreted. But at the center of these interpretations is still a community with its set rituals in which the individual unravels him- or herself and develops in interaction with his or her social surroundings. Learning continues to be regarded as embedded in a social context and constituted by a process of social interactions between the student and the teacher, in which the student is acculturated into a pattern of personal growth through developing connections to his or her social environment. This chapter examines the role of the individual in the Chinese educational context, including how it compares with the individual in American education and the transcultural adaptability of the Chinese educational model in America.

A flexible, dynamic, ritualized social context that gives high priority to education to reproduce the desired social outcome serves as the background to modern Chinese education. Understanding the role ritual plays in Chinese education helps explain different levels and outcomes that Chinese education achieves.

Ritualizing Chinese Education

In Confucian ritualized educational exchanges between the teacher and students, there is built-in anticipation wherein the teacher expects students to pay close attention to instruction and spontaneously attempt to absorb it without being told, and students expect the content of teaching to carry authority and be valuable without questioning it. A spontaneous corroboration between the teacher and the students is central to ritualized Chinese education. Sigurðsson notes: "Confucius's ideal students are those who elaborate on his laconic 'hints' and succeed in drawing the whole picture. . . . The method of 'hinting' certainly serves the purpose of inciting the students to reflect on the issue and develop their own understanding of it. But the key point consists precisely in 'their own understanding,' or, more appropriately, considering the practical nature of understanding in Chinese thought, 'realization'" (2015, pp. 111–112). The goal of such education was the full embodiment of tradition filtered through the aptitude and understanding of each student.

Therefore, learning is not just about the content of knowledge, but many related factors, including one's belief system and approach to knowledge, among other things. Research shows that for students to study science well, they need to be in possession of a proper attitude toward knowledge, for instance, believing that one's ability is incremental and can improve over time to tackle challenges in learning, be able to develop self-regulation in order to cope with work, and often, for those at a higher stage of achievement, develop an epistemic belief about science as doable and as a body of knowledge that constantly evolves (Chen, 2012). An instructor may teach content in a classroom but may not be able to convey the other layers that help students succeed in the study of science, including the "incremental nature of ability and the self-regulatory processes like hard work and effective strategies that are the hallmark of those who succeed in science-related fields" (Chen, 2012, p. 734).

Rituals form the cultural context that enables the instructor to teach through a medium students are often familiar with and, in the process, reinforce values and attitudes with those students. Modern education in China is conducted on the premise of a reified body of knowledge with well-defined content and boundaries and teachers who, by association with this knowledge, have the authority students must look up to, within a discursive context where both teachers and students have agreed to their respective roles and goals in education. Even though Confucian rituals are no longer enforced in China, a ritualized form of teaching laden with such assumptions about knowledge and the respective roles of teachers and students has continued in China, serving as the conduit of education in classroom today. And the impact of such ritualized education could not be ignored. Research shows a connection between teacher beliefs, instructional practices, and student learning (Correa et al., 2008, p. 140). On the one hand, teachers' attitudes toward students can have an impact on both the style of teaching and the outcome of student learning. Teachers' beliefs and teaching activities are consistent with broader values within a culture, or shared primordial values such as individualist, communal, or collectivist orientations (Correa et al., 2008, p. 141). Many primary-grade Chinese math teachers believe it is their responsibility to cultivate students' interest in math and hold interest as a prerequisite to mastery of math (Correa et al., 2008, p. 145). In higher-level primary school math instruction, Chinese teachers seem to be particularly aware of the importance of students' prior knowledge (Correa et al., 2008, p. 142). And this mindfulness of the students' learning abilities at different age levels constitutes a meaningful teacher-student relationship in which teachers guide student learning (Correa et al., 2008, p. 146). Good math teachers in China emphasize the importance of inspiring and guiding the student (*qifa youdao*). Both Confucius and Mencius advocated a method of inspiring and guiding the student to enable the student to be actively interested in the subject of learning (Song, 2006, p. 65). Math instruction in China is in accordance with a traditional approach to Confucian rituals that championed a dynamic interaction between individuals and social rituals.

But math instruction is regarded more as the instruction of reified knowledge, with rather fixed content, rules, and boundaries. Therefore, good Chinese math teachers emphasize a set procedure to tackle content, including constant practices, with the argument that practice makes perfect (*shu neng sheng qiao*), combining practice with proactive study habits by the students. Because of the abstract nature of math, instruction would emphasize gradual progression both for immersion and consolidation of a math knowledge structure (Song, 2006, pp. 66–68). The ideas are close to a Confucian approach to knowledge: Acknowledge students' inherent ability to learn, but, with the assumption that math knowledge is largely an external and self-contained system, the responsibility of the teacher is to create conditions to facilitate students' reception of this body of knowledge. In this relationship, the teacher is always mindful of students' level of math knowledge and provides encouragement, guidance, and supervision for students to build new knowledge on that basis. The relationship centers on the student, but largely proceeds from the teachers' initiatives, which focus on the knowledge that needs to be mastered, with students treated as receptacles who need to be prepared for the reception of knowledge. Student interest and prior math knowledge help prepare students for the new math knowledge. To establish student receptiveness to knowledge, a healthy relationship must be established so that students invest faith in their teachers and, subsequently, the knowledge they transmitted (Correa et al., 2008, p. 147). In the ritualized teacher-student relationship, Chinese teachers anticipate students' starting points and attitudes and cultivate student interest for the transmission of knowledge.

In contrast to Chinese teachers' self-perception as transmitters of a fixed body of knowledge, American primary school math teachers seem to focus more on students as individuals and integral entities, while knowledge is malleable and can be manipulated to cater to students at different stages of development. Math knowledge is treated less as a system as in China, but rather as an open-ended assortment that is subject to the students' manipulation (Correa et al., 2008, p. 148). The mastery of math is not meant to be the mastery of a system but whatever pieces that can be incorporated by each individual student. Instead of a systematic pursuit, math learning becomes piecemeal, which also helps to explain the spiral nature of math education in American primary and secondary schools. The idea is that students are not expected to have a systemic mastery of a particular area of math, and with the rotation of math curriculum, students will reinforce an area they did not previously master. American students, in this context, are treated more as knowledge builders rather than mere receptacles of knowledge. In learning math, they must first build individual conceptual frameworks of math, which the teachers cannot do for them. This, in a way, constitutes the American ritual of learning, which treats students, even when they are in primary school, as independent and individual thinkers who construct their own thinking processes. They will be molded by external knowledge, which only comes as bricks that are subject to the nature and structure of the cognitive and emotional systems the students build. The different approaches to student learning and outcomes led to different philosophies behind seemingly similar pedagogical activities. In the case of repetitive activities, Chinese teachers use the strategy to reinforce concepts for better student reception, while American teachers may do it to give students of different learning styles more opportunities to find the best ways to approach knowledge, and it is especially beneficial for students at the low end of knowledge acquisition (Correa et al., 2008, p. 149). Arguably, the Chinese educational model fosters systemic absorption of knowledge in China, and the American one encourages the development of individual enclaves of knowledge in the United States.

This ritualized relationship between teachers and students in China creates learning outcomes that cannot be explained with the American educational models. The highly interventionist teacher in the Chinese classroom can be easily interpreted as authoritarian by American standards. But Chinese students do not particularly mind authoritarian teachers so long as the outcome is good, because they usually regard individuals as incomplete beings without education. The ritualized teacher-student relationship is seen as facilitating student acquisition of knowledge. Because acquisition of knowledge is seen as decisive to the student's growth, and, as incomplete beings, students' capacity is limited by their own ability to acquire knowledge early on, internalization of the teacher's demands becomes of paramount importance to students before independent knowledge acquisition (Zhou et al., 2012, p. 1164). This contrasts with the American classroom, where the teacher encourages students to build their own structures to accommodate external knowledge. And student autonomy means students develop structures of knowledge independent of the teacher's.

Consequently, while a high social-emotional relatedness between students and teachers leads to higher academic performance on the part of students in both countries, in China higher levels of teacher academic intervention is often interpreted as a positive force, whereas higher teacher intervention in the United States is often viewed negatively. The ritualized teacher-student relationship directs student expectations in China, facilitated by traditional cultural values such as respect of authority, deference to parents and teachers, hard work, and gratitude and indebtedness to authority figures who are perceived as positive and facilitating individuals in reaching their goals. Moral obligations from students to teachers are an important component of this ritualized process (Zhou et al., 2012). Going back to Jason Chen's argument cited earlier, the ritualized Chinese teacher-student relationship and students' internalization of science knowledge and approaches help build resilience and confidence in knowledge acquisition, intellectual dispositions that are deemed vital to a mastery of science knowledge that is routinely drilled in Chinese classrooms, while, however, left to the schemes of individual students in U.S. classrooms. And in the U.S. classroom, if a student does not like science from the start, there is no ritualized procedure for that to be reversed.

If the expectations of the teachers are too high, the individual will need to go through greater self-adaptation to internalize the external expectations, which seems to be the case with Chinese junior high and high school students. In a recent study, a creativity slump is found among Chinese students between the ages of 10 and 16, and especially between 12 and 14, the junior high school years. The authors suspect the pressure of college entrance examinations has caused high school academic pressure to filter down to the junior high level (Yi et al., 2013).

The ritualized Chinese teacher-student relationship has a social context to sustain it. Besides the aforementioned cultural traditions of obedience to authority, Chinese culture's focus on the other encourages teachers to display greater levels of empathy to students to promote interdependent self-identity, whereas individualistic Americans tend to express self-focused emotion to affirm independent identities. And Chinese have been found to be more compassionate and less angry than their U.S. counterparts in interpersonal conflict. Chinese teachers, though, are generally perceived as less accessible than U.S. counterparts, and Chinese students are more apprehensive than their U.S. counterparts because of their culture's emphasis on teacher authority and student obedience. So one would assume that in China teachers would routinely provide compassionate guidance to the students, and students would defer to teachers. This ritualized pattern of relationship between teacher and student, in a way, provides a relatively stable academic environment that functions relatively independently of the teacher's demeanor on a particular day. That explains the surprising result of a comparative experiment in classrooms in the United States and China in which the effect of teachers' positive attitude on student learning was tested: While in the United States classrooms the teacher's positive attitude did impact student learning, it did not enhance cognitive learning in a Chinese classroom (Zhang & Zhang, 2013).[1] One could assume that the routinized rituals of academic learning in China already established a social-emotional bond between teacher and students, who did not need the extra motivation from an animated teacher in the classroom or an encouraging parent because the ritualized interpersonal bond was already there. The Chinese concepts that often equate the term "to govern" (*guan* 管) with responsibility and love also testify to this ritualized teacher-student relationship.

The ritual was also based on socialization between parents and children: Chinese parents tend to routinely and ritualistically display a range of interrelatedness to their children, from control to social connectedness, from academic encouragement to demands for improvement in particular academic areas, which is why children do not respond significantly with academic achievement to parents who suddenly become open and more encouraging in China, but they do significantly respond academically to parents who enact ritualized roles of authority (Leung, 1998). That is why Chinese children tend to interpret their parents' pressures and demands differently from American children. It is also this interpersonal dependency that leads Chinese mothers to base their self-worth on their children's performance more than American mothers. Even though Chinese children might not be as fully developed as American children in terms of emotional functioning in the long run, the emotional reciprocity they develop with their parents enables them to see parental control in a more positive light (Pomerantz, 2014). And the viability of this ritual might simply be due to the cultural values that set education on a pedestal, which eliminates a critical perspective on learning from a societal point of view. Indeed, Chinese parents often encourage or cultivate the idea of learning as a personal trait, with knowledge treated as an independent object that one has to adapt oneself to, as reflected in the term *haoxuexin* 好学心 (heart and mind to learn) (Cheung & McBride-Chang, 2008). Societal approval of education and the independent value assigned to education help constitute the social context for the dynamics of the ritual between teachers and students and parents and children.

Ritualizing teaching becomes a good way to convey new knowledge through the traditional method, with proper veneration, be it classical music, science, or other types of learning from abroad that are deemed authoritative.

John Dewey, Confucius, and Ritualized Learning

Ritualized Chinese teaching assumes an expansion of human growth and more meaningful connections between an individual and aspects of society. In that way, it resembles Dewey's flexible and expansive personhood, developed to mediate the individual and corporate culture and to resolve the inhumanity of corporatism in America. Dewey emphasized the proactive culture of labor. For Dewey, "humanity's subjectivity is not some fixed and immutable essence; it is something continually being mediated by a person's relations with nature and with other human beings. A human being is seen as both a social and a natural being whose subjectivity is continually being changed as social institutions and nature are transformed by human labor throughout history" (Shuklian, 1995, pp. 785–786). If ritualized teaching in China enabled the veneration of new sources of authority, for instance, science and classical music, and in that sense, a richer connection between humans and society, for Dewey, however, the expansive human being often altered knowledge as he or she discovered new things. Dewey became popular in China during the May Fourth Movement, when the Chinese tried to shake free of Confucian political orthodoxy. Dewey gave a thorough theoretical rationale for the free human being actively in pursuit of infinite new knowledge. This emphasis on infinite human adaptability and improvement and infinite knowledge provided the Chinese with a rationale to introduce new knowledge to China and to develop along more freely selected paths away from Confucian orthodox rituals that buttressed the authoritarian, patriarchal system.

On the other hand, there were also significant differences between Dewey and the New Culture thinkers. To render the human being infinitely adaptable to new situations, and to prevent preconceived knowledge from blocking such adaptations, Dewey set out to destroy all preconceived notions and situate all knowledge in specific social contexts. Therefore, even though his ideas of an expansive human being and expansion of human knowledge led many in China to call him "Confucius II," Dewey differed from his Chinese students in one important aspect: his rejection of the certainty of knowledge and strict placement of all knowledge in specific social contexts (Gavin, 1984, p. 17). For Dewey, the scientific method was not different from the specific content: Form does not rise above content. Logical forms are modifications of common sense: Scientific methods are incremental, adding on to the relational properties of common sense. For Dewey, thinking was a form of inquiry in life. Logical forms of inquiry directed people in the right way to think apart from the usual way they think (Gavin, 1984, p. 19). Dewey also relied on a functionalist approach to knowledge, which explained "the meaning of a concept according to which a whole is viewed in relation to its working parts," and which was to "be grasped only in and through the activity which constitutes it" (Buxton, 1984, p. 458). For Dewey, knowledge was never absolute. The parameters of truth and the context of knowledge changed with human experience. And for him, if logic became purely semantic and lost its ontological connotations, it would become meaningless (Dalton, 2002, p. 283). On the other hand, growth was both the goal and the process, the critical standard and the product of social intelligence. Social intelligence was the core of Dewey's individualism. Experience was an emancipatory act to free up individual potential and allow growth for Dewey. Dewey's new individualism was communicative, imaginative, and critical, rather than atomistic, acquisitive, and antagonistic (Dalton, 2002, p. 537).

It was Dewey's emphasis on human potential for growth and an integral connection between individuals and society that drew the Chinese close to Dewey. Both Dewey and Chinese Confucian-style educators privilege knowledge, and both link knowledge to social experience and social outcome. Dewey's knowledge and human growth, however, are both open. It would seem that Dewey wanted the acquisition of knowledge without sacrificing human freedom or individual growth. Chinese educators also wanted greater, and freer, human development than before, as well as the introduction of new knowledge and new social experience. The weakening of Confucian orthodoxy led to the untethering of many rituals and ideology so that rituals, both in content and format, became more freely interpreted and exercised. What seemed to be markedly different between Chinese educational practices and Dewey's theory was the more entrenched teacher-student relationship, the relatively fixed nature of knowledge, and the continued social conditioning of individuals who were still tied down to certain social relationships despite their fight for freedom and autonomy, as well as the relative absence of opportunities for individuals to really exercise the freedom and autonomy they sought. On the other hand, Dewey's ideas remained largely ideas. The extreme individual freedom and perfect harmony between individuals and society that he sought remained more an ideal than reality in the United States.

Dewey's greatest legacy to China was the affirmation of the social-minded individual whose pursuit of knowledge was to achieve positive social change. Dewey's two-year stay in China (1919–1921) inspired extensive Chinese educational reform. But the defense of the status of Chinese intellectuals in the new society and the continued treatment of accepted knowledge as reified truth in China led to the continued practice of rituals as a form of knowledge transmission, where teachers would be in control of the content and practice of rituals. The individual did gain greater freedom and room for development under the new Chinese educational system in the 1920s and beyond. There has been great emphasis on creative compliance with rituals and a dynamic interaction between children's initiatives and the enforcement of rules. Children are praised more for voluntarily performing as expected of them. There is a wide range of vocabulary in Chinese to indicate this, terms for which exact English equivalents are invariably hard to find, such as *guai* (乖), *tinghua* (听话), and *dongshi* (懂事), which imperfectly translate into nicely obedient, following the rules, and mature. Although there is the common denominator of obeying and following the rules in all three terms, the three are also characterized by an implication that the student praised knew what he or she was doing, that he or she was not just performing the rituals but also dynamically interacting with another party or other parties by constantly adjusting him- or herself to the circumstances. Although obedience is also praised, if a person is merely performing his or her social role without self-awareness and individual initiative in a dynamic social relationship, that praise will be lackluster compared with the aforementioned terms. The most common praise for this type of behavior is *laoshi* (老实), which can be translated into honest and trustworthy but lacks the positive connotations in the two English concepts. *Laoshi* often implies passivity compared with *guai*, or *tinghua*. If a person works very hard at his or her social role without caring about flexible adaptation to his or her circumstances, he or she could be referred to as *han* 憨 or *sha* 傻, the former meaning honest but a little dumb, and the latter meaning dumb, but not in a completely negative way. A typical hardworking woman who thinks she is performing her social role by helping others without observing the reactions of the recipients of her services is sometimes referred to as *sha dajie* (傻大姐) (dumb big sister).

The Transcultural Adaptability of Confucian Education in the United States

A ritualized educational style and reified knowledge are two major characteristics of contemporary Chinese primary and secondary, and to some extent tertiary, education today. Confucian rituals are no longer practiced as before, but learning remains highly ritualized in China today in the relationship between teachers and students, and in the reification of knowledge. This reification of knowledge, equating learning with a definite reality, was reflected in such traditional Chinese sayings as "In books there are houses made of gold, and in books there are girls whose faces are as beautiful as jade (*shuzhong ziyou huangjinwu, shuzhong ziyou yanruyu*)." Many Americans might look with wonder at how Chinese parents have their children recite poetry, study for Math Olympiad, and play the piano with a firm belief that the mastery of these subjects translates into a definite outcome. Chinese teachers continue to inspire students with such traditional sayings as "The boundless sea of learning can only be navigated through hard work (*xuehai wuya kuzuozhou*)." The reification of knowledge provides the continued ritualized authority of the teacher who imparts such knowledge to the students. The social authority of the teacher is also accommodated by more extensive ritualized social relationships where one has a definite, publicly defined social relationship with different people (older, younger, relatives, acquaintances of different levels of familiarity, etc.). These social relationships are also more or less reified, so that each is expected to play his or her role in that relationship at different times (e.g., a teacher is not expected to go behind a podium to talk about her boyfriend or his divorce or to become a transgendered person after the summer is over). These kinds of reified social relationships contrast with the relatively fluid social relationships and the generally more autonomous individuals in American society. If knowledge could be broken down and taught in more flexible ways to suit the different learning styles of students, as done in the United States, the reification of knowledge would disappear and so would the ritualized form of teaching. This would require a more autonomous definition of the Chinese individual and a greater role the individual could play in the acquisition of knowledge. In some ways, this is already happening with greater social and geographical mobility in China, more interaction between China and the outside world, increasing numbers of Chinese students studying abroad, and reforms in Chinese education.

On the other hand, the individual autonomy emphasized in American education may be modified to accommodate more ritualized teaching styles. Individual autonomy is not as universal a social value, even though it is one of the key assumptions in American education in light of the stratified social relationships found in many other aspects of American society, such as in corporate America, the military, and scientific research, where individual autonomy is significantly scaled back to accommodate rules specific to the discipline or profession. And some drills in math and science may be introduced. Even though this may compromise the idea of individual autonomy in learning, it is doable because individual autonomy always jostles with rules and disciplines in real life in American society.

Also, assuming individual autonomy, more could be done to encourage student initiatives by providing students with a stronger foundation of science. Instruction in the arts draws on the social, historical, and cultural milieu in the United States to aid student understanding of the subject matter, whereas such cultural backgrounds are not readily applicable to science instruction. Therefore, to facilitate science instruction, perhaps more background introduction of scientific and mathematical concepts would be useful in helping students develop a better grasp of otherwise abstract concepts. A history of science and technology may be included in the curriculum along with the instruction in science.

From the preceding discussion, it can be argued that an educational style that emphasizes individual autonomy and student-centered learning is not best suited to standardized educational testing, as the goal of education is not to promote a general standard but the best learning outcome for each individual student. Ritualized learning and reified knowledge have their shortcomings in that it is easy to render knowledge into something self-contained and ignore the changing nature of knowledge. That seems to be the case with Chinese science instruction, which largely has been focused on the improvement of the curriculum, compared with the Western science instruction premise of developing and testing general science theories (Liu & Zhang, 2014, p. 207). International educational conferences such as the one presided over by Xiufeng Liu in 2012 have been convened for the sake of integrating science instruction approaches internationally. At the 2012 conference, some Chinese teachers discussed experimenting with an inquiry-based approach to science (Liu & Zhang, 2014, pp. 207–210), which does not undermine a ritualized approach to knowledge so long as science as a whole is still reified to some extent. It is not impossible to incorporate elements of each into the educational system of the other.

Conclusion

In a discussion of the transplantation of Chinese and American approaches to education, one needs to take into consideration the different approaches to the individual in China and the United States. There is more autonomy accorded to the student in American schools compared with a much more socially situated student in the Chinese classroom. The Chinese student often assumes a situational role, be it a student, a child, or some other social role, before his or her role as an individual compared with his or her American counterpart, whose role as an individual is more often emphasized in the school environment. This social context prepares the Chinese student to easily step into the ritualized student-teacher role in the classroom and accept the teacher's treatment of knowledge as reified truth. Such an education system enables a degree of uniformity of achievement but deemphasizes creativity and innovation. Allowing more individual space for students and a less reified body of knowledge in Chinese education in the current system is possible so long as the ritual of teacher-student social responsiveness is maintained and some degree of reification of knowledge is retained. On the other hand, the mere introduction of more standardized examinations and standardized curriculum may not necessarily improve American education in the short run. Without a ritualized system, in which knowledge is reified and teachers' authority is augmented by the knowledge they control, many Americans would see this as an affront to the value of individual autonomy that is cultivated in the child from birth. For education to be more uniform, some degree of ritualized social relationship needs to be established between students and teachers, and knowledge needs to be more reified than it now is in the United States. A greater transcultural framework needs to be created in both China and the United States for each to incorporate elements from the other's educational system.

Notes

1. Kwok Leung et al. (1998) show that when parents encourage an open and egalitarian atmosphere in the family, it encourages academic achievement in American, but not Chinese, households.

References

Ames, R. T. (2002). Observing ritual "propriety (li 礼)" as focusing the "familiar" in the affairs of the day. *Dao: A Journal of Comparative Philosophy, 1*(2), 143–156.
Ames, R. T. (2011). *Confucian role ethics: A vocabulary*. Hong Kong: The Chinese University Press.
Buxton, M. (1984). The influence of William James on John Dewey's early work. *Journal of the History of Ideas, 45*(3), 451–463.
Chen, J. (2012). Implicit theories, epistemic beliefs, and science motivation: A person-centered approach. *Learning and Individual Differences, 22*, 724–735.
Cheung, Cecilia S., & McBride-Chang, Catherine (2008). Relations of perceived maternal parenting style, practices, and learning motivation to academic competence in Chinese children. *Merrill-Palmer Quarterly, 54*(1), 1–22.
Correa, C., et al. (2008). Connected and culturally embedded beliefs: Chinese and US teachers talk about how their students best learn mathematics. *Teaching and Teacher Education, 24*, 140–153.
Dalton, T. (2002). *Becoming John Dewey: Dilemmas of a philosopher and naturalist*. Bloomington: Indiana University Press.
Ebrey, Patricia. (1991). *Confucianism and family rituals in late imperial China: A short history about rites*. Princeton, NJ: Princeton University Press.
Eno, Robert. (2015). *The Analects of Confucius: An online teaching translation*. Version 2.2. Retrieved from http://www.indiana.edu/~p374/Analects_of_Confucius_(Eno-2015).pdf
Fingarette, H. (1972/1998). *Confucius: The secular as sacred*. Long Grove: Waveland Press.
Gavin, W. (1984). Dewey, Marx, and James' "Will to believe." *Studies in Soviet Thought, 28*(1), 15–29.
Hagen, K. (2003). Xunzi and the nature of Confucian ritual. *Journal of the American Academy of Religion, 71*(2), 371–403.
Ivanhoe, P. (1990). Reweaving the "one thread" of the *Analects*. *Philosophy East and West, 40*(1), 17–33.
Leung, K., et al. (1998). Parenting styles and academic achievement: A cross-cultural study. *Merrill-Palmer Quarterly, 44*(2), 157–172.

Liu, X., & Zhang, B. (2014). Editorial: Special Issue (SI): International conference on science education (ICSE). *Journal of Science and Education Technology*, 23, 207–210.
O'Dwyer, S. (2003). Democracy and Confucian values. *Philosophy East and West*, 53(1), 39–63.
Pomerantz, E. (2014). Raising happy children who succeed in school: Lessons from China and the United States. *Child Development Perspectives*, 8(2), 71–76.
Shuklian, S. (1995). Marx, Dewey, and the instrumentalist approach to political economy. *Journal of Economic Issues*, 29(3), 781–805.
Sigurðsson, G. (2012). Li 禮, ritual and pedagogy: A cross-cultural exploration. *Sophia*, 51, 227–242.
Sigurðsson, G. (2015). *Confucian propriety and ritual learning: A philosophical interpretation*. Albany: State University of New York Press
Song, X. (2006). Rujia jiaoyu sixiang yu zhongguo shuxue jiaoyu chuantong (Confucian educational thought and the tradition of mathematics instruction in China). *Gansu gaoshi xuebao* (Journal of the Gansu Normal College), 11(2), 65–68.
Wilson, S. (1995). Conformity, individuality, and the nature of virtue: A classical Confucian contribution to contemporary ethical reflection. *The Journal of Religious Ethics*, 23(2), 263–289.
Wu, Z., & Hu, M. (2010). Ritual hermeneutics as the source of meaning: Interpreting the fabric of Chinese culture. *China Media Research*, 6(2), 104–113.
Yi, X., et al. (2013). Is there a developmental slump in creativity in China? The relationship between organizational climate and creativity development in Chinese adolescents. *The Journal of Creative Behavior*, 47(1), 22–40.
Zhang, Q., & Zhang, J. (2013). Instructors' positive emotions: Effects on student engagement and critical thinking in U.S. and Chinese classrooms. *Communication Education*, 62(4), 395–411.
Zhou, N., et al. (2012). The Chinese classroom paradox: A cross-cultural comparison of teacher controlling behaviors. *Journal of Educational Psychology*, 104(4), 1162–1174.

Part 2

Confucian Insights on Teaching and Learning

5

Neo-Confucianism as a Guide for Contemporary Confucian Education

YAIR LIOR

> History doesn't repeat itself, but it does rhyme.
>
> —Mark Twain

It is frequently argued that the Confucian tradition has experienced three major historical epochs.[1] The classical stage is represented by Confucius (551–479 BCE) and his two influential students Mencius (372–289 BCE) and Xunzi (310–235 BCE), the Song period (960–1279 CE) by the emergence of Neo-Confucianism, and the modern period by the current Confucian revival of the 20th and 21st centuries.[2] The three-epoch theory assumes two major transformations of the Confucian tradition: its transformation from the classical period to Song dynasty Neo-Confucianism, and the transformation from the premodern period to what I refer to as "contemporary Confucianism."[3] I argue that these two historical transformations are unlike other changes the Confucian tradition has undergone in its long and tumultuous history, and that the striking similarities of these transformations are an excellent resource for comparison and mutual illumination. Following this rationale, the subsequent remarks represent an exercise in the creative interpretation of the Song dynasty transformation as a guide for the restoration of Confucian education in the 21st century. After analyzing the similarities between the two transformations in question, I discuss possible lessons we can draw from Neo-Confucianism's groundbreaking philosophy of education, followed by an examination of the textual reforms that unique historical transformations entail. Informed by the Song example, this chapter argues that one of the requirements for a successful contemporary rehabilitation of Confucianism is an eventual reorganization of the Confucian canon.

Paradigm Shifts and Structural Transformations

This chapter seeks to emphasize the fact that the Song and modern transformations can be seen as "structural" transformations and therefore as qualitatively different from other "ordinary changes" in the history of Confucianism. Thomas Kuhn's theory of scientific revolutions can help shed light on the distinction between these inherently different forms of change. Kuhn (1996) famously introduced the concept of scientific paradigms, which he understood as coherent and overarching interpretive frameworks that a community of scientists shares to guide its research agenda. Paradigms are a common explanatory foundation that provides a community of scientists with a sense of cohesion; without a common paradigm, it would be impossible to collaborate or even communicate in any meaningful way. It is an interesting fact that when a ruling paradigm begins to disclose shortcomings, scientists will strongly resist abandoning it. Instead, they will introduce ad hoc solutions and tentative alterations that only partially address existing inconsistencies. Kuhn referred to this as "patchwork" (p. 5) or "puzzle solving" (p. 144), designed to postpone or even avoid certain problems until better solutions present themselves.

Scientific paradigms are therefore extremely robust; they are supported by generations of indoctrinated students, established methodologies, powerful institutions, publications, and even political agendas. Members of the community are intellectually and emotionally invested in these grand worldviews, which are also the foundation for their careers and stature in a given research community. There comes a time, however, when a paradigm can no longer sustain an increase of anomalies. At this stage, alternative theories offering more elegant solutions to major problems begin to attract a growing amount of followers and eventually challenge the authority of the existing paradigm. The main problem arises when new theories cannot be added to the existing paradigm incrementally (p. 7). In other words, the two competing worldviews become "incommensurable." Such a nonconciliatory discrepancy of worldviews eventually leads to a scientific revolution in which the old paradigm succumbs to a new and more satisfactory explanatory framework (p. 103).

The dynamic of scientific revolutions is relevant to major transitions in cultural and religious systems.[4] Even more than scientific communities, religious groups are strongly invested in their long-standing modes of life. When a cultural or religious paradigm loses its explanatory power, authorities frequently resort to various commentarial and hermeneutical strategies that can help them rearticulate their tradition in light of changing circumstances. But, as in the case of science, there comes a time when cosmetic solutions can no longer conceal the crisis at hand. During these stages, commentarial strategies are no longer sufficient, and a more comprehensive reform becomes inevitable. Such radical changes represent projects of cultural restructuring that are very different from ordinary change. This is exactly the type of structural reform that took place during the Song dynasty and is taking place at present.

The question of interest is, what makes structural changes, or paradigm shifts, different from ordinary change? There are three features about these rare historical transitions that merit our attention: (1) alterations in socioeconomic structures, (2) institutional reforms, and (3) modifications in a tradition's informational networks, best exemplified by changes in canonical literature. In other words, while ordinary change requires a creative reframing of existing canonical information, structural changes entail a qualitative alteration of a tradition's conical body. In the following, I analyze how these three structural components are reflected in the Song and modern transformations.

Socioeconomic Transformations during the Song and Modern Periods

One of the greatest changes China experienced during what scholars refer to as the "Tang-Song transition" was a full-fledged social revolution. China's ruling aristocratic families, the *shizu* (士族), lost their long-standing hold on power to a new and dynamic class of scholar officials, the *shidafu* (士大夫) (Bol, 1992). This shift marked the appearance of a prosperous and increasingly confident middle class that replaced the deep-seated monopolization of government by old elites. In fact, Neo-Confucianism can be seen as a cultural movement that served the interests and rising power of this new intellectual elite. In other words, Neo-Confucianism was conducive to translating the growing cultural and economic prestige of new populations into political currency. These radical social changes were concurrent and intimately related to unprecedented economic changes. As Twitchett (Twitchett & Fairbank, 1979) famously argued, beginning in the ninth century a commercial revolution swept over China; by the time of the Song dynasty, in spite of lingering traditional biases against the merchant class, most legal restrictions against commerce and entrepreneurship were abolished. Greater division of labor, urbanization, private ownership, and technological breakthroughs profoundly reshaped and modernized the Chinese economy.

Similarities to the modern age are obvious. Economically, China has been experiencing the most profound transformation since the Song period. Deng Xiaoping's open-door policy, China's membership into the WTO, and the ongoing endorsement of Deng's pragmatic strategies by subsequent party leaders represent an unequivocal endorsement of the private accumulation of wealth. Socially, we are witnessing the emergence of one of the largest middle classes in documented history. As in the Song period, we see massive urbanization, growing division of labor, and a sharp rise in education and literacy. Present circumstances also suggest that China's sociopolitical changes have reached a crucial stage in which the new middle class is searching to convert its economic power into influence in the political sphere. Of relevance to our topic is the fact that both the Song and modern transitions were a result of profound structural transformations in Chinese society and its economy.

Reactions to Foreign Cultural Pressures

Before we proceed to look at the institutional and informational (canonical) components of structural transformations, it is important to highlight an additional reason for paradigm shifts. One of the most notable facts about structural transformations is that they are instigated by alternative paradigms that are highly attractive to a growing number of followers. In other words, as long as a tradition is not contested by an alternative worldview, there will be little incentive to doubt it, let alone abandon it. As in scientific revolutions, cultural revolutions can only take place when a new approach offers a viable alternative to a declining worldview. In the Song dynasty, Neo-Confucians were quite responsive to the escalating influence of Buddhism, especially the highly popular Chan

School (禅宗). The meteoric ascendency of Buddhism was facilitated by its powerful universalistic message, which resonated with the cultural sophistication of the new middle class. Chan Buddhism presented people with a highly attractive spiritual paradigm that profoundly challenged the rigidity of traditional Confucian hierarchies. More importantly, Buddhism undermined the old social structure by offering people from humble origins the prospect of reaching enlightenment regardless of social background. Instead of classifying them according to their ethnic or cultural affiliation, Buddhism's universal approach treated humans as equal by virtue of their common cognitive capacities.

An interesting fact about cultures that undergo structural transformations is that they are inevitably shaped and ultimately transformed by external pressures. In other words, paradigm shifts entail a creative manipulation of foreign influences and their systematic integration into native modes of living. Unsurprisingly, the Neo-Confucian reaction to Buddhism was founded on a broad range of borrowings that were unmistakably foreign. One obvious example is that the metaphysical dualism of *pattern* and *qi* (理/气) that stands at the foundation of the Neo-Confucian worldview was quintessentially Indian in character.[5] Neo-Confucianism also emulated Buddhist literary genres, as in the case of the influential *Recorded Conversation* literature (语录), and it followed Buddhist pedagogical methods based on a close interaction between master and student. In reaction to Buddhism's emphasis on the individual as a central channel for salvation, Neo-Confucians shifted toward a more introspective and personal form of spirituality. Song literati constructed a clear and relatively accessible method for achieving sagehood, which was focused on the individual and seen as a native equivalent to Buddhahood (Tillman, 1992). Without a doubt, the Buddhist worldview presented the greatest foreign challenge to indigenous Chinese culture prior to its modern encounter with the West. Buddhism's impact on Chinese culture was a real threat, leading many conservative Confucians to attack it as a "barbarian" culture threatening the very foundations of Chinese civilization.[6]

As in the Song case, China's current transformation is, to a great extent, a response to the challenges of Western culture. In both the Song and modern contexts, foreign paradigms proved highly appealing to a liberal and increasingly sophisticated middle class as well as to commoners in search of a more egalitarian worldview. The striking ascendency of Christianity in modern China, especially evangelical

Protestantism, can be seen as the religious manifestation of Western encroachment. The popularity of Christianity among officials, elites, and farmers is highly reminiscent of Buddhism's rapid ascendency between the 8th and 11th centuries. According to Yang Fenggang, there will be 250 million Christians in China by 2030 (Yang, 2012). One contemporary Confucian (Jiang, 2003) warns that if the spread of Christianity "is not arrested . . . China will become a Christian country, and Christian civilization will then displace Chinese (*Zhonghua*) civilization . . ." (p. 28). Whereas the rejection of Buddhism during the Song led to the emergence of Neo-Confucianism, today we see the emergence of contemporary Confucianism as a reaction to what many see as wholesale Westernization and the mounting domination of Christianity.[7]

The combination of the rise of a new powerful middle class and the escalating popularity of foreign ideologies led to a similar cultural crisis during the Song era and the present. Such periods of crisis are characterized by the inability of central authorities to dictate policy independently of new emerging elites. During the Song dynasty, uncertainty regarding national policy led imperial authorities to condone, and at times encourage, a more pluralistic cultural dialogue. This inevitably entailed conceding power to the emerging middle class. Looking at the modern situation, Lampton (2014) argues that a similar process is taking place in contemporary China, reflected by a shift in power relations between the once all-powerful Communist Party and an unprecedentedly influential middle class (p. 224). This new political reality entails the greater integration of public opinion into policy making and a more daring exploration of new visions for China's future among public intellectuals. In other words, although China is becoming increasingly powerful on the international arena, it is simultaneously experiencing a period of ideological uncertainty. China's leaders are very much aware of the declining stature of Marxist ideology and the growing need among the population to identify with an indigenous system of thought. Here again, the Song and contemporary transformations are strikingly similar; the combination of the rise of a new middle class, unprecedented economic prosperity, and strong cultural pressures exerted by foreign traditions lead to destabilization and ideological ambiguity that allow the type of intellectual experimentation needed for devising an alternative paradigm. As we shall see, a central characteristic of periods of transformation is the emergence of many contending schools of thought leading to intense ideological factionalism.

Institutional Revival:
The Song Academies in a Contemporary Context

One of greatest achievements of Song dynasty Neo-Confucianism was institutional—the second structural shift this chapter sets to examine. The sudden rise of the Neo-Confucian academies (书院, *Shuyuan*) beginning in the 11th century furnished the new middle class with a crucial institutional foundation for promoting its social, economic, and intellectual agenda. The Neo-Confucian academies fashioned themselves after Buddhist temples, with similar meditation halls and even architectural elements that were distinctly Buddhist (Walton, 1993). The main force behind the establishment of the academies were wealthy families that sought to become more involved socially and to project power locally by providing relatives and gifted scholars with the necessary resources to attain positions in government or establish careers outside government (Bol, 2008, p. 229). Not only did the Song academies create a complementarity between intellectuals and financial elites, but they also provided central authority with a regulatory mechanism that promoted social stability. Beyond the obvious fact that academies were oriented toward cultivating conscientious citizens, they were also instrumental in employing an unprecedented influx of talented intellectuals who could no longer be absorbed by governmental institutions (p. 39).[8]

Academies were therefore constructive on several levels; they were central in establishing a new cultural identity for the literati class, they provided many urgent social needs on a local level, and they were conducive to economic development and communal solidarity. Most importantly, academies were committed to the transformation of people through education *jiaohua* (教化) (Walton, 1993). The relatively aggressive dissemination of Neo-Confucianism during the Song period was designed to curtail the expansion of Buddhism. The missionary dedication to transforming the world through Confucian education fostered a greater awareness of China's indigenous identity among the public and strengthened patriotic sentiments at a time of military weakness and the sustained expansion of Buddhism.[9] As the preceding examples suggest, the emerging academies represented a major institutional development that played a central role in consolidating the power of the Neo-Confucian paradigm as an alternative to Buddhism. An important feature of this development was the ability of academies to promote a new model of private education that was supported by a powerful nongovernmental institution.

Turning to the modern period, there is an astonishing resurgence in the promotion of Confucian institutions in Mainland China. As in the Song period, modern institutions are conducive to the empowerment of a wealthy and increasingly educated class seeking to project power beyond the financial sphere. In common with the Song period, there are signs that these institutional changes in the private sphere are creating a network of interests between Confucian revivalists, China's booming business sector, and central authorities. As in the Song period, modern Confucian institutions can complement governmental institutions by engaging people in prosocial activism and promoting social stability with patriotic undertones. One of the major questions is what type of relationship will such organizations have with the Chinese government? Here again, the Song experience is a helpful mirror for contemporary reflection.

It has been observed that the long-term legacy of Neo-Confucianism was somewhat contradictory in that it was both traditionalist and nonconformist. Therefore, the widely held opinion that Neo-Confucianism was predominantly focused on serving the interests of the ruling elites is rather misleading. de Bary (1953) has noted that Neo-Confucianism contained a highly individualistic strand of thought that could be extremely critical of imperial order, the abuse of power, and the decline into shallow materialism (p. 87). The Neo-Confucian worldview infused many of its members with a stoic sense of social responsibility that was highly critical of political misconduct (Bol, 2008, p. 219). Despite these tensions, Song policy makers were increasingly sympathetic toward local initiatives as they realized these institutions played an important role in the new political and social model that was emerging. Before long, many academies began to enjoy governmental support, and some even turned into official government institutions (p. 256).

Reminiscent of Song Neo-Confucianism, modern Confucian academies are disclosing both conformist and nonconformist attitudes. Angle (2012) notes that "Confucian activists have started to take and publicize positions on matters of public interest, sometimes in direct opposition to governmental entities . . ." (p. 6). By contrast, many other organizations prefer a less confrontational approach toward state ideology; this helps them secure social legitimacy and even financial benefits (Billioud, 2011). An important point to stress is that exploring the fine line between political conformity and political criticism can be an important function of the emerging Confucian academies. In other words, new social and political ideas that do not conform to government policy can be explored within private Confucian institutions, thereby providing a more institutionalized way to enter dialogue with central authority.[10] One of the main things the Song experience might suggest is that contemporary Confucian institutions should ideally remain nongovernmental. It is the civic and private identity of these institutions that makes them potential channels for the empowerment of China's energetic middle class and an efficient platform for reevaluating education policy in China. The growing number of nonprofits and NGOs in China, many of which have Confucian characteristics, are an indication of a growing awareness of promoting social commitment and moral values outside government. As in the Song period, many contemporary Confucian institutions explicitly see themselves as dedicated to the mission of transforming the people through education (Billioud, 2011). The active promotion of a private model of Confucian education turns the new academies into hubs of experimentation for the development of a contemporary Confucian curriculum. As in the Song experience, the emergence of private Confucian academies and schools represents a major institutional development in the contemporary Chinese landscape that has far-reaching implication for the future of education. Examining the curriculum and pedagogy of the Song academies can provide us with an interesting model for the reconstruction of contemporary education in China and beyond.

Neo-Confucian Education and Learning

Neo-Confucianism was to a great extent an intellectual project based on a new approach to pedagogy and learning (de Bary, 1991; Gardner, 1990). It proposed a new educational model that sought to clearly articulate what to study, how to study, and the central objectives of learning. Indeed, there are valuable lessons contemporary education can draw from the pedagogical insights of Neo-Confucians. One of the greatest concerns among Song intellectuals was the heavy bureaucratization of education. Neo-Confucians were constantly critical of the imperial examination system, and they pointed out that bureaucratic advancement seemed to be the only reason people bothered to study. There was a widespread dissatisfaction in Confucian academies with the tyranny of exams as the focus of education and the lack of genuine learning with the objective of self-betterment. Under the famous Neo-Confucian slogan "learn for one's self" (为己之学), there was a strong push to reorient education toward the development of the moral integrity and spiritual depth of the individual. The oppositional "learning for others" (为人之学) was seen as a form of hypocritical opportunism that completely neglected the original goals of Confucian education. In our highly specialized and exam-based contemporary world, Neo-Confucian pedagogy is a reminder that a quantifiable grade-based model of education is not at all in the long-term interest of the individual. For Neo-Confucians, an obsessive focus on exam preparation was seen as the typical reflection of studying for others rather than oneself. More generally, the examination system was seen as a cynical political mechanism for indoctrination that marginalized the personal needs of students. This raises profound questions about the goal of learning. Is it too much to expect contemporary education, even in its early stages, to function as a tool for the exploration of one's psychological, moral, and creative resources? What should we make of what Weber (1968) referred to as the rationalization of education and the modern age's shift from character formation to the accumulation of objective knowledge? The Neo-Confucian solution was a form of pedagogical idealism, in which the objective of education was unapologetically oriented toward the lofty objective of self-transformation. Learning is not a means for the acquisition of technocratic skills, but a spiritual and intellectual activity that stands at the center of the human project. Authentic education is an ongoing process; it is what we do as a conscientious species that yearns for perfectibility. This position led Neo-Confucians to question the new meritocratic model that was emerging during the Song period. While the Song imperial court battled traditional nepotism and established strict rules for the objective recruitment of talent, Neo-Confucians pointed out that these new procedures completely neglected the evaluation of the moral stature of examinees (de Bary & Chaffee, 1989). The Neo-Confucian position asks that we question seemingly trivial concepts such as "merit" and "excellence" in our evaluation of students.

Beyond discussing the goals of education, Neo-Confucians were strongly invested in constructing systematic methodologies for learning. They asked questions such as: What mental states should a student be in during the process of learning? What does it mean to actually understand something rather than to superficially "know" it? Does the fact that we can read necessarily mean that we are reading properly? How do we integrate our fragmented knowledge into a holistic appreciation of the world? How do we introduce excitement and passion into learning? And how is knowledge translated into concrete and constructive behavior? Such questions raised by Song intellectuals are priceless resources for reevaluating contemporary education. According to Neo-Confucians, learning is the dynamic and creative process of becoming more fully human. Indeed, learning is related to the uniquely human ability to perpetuate civilization through the methodic transmission and active construction of culture. An important lesson we can draw from Neo-Confucian education is that rather than seeing learning as a means to an end, we should focus on the actual process of learning as an internal resource for moral growth and future development. Neo-Confucians trained their students to reach a mental state that was conducive to genuine learning motivated by passion and curiosity.

There are two more general points regarding education that are worth mentioning with regard to the Song revival. The first is that a reformed Confucianism must be tailored to the needs of the emerging middle class. To a great extent, the Neo-Confucian paradigm of the Song period offered a more universalistic and spiritual form of Confucianism that suited the yearnings and needs of a more sophisticated audience. It is in this sense that the transition from pre-Song Confucianism to Neo-Confucianism entailed the formation of a new and formerly unavailable "niche for operation." In other words, Neo-Confucianism provided an additional way of becoming a Confucian that was tailored to the middle class and provided a viable and attractive substitute to the competing Buddhist worldview.

Contemporary Confucian education should similarly be tailored to the needs of China's energetic middle class. The main consumers of contemporary Confucianism are likely to be entrepreneurs, corporate employees, factory and shop owners, and service providers in search of a more meaningful lifestyle. For the most part, these people have realized that their newly acquired financial stability has failed to deliver internal happiness. In the expanding marketplace of New Age spiritualities, techniques of self-improvement, and a widespread revival of traditional religions, it is crucial that contemporary Confucianism offer the middle class an accessible way to forge a meaningful lifestyle that is not overly intellectualized. While some strands of contemporary Confucianism, such as the very dominant Xiong Shili/Mou Zongsan lineage, will continue to explore self-cultivation from an elitist and intellectualist perspective, others trends should provide simple and general guidelines for infusing the lives of common people with a spiritual dimension. In fact, one of the most powerful features of Song Neo-Confucianism was its ability to successfully synthesize a sophisticated religio-philosophical system with a form of popular Confucianism that was oriented toward commoners (de Bary, 1984, pp. 14–16).

The second point worth mentioning is related to choices of learning material. Exciting attempts at constructing an official learning curriculum have been undertaken since the 1990s.[11] An interesting part of the current attempts to revive the Confucian textual tradition is the focus on the literary layers of Song Neo-Confucianism, especially the Four Books, which have also been incorporated into the official curriculum of many schools and other emerging Confucian institutions (Billioud, 2011; Yao, 2011). This chapter suggests that the Four Books, despite their partial relevance to contemporary needs, are not capable of addressing the large range of dilemmas that China is facing in the 21st century. This brings us back to the notion of paradigm shifts and their relationship to the restructuring of a tradition's classical canon. In the following, I explain why a potential shift in the textual resources of the Confucian tradition is a viable future possibility and how the Song period can help us understand and even plan this change.

The preceding analysis focused on commonalities between the Song and modern revivals of Confucianism, arguing that such resemblances are a reflection of similar structural transitions the Chinese tradition experienced in these distinct historical moments. In both cases, we witness socioeconomic transformations epitomized by mass urbanization, economic and political reform, and the emergence of an educated and wealthy middle class. And both Neo-Confucianism and contemporary Confucianism represent reactions to foreign civilizations. In both cases, we see Confucianism losing its spiritual relevance in the face of foreign systems of thought, leading to a profound identity crisis and a search for a relevant cultural paradigm. In both contexts, despite general prosperity, ideological uncertainty led to a proliferation of contending schools of thought offering different approaches to the reconstruction of Confucianism. Institutionally, the Song and modern revivals suggest a similar rise in grassroots organizations that served an important social, religious, and even political function. As these similarities suggest, the Song and modern transitions represent projects of comprehensive restructuration that are unparalleled in Chinese history. Never has China experienced such momentous transitions that were instigated by a similar and interrelated complex of social, economic, political, institutional, and ideological changes.[12]

Canonical Transformation

Traditions are composed of various sources and types of information: oral, written, popular, official, significant, and trivial. What is characteristic of premodern scriptural traditions is that at their core there is a central body of written information that is perceived as sacred or "particularly esteemed by the people in question" (Nakamura, 1997, p. 10). What makes such canonical literatures unique is that they represent the most stable and enduring informational foundation of cultural systems, a body of information that has a powerful impact on the patterns of life and beliefs of the people who subscribe to its contents. So foundational is this information that it is almost impossible to modify—it is therefore both unalterable and irrefutable (Rappaport, 1999). I refer to these texts as a tradition's "primary informational locus." In pre-Song China, this resilient body of information was represented by the Five Classics, which were seen as the sacred repository of sagely wisdom and the foundation of the bureaucratic system. The inalterability of canon is nevertheless problematic because it can easily become outdated in the face of changing circumstances. Because change is inevitable, commentary functions as a pervasive traditional strategy for adapting a culture's primary informational locus to shifting conditions. In this sense, commentarial traditions represent a flexible and alterable secondary layer that complements a more foundational primary informational layer. To our point, paradigm shifts are periods in which common commentarial strategies are no longer sufficient to deal with an acute cultural crisis. Such periods of ideological crisis require alterations in the most rudimentary informational foundation of a tradition. Although devising innovative hermeneutical strategies is certainly an important part of the process of restructuration, a bolder reform of a culture's main textual corpus becomes inevitable. Indeed, the reorganization of canon, or a tradition's main informational locus, is one of the three central structural components that compose paradigm shifts.

This is not confined to the Chinese tradition. Elsewhere, I have demonstrated that structural transitions in other scriptural traditions associated with the Axial Age have led to an extensive reorganization of their canonical literature (Lior, 2014). Scriptural reforms tend to entail the emergence of an additional textual layer as an extension and supplement to earlier canon. Naturally, supplementing traditional canon with new textual layers is never abrupt; it entails a long process of gradual legitimization that takes place over several generations. Nevertheless, because of the urgency of structural transitions and the fact that they are reactions to intense foreign pressures, these rare canonical shifts are noteworthy for their relatively rapid integration into orthodox culture. Let us return to the Song period as a guide for a possible future shift in the textual resources of contemporary Confucianism.

During the early stages of the Northern Song (960–1127 CE), conservative thinkers were advocating a return to native Chinese resources; they warned against the seductiveness of Buddhist philosophy and demanded that people "reject the foreign teachings of Buddhism and embrace anew the cherished values of the native tradition" (Gardner, 2007, p. xxi). As a result, Song intelligentsia "turned to the classics with an almost missionary commitment . . . the foremost intellectuals of the early centuries of the Song all dedicated much of their lives to studying the classics and writing commentaries on them" (p. xix). But as the revitalization of the commentarial tradition was taking place, a simultaneous trend of suspicion toward the authority of traditional canon was gaining momentum. Many intellectuals started distrusting the ability of the Five Classics to provide solutions to the urgent problems of the day. Some, like reformer Wang Anshi, claimed the Classics were an after-the-fact compilation (Bol, 2008). Others went further by promoting a trend known as "doubting the Classics," in which the Confucian corpus was conventionalized and seen as a product of different historical layers (p. 62).[13] Such tendencies reflect the exceptional rationalization that was taking over intellectual discourse in China during the Song. In Kuhn's terms, the Five Classics paradigm was undergoing a period crisis that led to an unprecedented trend of undermining its traditional authority.

All the different Neo-Confucian factions during the Song were wrestling with the Classics, and it was through the traditional channel of commentary that they sought to reform their tradition. What set the dominant Neo-Confucian School of Principle apart was its radical reformulations of the Confucian canon. Instead of confining itself to reinterpretation, this particular school initiated the historical textual transition to the Four Books. Zhu Xi (朱熹, 1130–1200), the main architect of the Neo-Confucian synthesis, redefined the traditional Confucian canon by establishing an engaging and coherent system of learning based on a new literary corpus that functioned as an extension to the declining stature of the Five Classics. Therefore, the Song revolution in education was predicated on a crucial informational shift in China's central literary corpus. The sudden prioritization of the Four Books over the Five Classics as the main material for Confucian bureaucratic advancement can be better understood as a result of structural reforms and a historical paradigm shift. One of the most interesting features about this transition is that it entailed not only a shift in content but also dramatic changes in formats of presentation and language.

In terms of language, the Neo-Confucian revival represented a full-fledged revolution. Neo-Confucian works were far more accessible than the dense and complicated language of the Five Classics. According to Zhu Xi, the Four Books were characterized by "ease, immediacy, and brevity" that ensured that the essential teachings of the Neo-Confucian tradition would reach the widest audience possible (Li, 1986, p. 249). Gardner (2007) argues that "to restore the Way (*dao* 道)—socially, politically, and intellectually—the Way had to be made accessible . . . the original Five Classics were too lengthy, linguistically archaic and challenging, and, in places, almost incomprehensible" (p. xxiv). Instead of the outdated language of the Five Classics, Neo-Confucian works were written in a semivernacular language that presented information directly to the individual, without assuming a prior understanding of the classical tradition.[14] As we shall see, the modern age represents a similar watershed moment in the transformation of written language. It will be argued that an additional phase of simplifying the Confucian canon is an important prerequisite for a full transition to a new literary paradigm in contemporary Confucianism.

In terms of presentation and structure, Neo-Confucians began to format information in a more analytic and systematic fashion that was very different from the lack of logical coherence characteristic of the Five Classics. The Four Books were meant to be studied in a linear order from the *Great Learning* (大学), to the *Analects*, to the *Mencius*, and finally to the *Doctrine of the Mean* (中庸). Zhuxi's pedagogy gave initiates a clear idea of how to progress through the new material methodically toward well-defined objectives. Even more systematic and rationalized were the Neo-Confucian introductory works to the Four Books, such as the *Xiao Xue* (Elementary Learning, 小学) and the *Jin Si Lu* (Reflections on Things at Hand, 近思录). The *Jin Si Lu* introduced the most central ideas of Neo-Confucian thought selected from the four early masters of the Northern Song in a highly logical order neatly divided into distinct chapters dedicated to specific topics.[15] Chen Chun's *Beixi Ziyi* (*Neo-Confucian Terms Explained*), a glossary of basic Neo-Confucian terminology, is another example of how Song intellectuals sought to make their philosophy more accessible to a rapidly growing pool of educated people. In this influential glossary, the most central concepts of Neo-Confucianism were clearly defined, functioning as a key for decoding earlier and less accessible layers of the tradition. In an age of extreme change, it became evident to Neo-Confucians that without a radical democratization of knowledge in terms of both language and formats of presentation, the middle class would potentially resort to competing ideologies, most notably Buddhism.[16]

The final point worth mentioning about the textual transition of the Song is the integration of a new contemporary link to the transmission of the Confucian *dao*, also known as the *daotong* (道统). Emulating the Chan school's lineages of transmission, different Neo-Confucian factions dedicated considerable time to the construction of new lineages of orthodox transmission. This was an efficient strategy of presenting their revolutionary form of Confucianism in an orthodox guise. An interesting characteristic of works in the new "recorded conversation" genre (*yulu*, 语录), or works such as the *Jin Si Lu*, was their incorporation of the familiar and admired philosophers of the very recent past. By constructing official lineages of transmission, these contemporary thinkers were presented as the legitimate torchbearers of an ancient orthodox "thread" (贯). Although the works of different contemporary thinkers were not necessarily compatible, Zhu Xi skillfully synthesized their different approaches into a coherent system that was seamlessly interwoven with the contents of the Four Books and Five Classics. There are therefore three central features about the textual transition of the Song period that can help us contemplate possible paths of development for contemporary Confucian education. The first was the transition to a more direct and vernacular language that was accessible to nonexperts. The second was a shift to more analytic and systematic formats of presentation. The third was the construction of lineages of transmission and the integration of recent and more relevant thinkers to the interpretation of antiquity. In the following, I explore how such characteristics can find expression in the contemporary Confucian revival.

In terms of language, we saw that the Song period represented a transition to more vernacular forms of writing that were conducive to a more effective dissemination of Neo-Confucian thought. Beginning with the May Fourth Movement in 1919, modern China has undergone one of its greatest linguistic revolutions, epitomized by the widespread adoption of *baihua* (白话), or written vernacular by progressive public intellectuals such as Lu Xun (鲁迅), Hu Shi (胡适), and Chen Duxiu (陈独秀). The modern vernacular represents an additional stage in the colloquialization of written Chinese. As argued earlier, historical transitions are primarily designed to serve new populations that are demanding participation in the construction of a new cultural paradigm. The democratization of knowledge in terms of linguistic accessibility is an important way to bring these new populations into a more participatory orbit of the Confucian tradition. On a more general level, because Confucianism represents the essence of Chinese culture, it is only natural that it be communicated in a language and terminology that reflect the spirit of its age.

In terms of structure, it was mentioned that Neo-Confucian literature was far more logically structured than the textual layers that preceded it. Similarly, the new literary layers of contemporary Confucianism should go a step further in the rationalization of their formats of presentation. Modern readers need a clear exposition of Confucian views regarding major contemporary topics that cannot be found in the contents of the Four Books. Perhaps one way of creating this additional textual layer is by editing a compilation of relevant passages from the Classics that can be divided topically into clear areas of interest, especially topics that are popular among a progressive readership such as gender equality, environmentalism, democracy, individual rights, and animal rights. These selections can be accommodated by a clear colloquial interpretation. Such a compilation can enable contemporary Confucianism to marginalize ideas that blatantly contradict modern sensibilities, while highlighting sections of the Classics that present a uniquely Confucian solution to present dilemmas. This was certainly the strategy that guided Zhu Xi and Lu Zuqian in the composition of the *Jin Si Lu*.

This is also where the integration of recent generations of contemporary Confucians is most relevant. Incorporating information from the 20th and 21st centuries is parallel to the integration of Song contemporaries into the lineages and texts of Neo-Confucianism. While old literary layers can only indirectly relate to modern issues, the thought of contemporary thinkers is crucial for addressing significant topics in a more sophisticated and specialized manner, written in a modern dialect. As in the Song period, these modern thinkers will also provide Confucianism with an air of relevance to the lives of potential enthusiasts.[17] As discussed earlier, the incorporation of recent thinkers into the Confucian canon is directly related to the construction of orthodox lineages of transmission (*daotong* 道统). During the Song, creating lineages of transmission was at the very heart of intellectual and political factionalism. Interestingly, there is a renewed and heated debate about the construction of new lineages of transmission in contemporary China. As in the Song, we are witnessing a process of incorporating contemporary thinkers into an orthodox lineage of transmission as a strategy for legitimizing their thought as a direct continuation of ancient lore (Makeham, 2008). This process will most likely provide certain lineages with the cultural prestige required for recognition as legitimate contributors to the Confucian canon.

The reconfiguration of the Confucian canon might seem like an unlikely possibility at the present. But there are initial signs that a bolder reevaluation of ancient texts is currently on its way. Mou Zongsan, perhaps the most prolific and influential contemporary Confucian, claimed that the *Great Learning*, the first of the Four Books, was not in concordance with the legitimate orthodox lineage of Confucius and Mencius. Instead, Mou highlighted the *Analects*, *Mencius*, *Doctrine of the Mean*, and the *Xici* (系辞) commentary to the *Yijing* as a preferable collection of texts (Makeham, 2003, p. 64). For very different reasons, Jiang Qing's political Confucianism attacks the misguided and idealistic interpretation of the *Great Learning* as a distortion of this text's original political and administrative function (Chen, 2009). The very fact that major Confucian revivalists are suggesting revisions to the classical corpus is an indication that a future restructuration of the Confucian canon is a likely possibility. Ironically, the intellectual output of those who suggest revisions to the Confucian canon might eventually become part of a modern supplement to the Four Books and Five Classics.

Conclusion

This chapter began by demonstrating why the Song and contemporary transitions should be construed in terms of paradigm shifts rather than ordinary change. The two periods witnessed historical social and economic transformations, far-reaching institutional changes, and significant changes in written communication. More importantly, both transitions were, to a great extent, a reaction to foreign cultural paradigms. Because of these similarities, it was argued that the present Confucian revival is likely to lead to a similar restructuring of the Confucian corpus and that there are initial indications that such a change is taking place. It is impossible to predict what the future textual transition of contemporary Confucianism will look like or when it will occur. What is clear is that classical

Confucian literature is no longer capable of adequately addressing the central dilemmas of modernity and that an updated body of information is likely to supplement old literary layers. Informed by the Neo-Confucian transition from the Five Classics to the Four Books, this chapter offered possible directions for constructing a new contemporary supplement to the Confucian classics in terms of linguistic simplification, changes in formats of presentation, and the incorporation of contemporary thinkers as legitimate transmitters of the Confucian tradition.

Finally, it was argued that the pedagogical idealism of Neo-Confucianism could teach us valuable lessons about the nature of education, its goals, and the learning process as a resource for character formation and moral awareness. Neo-Confucian learning was focused on the individual as the foundation for personal and social transformation rather than on insincere knowledge devoid of values. Moreover, in a quintessentially Confucian fashion, Song intellectuals repeatedly stressed the need to translate knowledge into concrete, prosocial behavior. It is in this sense that the preceding examinations of textual transformations and Neo-Confucian education are most interrelated. The pedagogical insights of Neo-Confucians were founded on the transition from the Five Classics to the more relevant content and linguistic accessibility of the Four Books. Similarly, alterations in canonical literature at present are a crucial step in equipping the modern individual with the relevant textual resources for the construction of a contemporary philosophy of education.

Notes

1. Tu Weiming was the main promoter of Mou Zongsan's theory of the three-epoch progression of Confucianism. See Mou Zongsan (1970, p. 62). Tu Weiming, "rujia chuantong de xiandai zhuanhua 儒家传统的现代转化" (The Modernization of the Confucian Tradition), in *Rujia chuantong de xiandaihua: Du Weiming xin ruxue lunzhe jiyao*, p. 69.

2. When referring to Neo-Confucianism, this chapter is concerned with the most dominant School of Principle (理学).

3. The frequently used term "New Confucianism" (新儒家) is problematic because some of the most influential approaches to Confucianism in contemporary China were established in response and contradistinction to New Confucianism. More inclusive, the term "Contemporary Confucianism" pertains to a broad range of philosophical, religious, popular, political, and even economic strands of the Confucian revival.

4. See more on the application of Kuhn's theory to culture and religion in Barbour (1974, 1997) and Hans (1988).

5. The Neo-Confucian *li/qi* distinction was modeled after Buddhism's similar distinction between *li* and *shi*, or *pattern* and *things*, or *affairs* (事). Such metaphysical dualisms can be seen as a Chinese interpretation of the Indian distinction between the separate spheres of Samsara and Nirvana.

6. Attacks began early with Han Yu's famous anti-Buddhist letter remonstrating to the emperor for allowing the ceremonial deliverance of the Buddha's bone relic to the imperial palace. For Song dynasty attacks, see Zhu Xi and Lu Zuqian, and Wing-tsit Chan (1967). *Reflections on things at hand: The Neo-Confucian anthology.* New York: Columbia University Press. Book 13(5), p. 283.

7. Organizations such as the Shenzhen Confucius Hall (*kongsheng tang*) conduct Confucian "services" that include singing "sacred songs," weekly sermons, and reading of sacred texts. Christian ideals regarding personal faith, prayer, morality, and religious ultimacy have also been a major source of inspiration for prominent contemporary Confucians such as Tu Weiming and Jiang Qing.

8. Academies and family-supported schools also functioned as an important safety net for young intellectuals, offering financial support and the promise of alternative career paths such as teaching locally; managing charitable estates (*yizhuang*, 義莊), shrines, and lineage buildings; and supervising printing projects and other private enterprises that were conducive to economic development (Bol, 2008, p. 39).

9. On military concessions to the foreign Liao and Jin dynasties, see Pulleyblank (1969, pp. 77–114) and Kuhn (2009, pp. 45–46).

10. Anna Sun seems to agree when she notes: "Confucian commitment to political activism could also become a source of positive political resistance and change" (2013, p. 178).

11. For example, the Beijing Four Seas Children's Recitation Center (Beijing sihai ertong duijing daodu jiaoyu zhongxin 北京四海儿童读经导读教育中心) promotes a recitation method that includes both Chinese and Western classics and includes CD-ROMs and supplementary reading material. In 2001, a group of academics supported by the Ministry of Education and strongly influenced by the controversial contemporary Confucian Jiang Qing offered a more orthodox and Confucian selection of texts that consisted of the Six Classics, Four Books, *Reflections on Things at Hand*, and *Instructions for Practical Living* (Makeham, 2003, p. 323). Beyond these initiatives, since its inception in the mid-1980s, the "reading the Classics movement" (读经运动) has become extremely popular across China.

12. Mark Halperin claims, "During the two millennia from the empire's unification in 221 BCE to its nineteenth century collision with the industrial West, no period saw more drastic change than the ninth, tenth, and eleventh centuries, from the late T'ang through the mid-Sung dynasties" (2006, pp. 5–6).

13. Su Xun, the father of the famous Su Shi, went as far as claiming that the *Yijing* (Book of Changes) "was merely a strategy aimed at mystification, a means of getting the populace to think that the order being imposed on them was not a political construction but somehow a natural one." *Su Xun Jiayou ji* (嘉祐集) 6.1a–2b. See Bol (2008, p. 63).

14. A. C. Graham (1989, p. 390) specifically highlights Chan Buddhists and Neo-Confucians as a new phase in which information was communicated in a highly colloquial form.

15. The four masters: Zhou Dunyi (周敦頤), Zhang Zai (张载), Cheng Yi (程颐), and Cheng Hao (程颢).

16. See more on the simplification of Neo-Confucian thought in de Bary (1984).

17. As an example, the Yidan Xuetang bases large parts of its ideology on the thought of modern thinkers such as Liang Shuming and Wang Fengyi (Billioud, 2011, p. 294).

References

Angle, S. C. (2012). *Contemporary Confucian political philosophy: Towards progressive Confucianism*. Cambridge, MA: Polity Press.
Barbour, I. (1974). *Myths, models and paradigms: The nature of scientific and religious language*. London: S.C.M. Press.
Barbour, I. (1997). *Religion and science: Historical and contemporary issues*. New York: Harper One.
Bell, D. (2008). *New Confucianism: Politics and everyday life in a changing society*. Princeton: Princeton University Press.
Billioud, S. (2011). Confucian revival and the emergence of "Jiaohua Organizations": A case study of the Yidan Xuetang. *Modern China, 37*(3), 286–314.
Bol, P. K. (1992). *"This Culture of Ours": Intellectual transitions in T'ang and Sung China*. Stanford: Stanford University Press.
Bol, P. K. (2008). *Neo-Confucianism in history*. Cambridge: Harvard University Asia Center.
Chan, W. T. (1957). *Chu Hsi and Neo-Confucianism*. Honolulu: University of Hawaii Press.
Chan, W. T. (1967). Neo-Confucianism: New ideas in old terminology. *Philosophy East and West, 17*(1–4), 15–35.
Chang, C. (1957). *The development of Neo-Confucian thought* (Vol. 1). New Haven: College and University Press.
Chen, M. (2009). Modernity and Confucian political philosophy in a globalized world. *Diogenes, 56*(1), 94–108.

de Bary, T. W. (1953). A reappraisal of Neo-Confucianism. In A. Wright (Ed.), *Studies in Chinese thought* (pp. 81–111). Chicago: University of Chicago Press.

de Bary, T. W. (1984). Neo-Confucian education and post-Confucian East Asia. *Bulletin of the American Academy of Arts and Sciences, 37*(5), 7–17.

de Bary, T.W. (1991). *Learning for one's self: Essays on the individual in Neo-Confucian thought*. New York: Columbia University Press.

de Bary, T.W., & Chafee, John W. (1989). *Neo-Confucian education: The formative stage*. Berkeley: University of California Press.

Fairbank, J. K., & Goldman, M. (1988). *China: A new history*. Cambridge: Belknap Press of Harvard University Press.

Gardner, D. (1990). *Learning to be a sage: Selections from the conversations of Master Chu, arranged topically*. Berkeley: University of California Press.

Gardner, D. (1998). Confucian commentary and Chinese intellectual history. *The Journal of Asian Studies, 57*(2), 397–422.

Gardner, D. (2007). *The Four Books: The basic teachings of the later Confucian tradition*. Indianapolis: Hackett.

Graham, A. C. (1989). *Disputers of the Tao: Philosophical argumentation in ancient China*. Chicago: Open Court.

Gregory, P. N. (1999). The vitality of Buddhism in the Sung. In P. N. Gregory & D. A. Gertz Jr. (Eds.), *Buddhism in the Sung* (pp. 1–20). Honolulu: University of Hawaii Press.

Hans, K. H. (1988). *Theology for the third millennium*. New York: Doubleday.

Foulk, G. T. (1993). Myth, ritual, and monastic practice in Sung Ch'an Buddhism. In P. B. Ebrey & P. Gregory (Eds.), *Religion and society in T'ang and Sung China* (pp. 147–208). Honolulu: University of Hawaii Press.

Halperin, M. (2006). *Out of the cloister: Literati perspectives on Buddhism in Sung China, 960–1279*. Cambridge: Harvard University Asia Center.

Jiang, Q. (2003). *Zhengzhe ruxue: Dangdai ruxue de zhuanxiang, tezhi yu fazhan* 政治儒学: 当代儒学的转向, 特质与发展 Political Ruxue. Beijing: Sanlian.

Kuhn, D. (2009). *The age of Confucian rule: The Song transformation of China*. Cambridge: Belknap.

Kuhn, S. T. (1996). *The structure of scientific revolutions* (3rd ed.). Chicago: University of Chicago Press.

Lampton, D. M. (2014). *Following the leader: Ruling China, from Deng Xiaoping to Xi Jinping*. Oakland: University of California Press.

Lee, T. H. C. (1989). Schools of education before Chu Hsi. In T. W. de Bary & J. W. Chaffee (Eds.), *Neo-Confucian education: The formative stage* (pp. 105–137). Berkeley: University of California Press.

Li Jingde (Ed.). (1986). *Zhuzi Yulei* 朱子語類 (The Conversations of Master Zhu Arranged Topically). Neijing: Zhonghua Shuju.

Lior, Y. (2014) Neo-Confucianism and Kabbalah: A comparative morphology of medieval movements (Doctoral dissertation). Boston University, Boston.

Liu, J. T. C. (1988). *China turning inward: Intellectual-political changes in the early twelfth century*. Cambridge: Harvard University Press.
Makeham, J. (2003). *New Confucianism: A critical examination*. New York: Palgrave Macmillan.
Makeham, J. (2008). *Lost soul: "Confucianism" in contemporary Chinese academic discourse*. Cambridge: Harvard University Press.
Nakamura, H. (1997). *Ways of thinking of Eastern Peoples: India, China, Tibet, Japan*. New York: Columbia University Press.
Mou Zongsan. (1970). *Shengming de Xuewen* 生命的学问 (Vital Learning). Taipei: Sanmin Shuju.
Pulleyblank, E. G. (1969). Neo-Confucianism and Neo-Legalism in T'ang intellectual life. In A. F. Wright (Ed.), *The Confucian persuasion* (pp. 755–805). Stanford: Stanford University Press.
Rappaport, R. (1999). *Ritual and religion in the making of humanity*. New York: Cambridge University Press.
Sun, A. (2013). *Confucianism as a world religion*. Princeton: Princeton University Press.
Tillman, H. C. (1992). *Confucian discourse and Chu Hsi's ascendancy*. Honolulu: University of Hawaii Press.
Tu Weiming. (1992) *Rujia chuantong de xiandai zhuanhua: Du Weiming xin ruxue lunzhe jiyao* 儒家传统的现代转化: 杜维明新儒学论者辑要 (The Modernization of the Confucian Tradition). Beijing: Zhongguo Guangbo dianshi chubanshi (China Radio Film & TV Press).
Twitchett, C. D., & Fairbank, K. J. (Eds.). (1979). *The Cambridge history of China, vol. 3: Sui and T'ang China 589–906, part 1*. Cambridge: Cambridge University Press.
Walton, L. (1993). Southern Sung academies as sacred place. In P. B. Ebrey & P. N. Gregory (Eds.), *Religion and society in T'ang and Sung China* (pp. 335–363). Honolulu: University of Hawaii Press.
Wang, X. Z. 王心竹. (2011). *Lixue yu fojiao* 理学与佛教 (The Lixue School and Buddhism). Changchun: Changchun Press.
Weber, M. (1968). *Economy and society* (3 Vols.). Totowa: Bedminster Press. (Originally published 1921.)
Yang, F. G. (2012). *Religion in China: Survival and revival under communist Rule*. Oxford: Oxford University Press.
Yao, X. (2001) Who is a Confucian today? A critical reflection on the issues concerning Confucian identity. *Modern Times: Journal of Contemporary Religion, 16*(3), 313–328.
Zurcher, E. (1972). *The Buddhist conquest of China: The spread and adaptation of Buddhism in early medieval China*. Leiden: Brill.

6

Learning as Public Reasoning (*gongyi*)

A Paradigmatic Shift of the Late-Imperial Confucian Educational Tradition in 17th-Century China

YANG WEI

> As for what is the most difficult to comprehend under Heaven, one person seeks it but may not attain it. If tens of thousands of people seek it, nothing is unattainable.
>
> —Huang Zongxi, *Huang Zongxi quanji*[1]

Education, in the Chinese Confucian tradition, consists of teaching (*jiao*) and learning (*xue*). The Confucian concept of learning has undergone diverse changes over the past two millennia. This chapter explores the redefinition of the Confucian notion of learning (*xue*) as public reasoning (*gongyi*) by examining change in the shared values among 17th-century Chinese scholar-officials. Between the 1590s and 1680s, a group of scholar-officials challenged the existing Neo-Confucian (*daoxue*) concept of learning as individualized comprehension of ancient classics and championed a new method of learning as open-ended, continual, inclusive, cumulative collective reasoning that aimed at congregating various ideas, opinions, and approaches. Fueling this new concept of learning was a rising populist attitude that saw individual observations and perspectives as inherently incomplete, limited, potentially biased, and inherently prone to errors. Questioning the preexisting Neo-Confucian claim of individual access to the ultimate truth of the cosmos, this new notion of learning believed that a collective remedy of individuals' deficiency is absolutely necessary, giving rise to a broad, inclusive aggregation of various opinions, views, and observations. The uncertainty about individual access to the ultimate truth also bred a popularist definition of the Way as publicly shared, spurring the florescence of encyclopedias, compendia, and collectanea marked by comprehensiveness, completeness, and diversity. The broad, indiscriminate aggregate of information and opinions in the various study manuals and guides compiled for students and scholars was deemed a remedy for the inherent deficiency of the individual perspective, making these comprehensive, erudite study guides "textual museums" available for readers to choose for themselves.

Orthodox Lineage of the Way and the Song-Era Neo-Confucian Tradition

The rise of Neo-Confucianism (*daoxue*) in the Song era (960–1276) significantly changed the landscape of China's intellectual world. Neo-Confucian scholars brought to the forefront the concepts of Heavenly Principle (*tianli*) and the Way (*dao*), understood as the ultimate and innate coherence of the cosmos and human society. These scholars believed that men can know, with absolute certainty, values innate to humans and integral to the processes of Heaven and earth. Learning was thus considered by Neo-Confucian scholars as a coherent, moral self-cultivation program aimed at the dominance of Principle in all dimensions of one's life against self-desires toward sagehood (Bol, 2009; Chen, 2010; Yu, 2003). In this moral philosophy, it was believed that only a handful of prominent individuals had comprehended the Way deeply rooted in the natural pattern of Heaven and earth, and these select individuals thus perfected their moral virtue. The transmission of orthodox learning concerning the Way through this enlightened minority was referred to as *daotong*.[2] Under the Ming (1368–1644), Song-era Neo-Confucian scholars' interpretations of earlier classical cannons were standardized as the official dynastic ideology; Zhu Xi and other Song-era Neo-Confucian scholars were deemed successors to the lineage of orthodox learning (Elman, 1997).

This Neo-Confucian stance restructured the aims, methods, and nature of learning (*xue*). *Daoxue* scholars, while elevating the importance of *gewu zhizhi* (investigating things and extending knowledge), particularly opposed "broad learning" (*boxue*), as the former is guided by pronounced moral purpose as opposed to the latter's aimless erudition (Bol, 1992). For Zhu Xi, the moral purpose of learning requires a universal approach to knowledge in search of the inherent coherence behind the variegated manifestations of all things, events, and phenomena (*gewu qiongli*). Zhu Xi's predecessor, Cheng Yi (1033–1107), feared that without moral guidance, "broad learning" would succumb to trifles of knowledge, and he particularly warns of the tension between the pursuit of the Way and an obsession with textual studies and book knowledge. The *daoxue* attitude entertained no free, extensive investigation of subjects of interest. Erudition and collective reasoning were not justified in the Neo-Confucian tradition of learning.

Epistemological Limits of Individual Learning

Under the Ming, scholarship of the former sages and worthies, including Song Neo-Confucian scholars, became authoritative, orthodox learning of the classical canons. However, this absolute certainty of the individual capability of accessing truth was challenged in the late 16th to 17th centuries. This section discusses the group of literati who questioned, from diverse perspectives, the *daoxue* confidence in the individual's ability to attain definitive knowledge through a moralist approach. These Ming scholars often disagreed with Song Neo-Confucian scholars with regard to specific interpretations of the Classics, but more important is their emphasis on the fundamental deficiency of an individual perspective that must be remedied through a collective orientation.

Xie Zhaozhe (1567–1624) was a Hangzhou-born literati-official who served in Zhejiang, Nanjing, and Beijing. His encyclopedic anthology, *Wuzazu* (Miscellaneous Writings of the Five), covers an extremely broad spectrum of knowledge, ranging from history, local gazetteers, local customs, poetry, geography, calligraphy, and astrology to book history, categorized into five main sections about Heaven, earth, humans, objects, and affairs with detailed analytical notes (Xie, 2007). Xie often argued against Song Neo-Confucian scholars on specific philosophical points (pp. 1472–1473), but he particularly stressed the epistemological limits of individuals. In discussing the hydrography of China, for instance, Xie cited a well-known observer who ranked the seven best springs under Heaven, but his ranking appears to conflict with an earlier evaluation. On this discrepancy, Xie remarked:

> Are these previous rankings really the final judgment? Are there really no better springs under the Heaven besides those tasted by these previous observers? I think these two observers' evaluations were only based on the reaches of their ears and eyes in their lifetime, and on their own personal experiences of tasting the water from the springs. . . . [It is impossible] for one person to examine thoroughly all the waters under Heaven. (p. 1532)

According to Xie, one individual's "hearing, vision, mind, and knowledge" is fundamentally insufficient to make a complete evaluation of springs under Heaven. The very limitation of personal observation is precisely the reason for his criticism of Zhu Xi's interpretation of passages from the Four Books—the most authoritative interpretations at that time. Regarding Zhu Xi's commentaries to the *Analects* about geysers in the area of Lu, Xie argued that it is wrong because: "Zhu Xi had never come to Lu in person. However, he made a judgment based exclusively on Principles. How could he do that?" (Xie, 2007, pp. 1533–1534).

Xie understood inference or deduction based purely on individualized comprehension of Principle as very untenable. An understanding of Principle does not replace direct, firsthand investigation of the concrete objects and affairs of the world. This attitude is shared by another mid-Ming scholar named Zhao Zhenji (1508–1576), who likewise questioned the fundamental Neo-Confucian premise on the coherence of the cosmos. Zhao's scholarly objective was to compile comprehensive, thorough, and all-encompassing encyclopedic works that merged theoretical knowledge and practical application. It is reported that he devoted much of his time to drafting lengthy compendia titled "Two Thorough Studies" (*er tong*) (Zhao, 1997). The first section of chapters, "Thorough Studies for Ordering the World" (*jingshitong*), offers thorough discussions on history, Classics, institutions, treaties, laws, conduct, arts, and miscellaneous methods and skills. The second section, "Thorough Studies for Transcending the World" (*chushitong*), contains extensive entries of knowledge about Buddhism and Daoism. As the title of his book series indicates, Zhao sought to conduct comprehensive studies encompassing all categories of knowledge known in his time. Unlike many 16th-century Neo-Confucian scholars, Zhao highlighted the textual approach to the Six Classics to attain knowledge of "ordering the world" (*jingshi*). He objected to the purely philosophical discussion of abstract concepts, such as mind and nature, and rejected the basic assumption of Neo-Confucianism regarding the coherence of Principle as encompassing all things and all aspects of human lives. For Zhao, it is impossible to talk about abstract, occult philosophical concepts before thorough investigation of individual objects and affairs one by one. Everything has its separate, unique natural order that cannot be easily translated into another. In understanding the distinctive attributes of each thing that is constantly changing like "a moving river," the Neo-Confucian concept of universal Coherence of all things hardly helps. It follows that the only way to obtain solid knowledge is to examine each individual object, affair, and phenomenon on its own right. Clearly, this position logically justifies erudition, a salient feature of Zhao Zhenji's own encyclopedic work.

This distrust of an individual's ability to comprehend Principle was shared by another 16th-century scholar named He Liangjun (1506–1573), a Songjiang native. Like Xie and Zhao, He was the erudite author of impressive encyclopedic works. Of the problems of his times, He said he was most troubled by the self-delegated authority of Neo-Confucians based on their essentially personal understanding of Principle and nature. He worried that this blind confidence, amplified by political power and accumulated over time, would result in a disastrous scenario of "killing all under Heaven through methods of learning" (yi xueshu sha tianxia)[3] (He, 1959, p. 30). He vehemently criticized the Neo-Confucian obsession with Principle and nature, arguing that it was worse than indulgence in sensory desires: According to He, the danger of the empty discussion of moral philosophy lies in the probability of one's bias and blind insistence on one's personal view (He, 1983, pp. 82b–83a).

He argued that scholarly opinions, like all opinions, are always prone to error and imperfection. What troubled him most was the absolute claim to ultimate truth by "those who discuss Principle." This distrust of any individual's infallibility led to He Liangjun's direct critique of the authoritative learning of Song Neo-Confucian scholars. For our Jiangnan scholars, these sages and worthies were no different from ordinary people in terms of their understanding of the Way. It follows that the words uttered and institutions invented by the sages are not complete, unchanging, and unmistakable. This popularist misgiving of the absolute authority of any individual prompted another late-Ming scholar, Lu Kun (1536–1618), to provide an alternative interpretation of the Way, challenging the Neo-Confucian concept of sagely learning. Lu argued that the infinity of the Way is far beyond the understanding of humans. Words uttered and institutions invented by the sages were also conditioned by historical contexts and contingencies and therefore situational, temporary, and incomplete (Lu, 2008, p. 642). Lu wrote: "The Way has no boundaries, and it cannot be limited by human words that are merely vehicles of the Way; affairs are conditioned by contexts and situations, and they would not be completed by the institutions established by sages" (Lu, 1962, p. 65). In another passage, Lu Kun noted that even Confucius's own words cannot be quoted as unquestionable, ultimate truth (Lu, 2008, pp. 645–646). That said, the problem of historical contingency and limits of language applies to everyone without exception. This viewpoint was echoed by Chen Que (1604–1677), another Jiangnan scholar in the late Ming, who asserted that the Cheng brothers and Zhu Xi, Neo-Confucian sages and worthies, were all wrong in their interpretations of the Classics. He wrote:

> We are not Yao and Shun [sage-kings]; who would never make mistakes? Mistakes are not what Gentlemen should try to conceal. The Cheng brothers and Zhu Xi were accidentally misled by the *Great Learning*. Thus, they misled themselves and then misled the others. If we saw this frequently and dared not to correct it, then this is no longer a mistake of Cheng and Zhu, but rather our own mistake. (Chen, 1979, pp. 565–566)

Chen Que hotly disputed the Cheng brothers' and Zhu Xi's authoritative commentaries to the *Great Learning*. Relevant to our discussion is not which interpretation of the *Great Learning* is closer to the original text, but rather the changing attitude toward the learning of classical canons (*xue*, see further discussion). According to Chen Que, we are in a world where everyone, including the sages and worthies, may err. The universal limits on our cognitive capability make problematic any individual's unquestionable authority in comprehending ultimate truth, even that of the sages and worthies. This distrust of the individual's infallibility bred a new popularist definition of learning as a collective, accumulative, and fluid process, in which all individual scholars partake.

The Importance of Diversity

This questioning of an individual's claim to ultimate truth logically gave rise to a greater tolerance of diversity, which gained refreshed philosophical attention from this popularist perspective. The same group of literati actively justified the importance of diversity of opinions and approaches, as well as broader communication among scholars who engage in collective reasoning.

Against the Neo-Confucian assumption of coherence in all things, our Jiangnan scholars stressed the particularity and distinction of each object, affair, and phenomenon. Zhao Zhenji, cited earlier, trenchantly pointed out the problem of the philosophical discussion of Principle and nature without solid, empirical investigation. In the face of a wide variety of worldly phenomena to be explored, other scholars underlined the necessity of diversity in approaches to the objects of examination. Such diversity of approach was justified in terms of the innately distinctive character of each person's nature. He Liangjun extrapolated this point through citations of the Classics:

> The *Book of Changes* says: "those who are benevolent see what is benevolent, and those who are wise see what is wise." This is to say that the material forces of humans differ in their purity, and the nature of their characters differs in quality. [These characters] each reach the maximum [of their potential] but cannot be all-encompassing. . . . The sages promised that people vary from each other; how can today's persons claim that they possess all the characters? (He, 1983, pp. 82b–83a)

It is natural, He argued, that humans differ in their distinctive qualities of material force and the unique nature of their character. The variegated natural qualities of people occasioned the diversity in approaches to learning. Another 16th-century Jiangnan scholar, Tang Shunzhi (1507–1560), particularly appreciated the variegated perspectives and methods scholars adopt based on their distinctive character; and he himself was also a practitioner of the encyclopedic approach to learning (see later discussion). Tang remarks: "[Confucius's disciples] differed from each other in their scholarly approaches. Some began [their learning] with moral virtues; some with the knowledge gained by hearing and seeing. They were simply following what are close to their different innate qualities" (Tang, 1997, pp. 133–138).

This acknowledgment of the innate diversity in human character was widely shared by many Jiangnan scholars in their justification of more tolerant, eclectic approaches to knowledge in the 16th century.

Tang's close friend Mao Kun (1512–1601), also a 16th-century Jiangnan scholar, championed the Confucian tradition of culture (*wen*) in contrast to the tradition of moral philosophy underscored by Neo-Confucians.[4] In the preface to his well-known *Annotated Selection of the Writings of the Eight Tang-Song Masters* (*Tang-Song badajia wenchao*), Mao remarked:

> Between Heaven and earth, humans endowed with distinctive material force and armed with necessary concentration can reach the utmost [of these distinctive qualities]. Linlun's musical talents, Bizao's divination skill, Yangyouji's archery techniques, Zaofu's talents of chariot-driving, Bianque's medical skills, Liao's mathematical talents, and Yi's talents of chess-playing, all, with the wisdom endowed by Heaven complemented by concentrated studies, gained their respective perspectives. (Mao, 1997, p. 648)

According to Mao, it is part of the natural order that Heaven endows people with distinctive talents and unique characteristics. Though having no intention to downplay the importance of *daoxue*, Mao sought to define it as only one trend of the great Confucian tradition; more importantly, other alternative traditions such as textual-literary studies of the Six Classics (*liujing*) were of equal importance. All these different approaches were equally valuable as associated with the grand Confucian tradition of learning now broadly redefined. Indeed, the Neo-Confucian attempts to make moral philosophy alone orthodox worried several Jiangnan scholars in the 16th century. Zhao Zhenji particularly criticized Song-era Neo-Confucian scholars' claim as the sole determiners of orthodoxy; instead, he called for a broader horizon and greater tolerance to facilitate more open and inclusive scholarly communication and exchange. He argued:

> When it came down to the northern and southern Confucian scholars during the Song period, they set up stricter barriers and exclusively defended their own territories [of scholarship], to prohibit communication. Chen Xianzhang sighed that the Song Confucian scholars were exceedingly rigorous in setting boundaries. It is precisely their rigor in setting boundaries that resulted in the inferior quality in [their methods of learning].

If objects are not connected, then their uses become insufficient; if [methods] of learning are not connected, then they appear to be inferior. (Cited in Huang, 1986, vol. 7, p. 882)

For Zhao, the progress of learning is hinged precisely on free, open communication and exchange, called "connection" (*tong*); this broader "connection" denies all boundaries of geographical origins, academic schools, or scholarly approaches. A broadened horizon and tolerance of diversity, according to Zhao, determines to a large degree the quality of learning. Zhao ridiculed those Neo-Confucian scholars who narrowed the scope of their reading but claimed absolute truth based on the coherence of Principle:

[These scholars] never travel beyond one hundred *li*, and never communicate with one single beneficial friend. They hold merely ten-odd old books of inferior learning, proud of being a leading figure among those who do not recognize a single character and have no knowledge. They say arrogantly: "I alone assume the transmission of this culture with no predecessor before me, and no follower after me." (Cited in Huang, 1986, vol. 7, p. 886)

To Zhao Zhenji, individual perspectives are inherently parochial, limited, and incomplete. These innate flaws must be overcome by broad dialogue with a variety of approaches and views. Unsurprisingly, Zhao was known for his zeal in finding common ground for varied approaches to learning, including those of Buddhism and Daoism. This syncretic attitude logically necessitates extensive textual study and inquiry as the foundation for progress of learning. Huang Zongxi (1610–1695) also stressed the importance of diversity in scholarly approaches. In the preface to his well-known study of Ming scholars, *Mingru xue'an* (Records of Ming Scholars), Huang wrote the following rebuttal to the Neo-Confucian claim to orthodox Confucian learning:

The diversity in methods of learning indicates precisely the infinity of the body of the Way. Unfortunately, today's gentlemen want all to derive from one single path. They follow the preexisting arguments to evaluate the past and the present.

> Anything that is slightly different is denounced as deviation from the Classics and betrayal of the Way. . . . The Way is like the ocean. Waters, whether it is from Rivers Jiang, Huai, He, Han, Jing, or Wei, or simply small water drops, flow, without exception, to the ocean day and night through routes with twists and turns. They are different waters on their own, but combined in one when reaching the ocean. (Huang, 2008, vol. 1, p. 7)

Like many Jiangnan scholars in the late Ming, Huang redefined the Way as a vast, open, all-encompassing entity universally accessible by all, in lieu of something vertically transmitted by a lineage of the enlightened few. Indeed, Huang Zongxi never agreed to the idea of *daotong*. In his eyes, the infinity of the Way ontologically necessitates the diversity of scholarly approaches. The unity of the Way is revealed only through broad, tolerant, indiscriminate inclusion of all scholarly opinions and methods that are sometimes conflicting, a decisively popularist attitude that justifies the encyclopedic approach to learning.

Redefining the Way

Consistent with the changing attitude toward diversity and tolerance, the concept of the Way became highly contested from the 16th century. The Song Neo-Confucian assumption of the lineal transmission of the Way was challenged. The new attitude redefined the Way as publicly shared by everyone across time and space. Wang Yangming (1472–1529) was one of the first in the 16th century to question the Cheng-Zhu Neo-Confucian school by promoting the concept of the Way as publicly shared. In challenging Zhu Xi's adaptation of the *Great Learning*, Wang Yangming argued:

> The Way is what is public to all-under-Heaven; learning is what is public to all-under-Heaven; these are not that which Master Zhu can obtain and privatize; these are not that which Confucius can obtain and privatize. What is public to all-under-Heaven must be discussed publicly by public speeches. (Wang, 1992, p. 78)

For Wang Yangming, there was never a lineal, vertical transmission of the orthodox Way through an enlightened minority. By contrast, the Way is horizontally shared by all-under-Heaven. It follows that the learning of the Way entails "open discussion by public speeches" (*gong yan zhi er yi yi*). One must participate in this public discussion with fair criteria for what is right and wrong, free from the distraction of emotions. Indeed, when Wang Yangming argued that "learning is what is public to all-under-Heaven, . . . what is public to all-under-Heaven must be discussed openly by public speeches," he was confident that the correct opinions would eventually prevail as a result of public reasoning—a procedure that fundamentally boosts the progress of "learning" (*xue*).

This notion of a "publicly shared" Way was widely endorsed by late-Ming scholars such as Zou Yuanbiao (1551–1624) and Liu Zongzhou (1578–1645). For instance, Liu redefined the Way as follows:

> The Way is the general Way under Heaven; the words on the Way must likewise be public words under Heaven. What was incomplete in the speeches by Confucius and Mencius were to be discussed by Masters Cheng and Zhu. What was incomplete in the speeches by Masters Cheng and Zhu were to be discussed by Master Yangming [Wang Yangming]. What is incomplete in the words by Master Yangming is to be discussed by later scholars.
>
> . . . The Way is the general Way under Heaven, and learning [depends on] the public words under Heaven (*xue zhe tianxia zhi gongyan*). (Liu, 2007, p. 187)

According to Liu Zongzhou, the fact that the Way is "publicly shared" innately prescribes the public nature of any learning about the Way. This logically requires a cumulative scholarly exchange and critical analysis of existing scholarship, including the speeches (*yan*) of previous scholars like Zhu Xi and Wang Yangming. No default submission to these authorities was assumed; instead, one must assume that even these prominent scholars may be "incomplete" (*buzu*) in their own learning. As Liu Zongzhou maintained that "learning [depends on] the public words under the Heaven (*xue zhe tianxia zhi gongyan*)," he anticipated generations of scholars contributing their own share of "words" to this ongoing, cumulative, collective process of "learning" that is open to all.

Learning as Public Reasoning: The Changing Idea of Xue

This idea of learning was further elaborated by Liu Zongzhou's disciples, Chen Que and Huang Zongxi, from a popularist perspective. To Chen Que and Huang Zongxi, learning was no longer a morally guided process in which one individual advances toward the ultimate coherence prescribed by Neo-Confucian programs, but rather a cumulative, fluid, inclusive, and open-ended process of collective reasoning in which all make their due critical contributions. Chen Que detailed the new concept of the Way and a popularist description of learning thereby as follows:

> The Way is that which has been commonly shared by thousands of sages and hundreds of kings, and that is commonly accessed and acknowledged by all-under-Heaven in tens of hundreds of generations. It is not that which one single person can obtain and privatize. We must say what is trusted, leave aside what is suspected, accept what is right, and abandon what is wrong. (Chen, 1979, vol. 2, pp. 565–566)

Chen Que maintained that his interpretation of the *Great Learning* was correct, while Chu Xi's was wrong; and he believed that the popularist approach to learning would ensure the prevailing of correct opinion through collective reasoning, in which scholars "say what is trusted; leave aside what is suspected; accept what is right; and abandon what is wrong." This idea of learning as public reasoning logically necessitates a set of commonly accepted and followed methods for academic investigations, so as to allow all to share a common methodological ground—the guiding principles of the Qing evidentiary scholarship (Chow, 1994; Elman, 1990).

This new definition of learning as public reasoning, stemming from a universal, egalitarian notion of the Way, was likewise central to Huang Zongxi's scholarly practices. In his preface to *Records of Ming Scholars* (*Mingru xue'an*), Huang Zongxi described the Way as an ocean that indiscriminately accommodates waters from all sources (Huang, 2008, p. 7). Huang argued that the diverse methods of learning and opinions (*xueshu*) must be valued in their own right. No enlightened minority can claim full comprehension of the truth and, thus, privileged access to it. It must be noted that Huang did admit that some opinions are better than others, and he made critical evaluations of previous scholarship. However, this does not offset his general popularist approach. The fundamental distrust of any individual's infallibility differentiates this popularist approach from the Neo-Confucian notion of orthodox learning, as the former entails juxtaposing one's critical opinions with competing opinions in an inclusive, open stream of debate, while the latter excludes heterodox opinions as intrinsically erroneous and worthless. In other words, the popularist approach to learning mediates various personal opinions and the general progress of learning through a more open, fluid, and dynamic process of public reasoning in which all partake and contribute their own critical studies, whereas the Neo-Confucian presupposes the rigid, monolithic, and absolute differentiation between orthodoxy and its opposition. The unity of the Way is thus believed, from the popularist perspective, as manifesting only at the collective level where various approaches and opinions are dynamically combined. In this regard, scholarly activities involving dialogue, exchange, debate, and synthesis are absolutely necessary for general progress of learning. In accounting for the discrepancy in scholarly opinion between Zhu Xi and Lu Jiuyuan, Huang Zongxi noted:

> Zhu Xi and Lu Jiuyuan debated thoroughly and repeatedly, and the discrepancies between the two scholars thus emerged clearly. . . . The two masters did not lightly agree with each other, in order to pursue the outcome that is most proper and optimal, and to show the Way to the following generations under the Heaven. . . . The Way is fundamentally a public Way. Each scholar pursues what is right to him respectively. (Huang, 1986, vol. 5, p. 277)

According to Huang Zongxi, the purpose of scholarly debate is nothing else but "to pursue the final outcome that is most proper and optimal." But to have this best result entails the coming together, debate, competition, exchanges, challenging, and synthesis of diverse personal opinions. This popularist approach championed by Huang redefined learning as a cumulative, fluid, open-ended, inclusive process of public reasoning. As Huang remarked:

> As for what is the most difficult to comprehend under Heaven, one person seeks it but may not attain it. If tens of thousands of people seek it, nothing is unattainable. As for what is the

most difficult to reach under Heaven, the investigation at one time would not complete it. If investigations go on for thousands and hundreds of years, nothing cannot be completed. (Huang, 1986, vol. 1, p. 48)

Clearly, the Way as described by Huang Zongxi is by no means that which was transmitted through the orthodox minority. Belonging to no single person or any single school, argued Huang Zongxi, it is a publicly shared entity that "disperses distinctively into the one hundred schools" (*shusan yu baijia*) (Huang, 1986, vol. 10, pp. 341–342). Its unity manifests only in the broadest inclusion of the great variety of the approaches to it. Such collective pursuits, marked by open debate and exchange and synthesis of diverse opinions, fundamentally surpass individual efforts and function as the prime mover for the progress of learning. According to Huang, learning must be a process of "public reasoning" (*gongyi*), a collective, open-ended, cumulative, and inclusive process in which all partake. Indeed, this is precisely how Huang Zongxi's historiography of scholarship contrasts with previous histories of scholarship embodying the Neo-Confucian idea of *daotong*, such as Zhou Rudeng's *Orthodox Transmission of Sacred Learning* and Sun Qifeng's *Orthodox Transmission of Learning of Coherence*. In his *Records of Ming Scholars*, Huang Zongxi applied the very popularist ideas of learning as his editorial principle, making this text a marketplace of ideas. If "the Way disperses into the one hundred schools," as Huang argued, then nothing is more proper than presenting the various scholars and academic schools in their own right. In fact, Huang also consistently applied this popularist editorial principle in his encyclopedic collection of Ming literature, the *Ocean of Ming Literature*. As he declared, the ultimate purpose of compiling these encyclopedic works is nothing but to "let the students follow and choose for themselves":

These various scholars approached learning not through one path. Their teachers' basic tenets may well split into several schools. Throughout their lifetimes, very often the teachings underwent changes after a long while. . . . Although these various scholars differ in the profundity and elaboration of their learning, we cannot say they did not contribute to the manifestation of the Way. Thus, I differentiate their basic arguments, categorize their learning's origins and developments, . . . and compile these chapters, so as to let the students choose for themselves. (Huang, 1986)

The attitude is highly consistent throughout Huang Zongxi's own scholarly engagements. In 1678, when Huang's students went to the Academy of History in Beijing to compile the *Standard History of the Ming* for the Qing court, Huang wrote them a letter suggesting that the category of *daoxue* be removed in the chapters discussing Ming Confucian traditions. Instead, "all" should be included in this standard history so as to "let the scholars in succeeding generations choose and select for themselves" (Huang, 1986, vol. 10, p. 215).[5]

In light of this popularist editorial principle, Huang Zongxi's encyclopedic works serve not only as a "textual museum" that preserves indiscriminately valuable primary sources for later generations, as it has been used by modern scholars, but, more importantly, it provides a "market of ideas" with Huang Zongxi's own shopping guides (his analytical notes) for students to choose what is most proper to their own education.[6] By making their own choices, readers in effect participated as well in this open-ended, cumulative public reasoning, which, as Huang argued, ultimately spurs the general advancement of learning.

Popularist Approach to Learning and Today's Education

The rise of the popularist approach reshaped the shared assumptions and agreed procedure of learning during the 17th century. Deriving from a deep skepticism of individual capability of accessing ultimate truth, the group of Jiangnan Confucian scholars examined earlier stressed the importance of diversity in scholarly methods and outlined a new notion of learning as a cumulative, inclusive, open-ended, and fluid process of public reasoning open to all. The idea of *daotong* and individual authority in comprehending the Way were thus undermined. Instead, a popularist orientation reconfiguring learning was buttressed, promoting the florescence of various encyclopedias, compendia, and anthologies that served as "textual museums" and a "market of knowledge/ideas" for readers/students to choose freely—a new intellectual strategy invented to advance the learning aspect of education (*xue*).

The significance of this study is twofold. Since the May Fourth/ New Cultural Movement (1910s and 1920s), Confucianism has been vehemently denounced by leading Chinese intellectuals who reduced this tradition to a stiff, monolithic, didactic, unidirectional, and authoritative inculcation of obsolete moral creeds. This case study casts into question this stereotypical misconception of the Confucian educational legacy. As evidenced in this chapter, the populist notion of learning emergent in the 17th century by no means promoted existing authority, suppressed individuality, and suffocated creativity. In fact, it called for the exact opposite. This chapter thus suggests the long-neglected flexibility and complexity of what we call the Confucian legacy. There is no singular "Confucian educational tradition"; there are multiple such "traditions" that are invariably being reconceived, reinvented, and refreshed.

But the late-Ming populist approach to learning has implications beyond a much-needed reevaluation of the Confucian legacy. It also provides insights for today's educators, especially those in higher education, in rethinking the nature of creative, active learning. What if we reconsider learning as a cumulative, fluid, inclusive, egalitarian, and open-ended process of public reasoning? For educators, then, it will require a strong awareness of the challenge of instilling of knowledge from the top down, and of the very deficiency of any one individual's observations. With this critical self-consciousness, a teacher is no longer an authority who provides undisputable truths, but must be a skillful moderator of dynamic dialogue, exchanges, and synthesis of competing viewpoints emerging from teaching and learning. The late-Ming populist approach also suggests that the classroom be turned into a marketplace of ideas where diverse approaches, arguments, and critiques compete with one another, allowing participants to choose, compare, and reevaluate for themselves. On the other hand, it requires learners to reevaluate critically with existing wisdom and appreciate diversity; more importantly, it prompts them to realize that the process of learning is *not* an isolated, lonely, individual adventure. While still encouraged to find answers to questions of their own making, students must be constantly aware of their personal, temporary conclusions and expose them to broader public reasoning for testing, improvement, and synthesis. They must be aware that no individual perspective may replace the type of productivity and creativity yielded by collective interaction. Hence this populist notion of Confucian learning would significantly enrich modern liberal educational practice that has sufficiently emphasized individual ingenuity instead of collective approaches. In this regard, this case study would not conclude our discussion of the millennia-long Confucian educational tradition;

it only urges us to rethink, collectively, the new possibilities of active learning this grand tradition may inspire in 21st-century classrooms.

Notes

1. English translations of original Chinese texts in this chapter, unless specified otherwise, are the author's.

2. In general, Neo-Confucian scholars imagined the genealogy of the transmission of the Way and orthodox learning from the sage-kings—including Yao, Shun, and Yu—to King Tang of the Shang dynasty, King Wen and King Wu in the Zhou dynasty, to Duke Zhou, and then to Confucius and Mencius. According to Song Neo-Confucian scholar Cheng Yi (1033–1107), the transmission of the Way was lost after Mencius. Zhu Xi further elaborated on this system by asserting that the Cheng brothers and Zhou Dunyi in the 10th to 11th centuries recovered the transmission of the way that had been discontinued since Mencius in the fourth century BCE. Zhu Xi implied that he himself was the one succeeding the transmission following his predecessors, the Song-era *daoxue* scholars. For literature on the Neo-Confucian concept of the transmission of the Way and orthodox learning, and its political impact, see Wilson (1995), Wood (1995), and Huang (2002).

3. It should be noted that this phrase was originally used by Mencius to describe the heterodox teachings of Yangism and Mohism in the *Mencius*—one of the most important Neo-Confucian texts—from 400 BCE. Now this line is appropriated by He to address the very problem of Neo-Confucian scholars themselves. Throughout his writings, He uses this phrase to describe the danger of Neo-Confucianism only; it is never applied to any other intellectual traditions.

4. The conflict between *wen* and *dao* has a long history that can be traced back to the Northern Song period. The rise of Neo-Confucianism in the Northern Song was, to a certain degree, based on the critique of the tradition of culture. See Bol (1992).

5. Huang's suggestion was taken, and in the standard history of the Ming compiled in the early Qing, there is no independent chapter devoted to Neo-Confucian scholars as in previous standard histories. All Ming scholars were included in one long chapter, and the differences in their approach and arguments are presented to let readers choose critically for themselves. Because of Huang's efforts, the Neo-Confucian notion of orthodox learning is challenged in the standard history of Ming.

6. Chu Hung-lam has pointed out that Huang Zongxi's intention of compiling the *Records of Ming Scholars* was mainly to provide a guide for students to find the best approach to learning for themselves. See Chu (1991).

References

Bol, P. K. (1992). *"This culture of ours": Intellectual transitions in T'ang and Sung China*. Stanford: Stanford University Press.

Bol, P. K. (2009). *Neo-Confucianism in history*. Cambridge: Harvard University Press.

Chen, L. (2010). *Song-Ming lixe* (Neo-Confucianism in the Song and Ming eras). Shanghai: Huadong shifan daxue chubanshe.

Chen, Q. (1979). *Chen Que ji* (The anthology of Chen Que). Beijing: Zhonghua shuju.

Chow, K. (1994). *The rise of Confucian ritualism in late imperial China*. Stanford: Stanford University Press.

Chu, H. (1991). *Mingru xue'an dianjiao shiwu* (Corrections of Errors in the Modern Punctuation of *Mingru xue'an*). Taipei: Academia Sinica.

Elman, B. A. (1990). *From philosophy to philology: Social and intellectual aspects of change in late imperial China*. Cambridge: Harvard University Council on East Asian Studies.

Elman, B. A. (1997). The formation of "Dao Learning" as imperial ideology during the early Ming period. In T. Huters, B. Wong, & P. Yu (Eds.), *Culture and state in Chinese history: Conventions, accommodations and critiques* (pp. 58–83). Stanford: Stanford University Press.

He, L. (1959). *Siyouzhai congshuo* (Categorical discussions in the Studio of Four Friends). In *Yuanming biji shiliao congkan*. Beijing: Zhonghua shuju.

He, L. (1983). *Heshi yulin* (The analects of Mr. He). In *Yingyin wenyuange siku quanshu* (Vol. 1041). Taibei: Shangwu yinshu guan.

Huang, C. The cultural politics of autocracy: The Confucius temple and Ming despotism, 1368–1530. In T. Wilson (Ed.), *On sacred grounds: Culture, society, politics and the formation of the cult of Confucius* (pp. 267–296). Cambridge: Harvard University Asia Center.

Huang, Z. (1986). *Huang Zongxi quanji* (Vols. 1–12) (The complete anthology of Huang Zongxi). Hangzhou: Zhejiang guji chubanshe.

Huang, Z. (2008). *Mingru xue'an* (Records of the Ming scholars). Beijing: Zhonghua shuju.

Liu, Z. (2007). *Liu Zongzou quanji* (The complete anthology of Liu Zongzhou). Hangzhou: Zhejiang guji chubanshe.

Lu, K. (1962). *Lu Kun zhexue xuanji* (The complete anthology of Lu Xun's philosophy). Beijing: Zhonghu shuju.

Lu, K. (2008). *Lu Kun quanji* (The complete anthology of Lu Kun). Beijing: Zhonghua shuju.

Mao, K. (1997). *Mao Lumen xiansheng wenji* (The anthology of Mr. Mao). In *Xuxiu siku quanshu. jibu* (Vol. 1344). Shanghai: Shanghai guji chubanshe.

Tang, S. (1997). *Lidai shicuan youbian* (The selection of histories from various dynasties). In *Siku cunmu congshu Shibu*, vol. 133. Beijing: Siku cunmu congshu biancuan weiyuanhui.

Wang, S. (1992). *Wang Yangming quanji* (The complete anthology of Wang Yangming). Shanghai: Shanghai guji.

Wilson, T. A. (1995). *Genealogy of the way: The construction and uses of the Confucian tradition in late imperial China*. Stanford: Stanford University Press.

Wood, A. (1995). *Limits to autocracy: From Sung Neo-Confucianism to a doctrine of political rights*. Honolulu: University of Hawaii Press.

Xie, Z. (2007). *Wuzazu* (Miscellaneous Writings of the Five). Shanghai: Shanghai shudian.

Yu, Y. (2003). *Zhuxi de lishi shijie* (The historical world of Zhu Xi). Taibei: Lianjing chubanshe.

Zhao, Z. (1997). *Zhao Wensugong wenji* (The anthology of Mr. Zhao Zhenji) in *Siku cunmu congshu*, jibu 100. Jinan: Qilu shushe.

7

The Confucian Philosophy of Education in Hexagram Meng (Shrouded) of the *Yijing*

Bin Song

The *Yijing* (易经, the Classic of Changes)[1] was traditionally crowned as the supreme Classic among the Confucian classics. The fact that there is an ad hoc hexagram, Meng (蒙, Shrouded), dedicated to the issue of education, deserves special attention from scholars who are interested in Confucian educational thought and the philosophy of education in general.

If we read the text of this hexagram in reference to both the Confucian classics that are synchronic to the *Yijing*,[2] such as the *Analects* and the *Zhong Yong* (中庸, Commonality and Centrality), and the diachronic major Confucian commentaries after the *Yijing*,[3] we may find five main points of the Confucian philosophy of education. Each is quite relevant to the contemporary situation of American and Chinese education:

> 1. *Education is divine.* It does not shape human personality from without but helps to rediscover and nurture people's innate good nature, which is bestowed by Heaven and enables human beings to have appropriate reactions to constantly changing cosmic realities.
>
> 2. *The best pedagogy is heuristic*, which requires both the initiative research of the student and the wise response of the teacher. It

targets the special talent and character of different students and meanwhile allows teachers and their students to be correlative and cooperate with each other to constitute the most opportune moment when good education could happen.

3. Learning by rote memorization and imitation, while simultaneously motivated by reward and punishment, is the pedagogy for elementary learning (小学). This method can make known the right norms of learning but can't foster creativity, so it can only be used in the first stage of education.

4. Learning creatively, while motivated by the goal of self-cultivation as grounded in the depth of the human heart-mind (心)—to be in trinity with Heaven and Earth and to co-create and nurture myriad things under heaven—is the trajectory for great learning (大学). Because elementary and great learning are different levels of education, any person at any age needs to upgrade his or her learning from the elementary to the great one. Because great learning always aims for creation and is thus without end, education is a lifelong project. A human being cannot stop learning.

5. The order of education challenges those in power. As long as the situation is demanding and the right ritual is obeyed, subjects have the obligation to educate the monarch, children ought to educate their parents, and students have great potential to inspire their teacher. The independence of personality of every human being is built from a divine foundation and is a guarantee for the right human relationship in education, as well as for the health of any other kind of human relationship.

In the text of Hexagram Meng, these points can be represented by the name of the hexagram (卦名), the statement of the hexagram (卦辞), and the *yao* (line) statement (爻辞) of Initial Six (初六).[4] In this chapter, I first compose a philosophical commentary of these parts of Hexagram Meng in the genre of a traditional Confucian commentary of the *Yijing*. Then I reflect on the current situation of American and Chinese education and discuss the educational implications of Confucian wisdom.

Commentary

The Name and Image of the Hexagram (卦名与卦象)

The first step for the commentary of a hexagram is to figure out why its name corresponds to its image.

For Hexagram Meng (蒙), ䷃, its trigram above is Gen (艮), ☶, which symbolizes mountain and abeyance[5]; its trigram below is Kan (坎), ☵, symbolizing water and danger.[6] Reading from top down, we get the combined symbolic meaning for the whole hexagram as: spring water flows from within a mountain. Because the land within a mountain is bumpy and rugged, full of thorns and thistles, a spring flowing from within must be hindered and thwarted at the very beginning. It is just like a naive and ignorant child. Before she or he finds a teacher and gets an education, she or he doesn't know how to deal with her or his life, especially how to live in a society. Therefore we can see how the name of the hexagram, "Meng" (蒙), resonates with this general imagery.

According to Xu and Duan (1981), the original character of "蒙" is "冡." "冡" is ideographic: The top radical "冖" means "to cover," a short line "一" reemphasizes this meaning, and "豕" is a pictographic character to represent a pig (pp. 100, 637). A pig is covered, therefore heading nowhere; this is the original meaning of "蒙"; so we translate it as "shrouded." It means to be shrouded by anything that could hinder someone's growth or something's movement.

However, water is bound to flow downward. That is its nature. Even if a spring is thwarted by the bumpy rocks in a mountain at the very beginning, as long as time passes and conditions are appropriate, it will eventually flow out of the mountain, maybe converging with other springs to form a huge and vigorous river. By the same token, no matter how shrouded and limited a person's intelligence was when she or he was young, after appropriate education, the shroud will be removed and she or he will be finally enlightened, capable of being a human in a society. So the future of "being shrouded" is to be "unshrouded" (启蒙). In Chinese, "unshrouded" also means enlightenment and education. The most famous beginning sentences in *Zhong Yong* enunciate this cornerstone of the Confucian philosophy of education quite accurately: "What Heaven (天) bestows is called nature. To follow the nature is called the Way (Dao). To build up the Way is called education" (Chan, 1963, p. 98). Whether it is a pig, a spring, or a human, to be shrouded is to lose its way, so only through a process of unshrouding could the way be rebuilt up. For humans, it is through education.

Statement of the Hexagram

> 4.1 The Hexagram of Shrouded leads to unshrouding. 4.2 It should not be I who seeks the shrouded youth, but the shrouded youth who seeks me. 4.3 A diviner should tell the result of the first divination, but a second or a third divination about the same thing would result in blasphemy; if there were such blasphemy against divination, the diviner should not inform of anything. 4.4 Beneficial to persevere.[7]

The *Yijing*'s hexagram statements explain the meaning of each hexagram as a whole. In the context of divination, they also prognosticate the process of a life-event that a hexagram intends to address.

The statement of Hexagram Meng is made up of three parts. The first one, which is 4.1 in my translation, prognosticates the result of the life-event that Hexagram Meng intends to address. The second one, which includes 4.2–4.3, prescribes the conditions under which the prognosticated result could come true. The third one gives a warning that the prescribed conditions must be conformed to. Let's interpret these three parts one by one.

亨 in 4.1, whose Xiao Zhuan is 亯,[8] is pictographic. It represents a utensil for sacrifice; above is the cap, below is the vessel and the leg, and in the middle are two stacked boxes representing numerous rarities to be sacrificed. Therefore, its original meaning is to be rich or prosperous, which is further extended into "to go smoothly," penetrate, permeate, and so on.[9] In the context of Hexagram Meng, it means that given the right conditions, the obstacle to an emerging life will finally be removed, as the life is bound to be free and thriving by its nature. Because of the changes gone through by the growth of the life, being shrouded would lead to being unshrouded, so I translate 亨 as "unshrouding" in conformity with the name of this hexagram.

The condition for an emerging life to be unshrouded is prescribed in 4.2–4.3. These two sentences are a phenomenological description about what the best education could be. From the perspective of *Yijing* symbology, both Nine Second and Six Fifth are central[10]; they are resonant with each other,[11] and Nine Second is the main *yao*.[12] All these factors lead to the fact that they could cooperate to realize a good education at the right moment. So what does a good education look like?

"The shrouded youth" (童蒙, or an uneducated child) in 4.2 refers to Six Fifth. It is "young" because Six Fifth is in the trigram above Gen, ☶, while Trigram Gen symbolizes the youngest son in the family of trigrams (Wang, Han, & Kong, 1999, p. 330). Meanwhile, Six Fifth is in Hexagram Meng, shrouded and thwarted in its initial development. With the combination of these two images, the statement accordingly depicts Six Fifth as "a shrouded youth." The character 童 (young, childish, or juvenile) denotes both the ignorance and the purity of mind of Six Fifth as an earnest student. It is ignorant, so it must seek a teacher to learn, just as Six Fifth as a *yin yao* is resonant with Nine Second and thus must treat this central *yang yao* as its teacher. It is pure, so it can be humble and active in the aforementioned seeking whether or not it has a higher official position. In Hexagram Meng, Six Fifth occupies the position of a monarch, while Nine Second's position is lower and thus ought to be counted as one of Six Fifth's subjects. The fact that Six Fifth is, by contrast, eager and active in pursuit of Nine Second as its teacher is a perfect example of the humility and purity of a good student. Based on these credits, the statement of Six Fifth is as simple as "4.28 The shrouded youth; auspicious," and the commentary of Small Image (小象传, one of the *Ten Wings*) interprets this statement as "4.29 The good fortune of the shrouded youth comes from its compliance and obedience."[13] Note the fact that Six Fifth is also the top *yao* in the interlaced trigram Kun ☷, which is made up of Six Third, Six Fourth, and Six Fifth.[14] Trigram Kun symbolizes "obedience" (Wang, Han, & Kong, 1999, p. 329), while being on the top of Trigram Kun symbolizes being extremely obedient. This is the reason why 4.29 uses two characters that basically have the same meaning to describe the behavior and mentality of Six Fifth: 顺 (compliance) and 巽 (obedience). As indicated, the fact that Six Fifth is a monarch but eager and active to learn from its subject is a graphic illustration of this "compliant and obedient" mentality. Therefore, in the Confucian view of education, humility and thus eagerness to learn on the student's part is the first prerequisite of a good education.

"I" in 4.2 refers to the shrouded youth's teacher, Nine Second. In the formation of a hexagram, the six *yaos* making up the hexagram are drawn one by one from the bottom up during a divination. It entails that the trigram below is the first one formed and thus closer to the diviner in comparison with the trigram above. In this sense, the trigram below is also considered the inner trigram (內卦), and the trigram above is the outer one (外卦). The behavior of Six Fifth as a central *yin yao* in the trigram above to come down and learn from Second Nine, his teacher as a central *yang yao* in the trigram below, could also be thought of as a movement from outside to inside. So Nine Second is represented as "I," seated in the inner trigram and awaiting his students.

The appropriate sequence in the initiative of seeking described in 4.2, which corresponds to the relationship of resonance between Six Fifth and Nine Second as illustrated earlier, both emphasizes the respect for the teacher and indicates a deep pedagogical rationale. It is a notion particular to Confucian education that although a close relationship with a good teacher is a determinative factor for a student to be well educated,[15] it is the obligation of the student to find his or her teacher to obtain the education, not vice versa. As the chapter "Summary of Rituals" (曲礼) in the *Li Ji* (礼记, The Classic of Rites) says: "It is heard that it is in accordance with the rules of propriety that students come to learn; it is never heard that the teacher is supposed to go teach" (Zheng & Kong, 1999, p. 13). The primary rationale for this advocacy is to show respect for the teacher. If a teacher took his or her initiative to teach regardless of the will and receptive ability of the student, the teachings would be obtained too easily, they would not be respected, and the relevant educational activities could not be set in order. Meanwhile, for a specific round of question-and-answer between a student and teacher to be effective—able to transform the intelligence and personality of the student—the student him- or herself must take full initiative to try to figure out what the answer is even before questioning. Similarly, in order to remove the obstacle of a spring flowing from within a mountain and help it find its way to flow down, it is better to overview the whole itinerary and then find the most obstructive point to finally give the spring water a releasing prompt. Therefore, the best pedagogy is heuristic: The teacher can discern what is really needed by the student from his or her initiating learning behaviors, and then inspire the student to find the answer him- or herself on the basis of the teacher's comprehensive knowledge. This heuristic pedagogy is illustrated by Confucius's own teaching method: "If a student is not thwarted in the process of finding an answer by himself, I would not give him a clue; if a student does not stammer in expressing himself, I would not provide a help. When I have presented one corner of a subject but do not receive the other three in response,[16] I teach no further" (*Analects* 7.8, Eno, 2012, p. 30).

Nevertheless, this heuristic pedagogy will have nowhere to be applied if the student doesn't take the initiative. This is another reason why 4.2 emphasizes the initiative of the shrouded youth to find a teacher.

From this emphasis on heuristic pedagogy, we also know that respect for the teacher is not ultimately for the sake of the teacher. It is for the transmission of the teachings and for the transformation of the student. In spiritual terms, we would say it is to fulfill a specific human responsibility to help Heaven and Earth to co-create and nurture myriad things under Heaven, as instructed in chapter 22 of the *Zhong Yong* (Chan, 1963, pp. 107–108). Or, simply, we could say it is for the sake of Dao. The existence of this third, transcendent, and luring element endows educational activities with a specific glamour of holiness and mystique. When the *Zhouyi* was composed, nothing was more religious and educational than divination. So after 4.2, 4.3 uses the imagery of divination to foreground the holiness of education and reemphasize the pedagogical correlation between the student and teacher.

There is an unwritten rule for divination in Chinese people's daily religious practice: If someone is not sincere, do not divine (不诚不占) (Fu, 2010, p. 24). It implies that if anyone wants to ask a diviner to divine for him or her, he or she must be fully prepared to accept any result and thus sincerely believe in whatever the diviner will say even before divination. Otherwise, someone could request further divinations until a good result is obtained, and this would be devastating to divination. This is the reason why 4.3 says a second and third divination about the same thing will be a blasphemy and warns the diviner not to tell anything in this case. In relation to education, the instruction in 4.3 in the form of divination poses special requirements for both the student as the questioner and the teacher as the answerer to effect the most opportune moment of education.

As already instructed in 4.2, the student must be humble and take initiative. He or she must know exactly what he or she needs and thus ask a question concise and definite enough to accommodate a pertinent answer. Meanwhile, what 4.2 has not instructed and 4.3 emphasizes, by contrast, is that the teacher also must deliberately think about whether and how to answer the question. If the content of the question strays too much from the point, or the method of questioning doesn't comply with the rule of propriety, perhaps showing irreverence for both the teacher and the Dao that the teacher tries to inculcate, the teacher ought not to answer. Furthermore, the teacher's answer ought to be succinct, adequate, and resolute enough to target the weakest point of a student's acquired knowledge. This point may be very easy, or it may be the most profound one for the relevant subject. Regardless, the teacher's answer ought to be so pertinent as to be both in line with the receptive ability of the student and meanwhile to inspire him or her. The most desirable result is to have the student find his or her own way to acquire a comprehensive grasp of the subject based on the teacher's pertinent answer. In the *Analects*, Confucius gives different answers about the meanings of "humanity" (仁), the virtue of virtues in Confucian moral philosophy, regarding different personalities and different situations of his students who ask the same question. He also refuses to answer an inappropriate question posed by a nonvirtuous monarch who is more interested in winning a war against other states than in bringing peace and humanity to his own society through the practice of ritual (*Analects* 15.1, Eno, 2012, p. 82).

These are examples of the best question-and-answer method instructed by 4.2 and 4.3. These texts demonstrate that the Confucian philosophy of education is a mode of correlative thinking from the very beginning. Both student and teacher have indispensable roles in co-creating the most opportune moment for a good education. As indicated, in Hexagram Meng, Six Fifth and Nine Second are both central and resonant; one is humble, receptive, and initiating, and the other is firm, erudite, and circumspect, the qualified *yaos* that can make the best education happen. As a result, everyone who is eager to learn should take these two *yaos* in the context of Hexagram Meng as a model to facilitate specific adaption for their own education. This is also exactly what the *Yijing* as interpreted in the Confucian tradition intends to do: to develop people's morality under the enlightenment of the pattern-principles (理) of things-in-change in the world.

After describing how the situation of the second *yao* as a teacher and the fifth *yao* as a student could represent the most opportune moment for a good education, 4.4 warns that it is "beneficial to persevere" (利贞). The original meaning of 贞 is to divine by a holy tripod.[17] But in the context of the *Zhouyi*, to divine is to search for a principle that regulates the action of a confused and hesitant person, so the extensive meaning of 贞 is 正, to be upright, to persevere in principle. The reason why there is such a warning (戒辞) in the statement of Hexagram Meng is that neither the second nor the fifth *yao* is "upright" according to *Yijing* symbology. The second one is a *yang yao*, which occupies a *yin* position, and the fifth is a *yin yao*, which occupies a *yang* position.[18]

It implies that although from a structural point of view the situation in these two *yaos* could represent the principle of good education, the persons represented by them are liable to lose their grit to carry out the principle because they are not quite upright and trustworthy. Thus, the only way to correct this character flaw of either the second as a teacher or the fifth as a student and thus make education beneficial is to warn them to persevere.

The Statement of Yao and the Commentary of the Small Image: Initial Six

The statement of *yao* posits the specific situation of each *yao* in its relationship to the whole hexagram. In the context of Hexagram Meng, the statement of the first *yao* and its related commentary describe the specific situation of education for the novice.

> 4.12 Initial Six begins to lift the shroud. 4.13 In order to remove the shackles and fetters, it is favorable to establish the rule and apply punishment. 4.14 Nevertheless, this method can be barely applicable in the long run.
>
> 4.15 "It is favorable to establish the rule and apply punishment"; this is to set up the right norm.[19]

Initial Six is a *yin yao*, which sits at the bottom of Hexagram Meng. This implies that it is the youngest of all the shrouded (the four *yin yaos*: Initial Six, Six Third, Six Fourth, and Six Fifth) who strives for Nine Second to get a good education. It is a novice, the most ignorant, immature, as well as the most undisciplined in his or her behaviors. 4.12 affirms that Initial Six will receive a good education appropriate to its situation. Generally speaking, whether a *yin yao* in Hexagram Meng could get a good education depends on whether it is proximate[20] to Nine Second and whether it can accordingly match its good will to learn. Initial Six is proximate to Nine Second, it is not resonant to any other *yang yao*, and it is a *yin yao* that occupies the basest position in the hexagram. These points mean that Initial Six could quite easily find its teacher and also be quite willing and obedient to be educated. Nevertheless, because Initial Six is the youngest and most ignorant student, even if it can get an education that is suitable for its specific situation at this initial stage, the shroud that covers its mentality and physicality cannot be totally removed. After finishing this elementary learning, it must adapt to a new set of pedagogical rules and continue to be educated and self-cultivate. Therefore, 4.12 describes the result of Initial Six's education as "Initial Six begins to lift the shroud."

4.13–4.15 give the method that is taken by Nine Second to teach Initial Six, a specific pedagogy targeting beginners and elementary learning.

Initial Six is in Trigram Kan ☵. One basic symbolic meaning of Kan is "sinking and being trapped" (陷) (Wang, Han, & Kong, 1999, p. 329), because the only *yang yao* is trapped in the middle of two *yin yaos*. As indicated, Kan also symbolizes water, which by nature sinks in the earth like a river. "Shackles and fetters" always trap, and to "establish the rule and apply punishment" is also another way to restrict; both images are extended from the fact that Initial Six sits in Trigram Kan. Therefore what 4.12 says is that Nine Second as a teacher uses the pedagogical method of "establishing the rule and applying punishment" to remove the "shackles and fetters" of Initial Six as a student. These shackles and fetters are in fact a set of very weak mental and physical conditions that make people in their youth extremely vulnerable to negative external influences.

This method is quite different from heuristic learning (4.2–4.3), which is applied between Nine Second and Six Fifth: There, the student is humble and inquisitive, knowing what is really needed and how to ask, and the teacher is firm, erudite, and circumspect, knowing how to answer, inspire, and transform. Compared with this most opportune moment of education to which the initiative of the student contributes a lot, this method (4.13) cannot be said to occur without coercion. Because the mentality of youngsters in their initial stages of education is too immature to understand the rationale behind what they are taught, it is ridiculous to expect them to have a command of the teachings beyond the level of rote imitation. Meanwhile, also because these young kids are too immature, they are quite susceptible to negative influences from outside, and thus it is quite easy to form bad habits that will be difficult to rectify if not corrected as they emerge. Therefore, the only viable way to educate beginners is to establish the rule, have them know what is the right norm (4.15) by rote, and do what is right by imitation. If someone "knows" and does well, he or she will be rewarded; if not, he or she will be punished. This quite utilitarian and authoritarian pedagogy specifically targets the first stage of education, which can correct beginners' wrong behaviors, prepare them for higher levels of learning, and meanwhile doesn't elevate the level of discourse beyond what their mentality can accommodate. Surely it can't be applied in the long run as said in 4.14. Humans are bound to be curious, explorative, and creative, so that in the long run only the kind of pedagogy described in 4.2–4.3 can be viable, which makes use of and nurtures, rather than blocks, human nature. Compared with this heuristic pedagogy that aims to inspire people's moral consciousness and transform their behaviors by their own will, the one symbolized by Initial Six can only be counted as "elementary learning" (小学).

In the Confucian philosophy of education, "elementary learning" (小学) and "great learning" (大学) do not only address two different periods of learning; they are also two levels of learning. If anyone intends to learn anything in any age, he or she will be responsible to upgrade his or her learning from an elementary level to a great one. In the context of the Yijing, there are two venues where these two kinds of learning are best illustrated and contrasted. They are the commentaries of the Great Image (大象传, one of the Ten Wings) of Hexagram Xiaoxu (小畜, lesser domestication) and Hexagram Daxu (大畜, great domestication). The core topic for both hexagrams is self-cultivation. The Great Image of Hexagram Lesser Domestication defines the content of lesser self-cultivation as "The virtuous person refines his or her outward virtue of culture."[21] The Great Image of Hexagram Great Domestication defines the content of great self-cultivation as "The virtuous person comprehends lots of what has been said and done in the past to nurture his or her own virtue."[22]

The wisdom implied in the Yijing is that human beings are born with a power to self-aggrandize, which is symbolized by the solid line of yang and is analogical to libido in Freud and the will to power in Nietzsche. This power makes humans always aspire to mark their own existence on their surroundings and thus thrust themselves into an insatiable process of self-aggrandizing. If this power is not adjusted and facilitated by another, the supportive and receptive yin power that is always caring for the welfare of others during the process of someone's self-realization, it will lead to unmanageable conflict and disharmony, which is akin to the "war of everyone against everyone" in Thomas Hobbes (Hobbes, 1651, p. 80). So the curriculum of lesser self-cultivation suggested by the Great Image of Hexagram Lesser Domestication is to "refine the outward virtue of culture." It means to provide disciplines, such as literature, music, sport, and ritual, among others, to help consume and adjust the ever-aggrandizing *yang* power within human nature, to channel and mix it gradually into the compassionate *yin* power that is also indispensable to human nature and thus prepare a human to be a fully autonomous and civil being after an arduous process of self-cultivation. Because the self-cultivation that happens in this stage stays at the level of art and technique, people who are able to perform these arts of civilization well by imitation and repetition can embellish their behavior outwardly and thus appear cultured when in fact they can't fully comprehend the rationale, the Dao, that underlies these arts. As a result, they can't correlate these rationales as the principle of reality with every detail of their ordinary life and then creatively transform things that are sorely in need of change for the better. Therefore, this curriculum of self-cultivation could only refine people's "outward virtue of culture" and is indeed of a lesser and minor type. Correspondingly, the pedagogy of elementary learning addressed in Initial Six of Hexagram Meng belongs to this type of self-cultivation. It can't be expected that learning by memory and imitation and motivating through reward and punishment could inspire and nurture students' creativity. That is also the reason why 4.14 is quite explicitly against the application of this pedagogy in the long run. In contrast, what the great self-cultivation requires in the Great Image of Hexagram Great Domestication is a full comprehension from within the depth of the heart of what has been said and done in human history. The virtuous person, committed to such a great self-cultivation, seeks to master the principles of reality revealed in the rich heritage of human culture, tries to flesh them out in practice, and thus contributes to transforming the world into the best possible. As the Great Learning (大学), one of the Confucian Four Books that lays out a systematic curriculum for the virtuous person's self-cultivation, says in its opening chapter: "The Way (Dao) of great learning consists in rediscovering and manifesting the innately bright human virtue, loving and renewing the people, and in achieving and abiding in the highest good."[23] As an example, the heuristic method of question-and-answer addressed in the statement of Hexagram Meng ought to be subsumed into the pedagogy of this great self-cultivation and great learning.

Understood as such, it can be discerned from above how this differentiation between the pedagogies of elementary and great learning is of paramount importance for the Confucian philosophy of education. In fact, in the millennia-long history of Confucian education, generations of

Confucian educators quite consciously maintain this differentiation and try to address these two different levels of education through designing and implementing different curricula and pedagogies. The goal of Confucian education is always about transformation and creativity, either of human beings or of the world, on which all the other minor details of Confucian pedagogy pivots. I believe contemporary educators are still obliged to design their own methods for realizing this Confucian ideal of education in a way that accommodates the technology and realities of the modern age.[24]

Reflection on Educational Implications

Based on this commentary of a significant part of Hexagram Meng, and those points of the Confucian philosophy of education I have summarized at the beginning of this chapter, we can have a brief discussion about contemporary American and Chinese education.

On the first page of the website for the International Conference on Confucianism and Education (Buffalo, 2014), it declares that the conference's interest in Confucian educational thought is partially motivated by "Chinese students' outstanding academic performances, particularly in Science, Technology, Engineering and Mathematics (STEM)" as they contrast with educational reforms that are stressed in Western countries, especially the United States. The logic implicit in this assertion seems to be that, by absorbing ideas from Confucian educational philosophy, Western countries may figure out why Chinese students have such outstanding performance in these subjects and how Western students might catch up with their Chinese counterparts after a series of timely and efficient educational reforms. But I think this logic makes a mistake along the lines of "the fallacy of misplaced concreteness" expounded by Whitehead: It mistakes an abstract theory for concrete reality (Whitehead, 1926, p. 64). I think Confucianism, as the most prominent influence on Chinese intellectual history, could indeed help explain why contemporary Chinese students have such high academic performance in these areas. But it doesn't mean Confucianism values this performance as much as people think it does. Neither does it mean that Western reformers should imitate what Chinese education has done to improve their students' academic performance—or think then that the reason for the imitation is due to Confucianism.

As is well known by Confucian scholars, the main subject of the Confucian curriculum is ritual, and ritual, in the broadest sense defined by the *Yijing*, refers to all the cultural products that facilitate human beings' creative reaction to human and cosmic realities-in-change (Wang, Han, & Kong, 1999, p. 275). This includes the knowledge of STEM, of humanities, and of social sciences. If Confucian educational philosophy does indeed play a dominant role in Chinese students' academic performance, the students should excel in STEM and all other subjects, and the "excellence" mentioned here must be defined together with "creativity." But the fact is, although Chinese students historically have achieved high scores in tests related to STEM, they are not equally creative. In 2005, when former premier Wen Jiabao visited one of the most famous scientists in China, Qian Xuesen, the latter asked why none of the students raised in the contemporary Chinese educational system were on a par with the many great masters of science educated during the period of the Republic of China (1911–1949), some of whom even won the Nobel Prize in some cases in the area of basic sciences such as theoretical physics. This is named the "Question of Qian Xuesen." It has been a hot issue in Chinese public media in recent years. It indicates that the Chinese people are very aware of the defects hidden behind the remarkable test scores of Chinese students. Furthermore, most of the humanities and social sciences are not as easily standardized and testable as STEM. Good performance in these areas relies heavily on the diversity and creativity of students' intelligence and personality. I believe a college student from China will immediately understand how Chinese education is lacking these areas once he or she steps onto the campus of an American university and has a chance to study there for a while.

Why does contemporary Chinese education have such one-sided excellence in STEM? In Confucian terms, it's because the essentially test-oriented educational system in contemporary China is stuck in the stage of "elementary learning." This is far from the "great learning" that aims to cultivate the person and nurture creativity so as to construct a vibrantly harmonious and humane society. As shown earlier, elementary learning requires memory and imitation, and motivation by reward and punishment; its aim is to set up the right norms without students' real understanding of them at the earliest stages of education. Correspondingly, STEM subjects are highly standardizable. If the same textbook, the same test, and the same group of people are taken to teach, the resulting boredom of the process of learning can only be offset by a ranking system that provides such an incentive to say that the competitors with higher scores can go to better universities and find better jobs. The most efficient way to get a high score in this system will be imitation, repetition, and endless practice without much hope of releasing the creativity innate in every individual. This is exactly what has happened in most Chinese public schools with regard to teaching and learning STEM. Actually, these schools also use the same pedagogy to train students in other subjects, but unfortunately humanities and social sciences can't succumb to standardization. As a result, a high score in these subjects would barely mean anything in any international competition. In a word, I think the general political, economic, and social structures of contemporary China are not yet able to create a platform to allow the level of education in its public educational system to be upgraded from elementary learning to great learning.

By contrast, American education seems to be in line with Confucian great learning from the start. American students rarely experience what Chinese students have suffered under the strict ranking system. Individuality, diversity, and creativity seem to always stand in the forefront of values that American education cherishes and pursues. But, according to recent observations, under the pressure of intensifying political and economic global competition, the United States now tends more and more to follow the example of China and some other East Asian countries to reform and standardize its public education, thus giving its students more tests. Zhao (2009) aptly notes: "American education is at a crossroad. Two paths lie in front of us: one in which we destroy our strengths in order to catch up with others on test scores and one in which we build on our strengths so we can keep the lead in innovation and creativity" (p. 178). In the Confucian view, I think American educational reformers need to proceed nimbly through this crossroads.

On the one hand, standardization of education in the genre of Confucian elementary learning is not totally without value. The practice in China has proved that people who are trained in this genre of education are favorable to the implementation of grand national programs that value the power of collective execution more than the strength of innovation from individuals. In this sense, they are also quite adaptable to the quick import and absorption of the most up-to-date techniques to enhance the competitive power of the national economy. But the cost is also very high. As 4.14 has formulated, this pedagogy can be barely applicable in the long run. Over time, it not only damages the cornerstone of a nation's power—the thriving and creativity of individuals—but it also goes against the goal in the Confucian philosophy of education: the construction of a vigorous, harmonious, and humane society on the basis of the full moral self-consciousness and unfettered self-development of each individual. Taking these points into consideration, it would not be totally counterproductive to give some testable discipline to American students in their initial stages of education, especially in the area of STEM, because that will help to refine their mental receptivity and prepare them for deeper and further study. It is not useless for the execution of a national strategy either. The consciousness of norm and authority fostered in the genre of Confucian elementary learning could enhance the solidarity of human community on which the functioning of any political system undoubtedly relies. This is especially applicable to the United States, as it is such a multicultural nation. Some discipline given to young students and newly enfranchised citizens about a basic set of values that is necessary for the maintenance and improvement of a good democratic polity would be more than helpful. However, if American education really needs such an adjustment toward the genre of Confucian elementary learning, concerned educational reformers must take a special precaution that this can't be counted as the ultimate direction of education. As the Confucian great learning quite clearly endorses, the real power of a nation consists in the creativity of its citizens as individuals and the vibrant harmony of its society based on that.

Therefore, a special balance needs to be achieved between the traditional advantage of American education in fostering the creativity of individuals and its growing need to enhance its society's solidarity on the basis of some sense of authority that must be inculcated into an individual's moral consciousness through education. We will be more than happy to see how this balance can be achieved under the inspiration of Confucian educational philosophy, especially its idea of the structural differentiation between elementary and great learning.

Notes

1. Following the traditional usage of the term, I use the *Yijing* in this chapter to refer to the Confucian classic that comprises the *Zhouyi* (周易, The Zhou Book of Changes) as the original text and the *Ten Wings* (十翼) as its

earliest commentary. My analysis of the *Yijing* will be based on its received version in Wang, Han, and Kong (1999).

2. It is beyond the purpose of this chapter to discuss the authorship of the *Yijing*. All we need to know is that its commentarial part, the *Ten Wings*, was presumably written by Confucian scholars during the Spring and Autumn and the Warring States periods (770–221 BCE). Therefore, it can be read together with the other Confucian classics, which were composed around the same period. Please refer to Zhu (1993, pp. 3–53) for a philological analysis of the authorship of the *Yijing*.

3. It is beyond the purpose of this chapter to take a survey of relevant resources in the Confucian commentarial tradition of the *Yijing*. However, note that my philosophical commentary of Hexagram Meng is mainly inspired by the school of "meaning and principle" (义理派) in the study of the *Zhouyi*. Major commentators in this school include Wang Bi (226–249 CE), Kong Yingda (574–648 CE), Cheng Yi (1033–1107 CE), and Zhu Xi (1130–1200 CE), among others. Some of their works have been listed in the references.

4. Every hexagram is made up of six lines, which are called *yao* (爻, imitation). Each of the *yaos* is either a solid or a broken line symbolizing either *yang* or *yin* as two basic forms of reality. The nomenclature of these *yaos* is as follows: From bottom up, each *yao* occupies the first, the second, the third, the fourth, the fifth, and the top positions one by one. In relation to the method of divination described in Wang, Han, and Kong (1999, pp. 279–282), the number "six" represents *yin* and "nine" represents *yang*. Therefore, the *yao* of Initial Six in Hexagram Meng means that it is the *yin yao* (the broken line) that occupies the first position.

5. These basic symbolizations are not without reason. There is one yang yao on top of the other two yin yaos in Trigram Gen. According to the correlative and symbolic thinking in the *Yijing*, yang is high and yin is low just as yang is strong and yin is weak; so from the shape of this trigram you can tell it could represent that something very high stands far above the other things. Then Wang et al. (1999) says: "Gen is a mountain" (p. 333). Because all the yaos in a trigram are generated from bottom up during the process of divination, within a trigram there is a dynamic cause of every yao striving to move from bottom up (this rule also applies in the hexagram). But if a very high thing like a mountain stands in front of you, your movement must be stopped by it. So Wang et al. (1999) says the other basic symbolic meaning of Trigram Gen is abeyance: "Gen symbolizes abeyance" (p. 329).

6. The midstream of a river is usually much stronger than its side streams, so a trigram with a yang yao in the middle and two yin yaos in both sides symbolizes water: "Kan is water" (Wang et al., 1999, p. 332). A river sinks in the field. For ancient people who have no advanced means of transportation, to

cross a river is extremely dangerous. So Wang et al. (1999) thinks that Trigram Kan is also symbolic of sinking and being trapped in danger: "Kan is sinking and being trapped" (p. 329).

7. Translation adapted from multiple resources. The original text is in Wang, Han, and Kong (1999, p. 37). Verses are numerically noted according to their position in Hexagram Meng, which is the fourth hexagram in the received version of *Yijing*.

8. Please refer to the online database 汉典 (The Dictionary of Chinese Characters, n.d.), retrieved from http://www.zdic.net/z/15/xs/4EA8.htm

9. All etymological discussions are based on Xu and Duan (1981) and other online databases such as that listed in note 8. Like other similar discussions in philosophical reasoning, they are tentative rather than definitive. I intend through the discussion to foreground the relevance of the literal meaning of each character with its philosophical implication.

10. The second and the fifth positions in a hexagram are central (中), because each stands in the middle of the two constitutive trigrams. If a *yao* occupies a central position, that usually means that it is in a good situation. The *Yijing* symbology is developed by the *Yijing* scholars when they try to figure out what the relationship is between the *Zhouyi* symbols and its texts. Nevertheless, there is no consensus about its authoritative version. Different scholars in different historical periods usually have extremely diverse opinions of it. I abide by the principle of "minimalism" in this regard, which means that I try to use the simplest version of *Yijing* symbology to articulate the aforementioned relationship as long as it can provide a rationale for my commentary. Please refer to Huang and Zhang (2007, pp. 460–479) to see the main points of *Yijing* symbology to which the commentarial tradition of the *Yijing* most frequently refers.

11. If two *yaos* occupying the initial and the fourth positions are of different genders, they resonate (应) with each other. The same situation could happen between two different *yaos* when they are respectively in the second and the fifth positions, or in the third and top positions. If two *yaos* resonate with each other, that usually means they are mutually supportive.

12. The nature of a main *yao* determines that of the hexagram to which it belongs. Quite often, whether a *yao* is the main one for a hexagram can be told from the semantic similarity between its statement and the statement of the hexagram.

13. Translation adapted from multiple resources. The original text is in Wang, Han, and Kong (1999, p. 41).

14. An interlaced trigram (互卦) is made up of the second, the third, and the fourth *yaos*, or of the third, the fourth, and the fifth *yaos*. Obviously, each hexagram contains two interlaced trigrams. The symbolic meanings of these trigrams are sometimes referred to in the *yao* statement.

15. For example, Xunzi (1988) says: "Therefore in learning, no method is more advantageous than to be close to a man of learning" (p. 140).

16. There are altogether four corners in a house. Here Confucius likens the complete understanding of a subject to a four-cornered comprehension of it.

17. Please refer to Shaughnessy (2014, pp. 1557–1580) to see the philological discussion.

18. The initial, the third, and the fifth positions are *yang*, and the rest are *yin*. Only a *yang yao* occupying a *yang* position is upright. The same rule also applies in the *yin* case.

19. Translation adapted from multiple resources; the original text is in Wang, Han, and Kong (1999, p. 39).

20. Two *yaos* in a hexagram are proximate (邻) to each other if they occupy the proximate positions, such as the first and the second, or the second and the third.

21. Translation adapted from Wilhelm (1977, p. 432).

22. Translation adapted from multiple resources. The Chinese text is in Wang, Han, and Kong (1999, p. 120).

23. Translation adapted from Chan (1963, p. 86).

24. Through this analysis, I also explicitly deny the charge that Confucianism intrinsically promotes rigid hierarchy and totalitarianism. This charge was initially made by early modern Chinese intellectuals under the impact of Western colonialism. They intended to import advanced elements from Western culture to reform traditional Chinese culture, mainly Confucianism, to overcome the aforementioned impact. In my view, the form of Confucianism this charge targeted was the sociological and political expressions of Confucianism, which had been somewhat rigidified by the authoritarian power of the Ming (1368–1744 CE) and Qing dynasties (1616–1912 CE). By contrast, the philosophical and spiritual kernel of Confucianism, as manifested in this chapter with regard to its educational thought, has an intrinsic impulse to break through any rigidified social reality and, thus, to promote human creativity. In other words, Confucianism is a progressive tradition that has great potential to be revived authentically in the contemporary context.

References

Chan, W. (Trans. and Ed.). (1963). *A source book in Chinese philosophy*. Princeton: Princeton University Press.

Eno, R. (Trans.). (2012). The *Analects* of Confucius: An online teaching translation. Retrieved from http://www.indiana.edu/~p374/Analects_of_Confucius_(Eno-2012).pdf

Fu, P. 傅佩榮. (2010). 易想天開看人生 (To see human life through the *Yijing*). Taiwan: Shi Bao Chu Ban.

Hobbes, T. (1651). *Leviathan*. London: The Green Dragon in St. Paul's Churchyard.

Huang, S., & Zhang, S. 黃寿祺, 张善文. (2007). 周易译注 (A translation and commentary of the *Zhouyi*). Shanghai: Shang Hai Gu Ji Chu Ban She.

Shaughnessy, L. (2014). *Unearthing the Changes: Recently discovered manuscripts of the Yijing and related texts*. New York: Columbia University Press.

汉典 (The Dictionary of Chinese Characters). (n.d.). Retrieved from http://www.zdic.net/

Wang, B., Han, K., & Kong, Y. 王弼, 韩康伯, 孔颖达. (1999). 周易正义 (A justified commentary on the *Zhouyi*). In L. Xueqin 李学勤 (Ed.), 《十三经注疏》 (The commentary of thirteen classics). Beijing: Beijing University Press.

Whitehead, A. (1926). *Science and the modern world*. Cambridge: Cambridge University Press.

Wilhelm, R. (Trans.). (1977). *The I Ching or Book of Changes* (C. F. Baynes, Trans.). Princeton: Princeton University Press.

Xu, S., & Duan, Y. 許慎, 段玉裁. (1981). 說文解字注 (A commentary on *To Explain and Analyze Characters*). Shanghai: Shang Hai Gu Ji Chu Ban She.

Xunzi. (1988). *Xunzi: A translation and study of the complete works* (J. Knoblock, Trans.). Stanford: Stanford University Press.

Zhao, Y. (2009). *Catching up or leading the way: American education in the age of globalization*. Alexandria: Association for Supervision & Curriculum Development.

Zheng, X., and Kong, Y. 郑玄, 孔颖达. (1999). 礼记正义 (A justified commentary on the *Li Ji*). In X. Li (Ed.), 《十三经注疏》 (The commentaries of thirteen classics). Beijing: Beijing University Press.

Zhu, B. 朱伯崑. (1993). 易学哲学史 (A philosophical history of the studies of the *Zhouyi*) (Vol. 1). Beijing: Hua Xia Chu Ban She.

8

Facilitating Critical Thinking Skills of Chinese Students

A Confucian Perspective

YIN WU

Confucianism, as one of the main philosophical systems in the world, has had a profound impact on how billions of people think and act for centuries. Education in Confucian countries (especially China, but also South Korea and other East Asian countries whose culture has been highly influenced by Confucian principles) (House et al., 2004) is greatly shaped by Confucian thought. In general, several scholars, such as Egege and Kutlieh (2004), Atkinson (1997), and Fox (1994), argue that critical thinking is incompatible with Asian cultures. Some scholars specifically state that Confucian education is more likely to produce the kind of students who are diligent and knowledgeable yet obedient and lacking the skills of critical thinking (Biggs, 1998; Durkin, 2008; Flowerdew, 1998; O'Sullivan & Guo, 2010; Paton, 2005; Zhu, 2015).

However, Asian students' lack of critical thinking skills cannot be entirely attributed to the influence of Confucianism. In fact, critical thinking is highly emphasized in Confucianism. Yet few studies have comprehensively examined the cultivation of critical thinking from a Confucian perspective. Unsurprisingly, little is known about how Confucian principles can be applied to enhance students' critical thinking. To address this gap in the literature, the present chapter explores how Confucian thought approaches the cultivation of critical thinking.

Critical Thinking: An Overview

The concept of critical thinking has a long history of 2,500 years. The word "critical" derives from the Greek word "kritikós." Its original meaning is to find the nature of things and make an analysis (Chaffee, 2014). The definition has been refined and enriched mainly in the United States during the past two centuries. In the 1930s, Dewey described critical thinking as "reflective thinking" (1933, p. 13). He suggested a critical thinking model that includes the following five phases: suggestion, problem definition, hypothesis generation, reasoning, and hypothesis testing. The greatest contribution of Dewey's definition is that critical thinking is related to thinking rationally, generating reasons, and evaluating reasoning effectively and efficiently. In other words, skillful reasoning is a key element of critical thinking (Fisher, 2011).

Another important contributor in defining critical thinking is Ennis, who defines critical thinking as "reasonable, reflective thinking that is focused on deciding what to believe or do" (1996, p. 166). In the late 20th century, further expansion of the meaning of critical thinking was influenced by postmodernism, suggesting that questioning and challenging the existing knowledge and social habits are essential to critical thinking (Scriven, 1985).

Despite the different emphases in various scholars' definitions of critical thinking, the consensus is that critical thinking includes not only processes of thinking involving analysis, interpretation, inference, explanation, evaluation, and self-regulation, but also thinking dispositions, such as clarity, accuracy, precision, consistency, relevance, sound evidence, good reasons, depth, breadth, and fairness (Paul et al., 1989). In short, critical thinking is "the art of thinking in such a way as to: 1) identify its [the objective's] strengths and weaknesses, and 2) recast it in improved form [where necessary]" (Paul & Elder, 2005, p. 22).

Furthermore, Paul and Elder (2006) highlight that critical thinking requires a thinker to possess skills for analysis and evaluation (Paul & Elder, 2006). Figure 8.1 shows the characteristics of a critical thinker (Paul & Elder, 2006; PART, 2012).

Accordingly, the skills that a person needs to think critically are various and include analyzing, discriminating, information seeking, interpreting, logical reasoning, predicting, transforming knowledge, problem solving, and decision making (Paul & Elder, 2006; PART, 2012; Scheffer & Rubenfeld, 2000; Vyncke, 2012).

Figure 8.1 What Is a Critical Thinker?

Confucianism and Critical Thinking

Some educational researchers maintain that Confucianism prevents students from developing critical thinking skills (Atkinson, 1997; Durkin, 2008; O'Sullivan & Guo, 2010; Paton, 2005; Zhu, 2015). A major reason may lie in the highly centralized Chinese educational system and test-oriented policies that support centrality and tight control (Guo, 2013), which are considered to be based on Confucian traditions (Flowerdew, 1998; O'Sullivan & Guo, 2010). The national examination system, which is treated as an important aspect of education and a major way to select talent in China, stems from the Chinese imperial examination system established in the Sui dynasty in the seventh century through which government officials were selected. By the Song dynasty, the content was narrowed and fixed on texts of Neo-Confucian orthodoxy, that is, the Four Books and the Five Classics. The prerequisite for attending the imperial examination was to entirely memorize and recite the nine books. This system remained in place for more than 1,000 years until the beginning of the 20th century (Kracke, 1957; Yang, 1961). Although the imperial examination system no longer exists, under its profound influence on education systems, education in China is still extremely oriented toward rote memorization for tests (Guo, 2013). Contemporary elementary and secondary education in China is criticized for paying far too much attention to students' learning outcomes as lower-order thinking skills (e.g., remembering) (Anderson & Krathwohl, 2001). Every student in China is required to memorize a great amount of knowledge in textbooks for test taking, but not necessarily required to understand or be able to make connections between knowledge and practice. This type of memorizing without understanding does not help students learn how to think critically (Paton, 2005; Zhu, 2015). In summary, the Chinese system does not place enough emphasis on higher-order thinking skills, such as analyzing, evaluating, and creating, which are components of critical thinking that both Western and Eastern educators should promote (Anderson & Krathwohl, 2001).

In addition, in the context of Confucian tradition, keeping a sense of shame (*chi*, 耻) is one of the basic principles.[1] Students are expected to keep an appropriate level of humility and to refrain from raising critical questions within group settings (Flowerdew, 1998). The applications and interpretation of shame are diverse: For example, students who challenge the teacher in public may end up appearing disrespectful, whereas the teacher may lose face and feel ashamed. Therefore, students may avoid challenging and critiquing the teacher to save "face"—both their own and the teacher's. In addition, students avoid expressing their personal opinions in class to avoid embarrassing themselves (Flowerdew, 1998; Hofstede & Hofstede, 2005). Accordingly, these scholars conclude that East Asian students in a traditional Confucian context are more likely to be diligent yet obedient and lacking critical thinking (Durkin, 2008; O'Sullivan & Guo, 2010; Paton, 2005; Zhu, 2015).

However, contrary to this popular belief in the West, critical thinking is highly emphasized in Confucianism (Kim, 2003; Lam, 2016). The characteristics of a critical thinker are embedded in Confucian principles.

Corresponding to each aspect in figure 8.1, development of students' important skills for thinking critically is encouraged by all Confucian classics, including the *Analects*, the *Works of Mencius* (孟子), *Zhongyong* (中庸), the *Great Learning* (*Da Xue*, 大学), and the *Book of Rites* (*Li Ji*, 礼记).

A critical thinker should be open to new information, and seek and consider alternative hypotheses (Paul & Elder, 2006; PART, 2012). In the Confucian classics, a similar issue is frequently discussed as a requirement for an ideal learner. For example, in the *Analects*, Confucius states: "I use my ears widely and follow what is good in what I have heard; I use my eyes widely and retain what I have seen in my mind. Knowledge will follow if we consistently do it" (*Analects* 7.27: 多闻, 择其善者而从之; 多见而识之; 知之次也). That is, as a learner, one should always seek new information by different means; at the same time, one should consider the reliability of the information and only learn the truth from that information. Moreover, being open-minded and considering any possible hypothesis is the pathway to self-improvement (Scheffer & Rubenfeld, 2000). Consistent with this, Confucius also states: "If you can improve yourself in a day, do so each day, forever building on improvement" (*The Great Learning* [*Da Xue*] 3.8: 苟日新, 日日新, 又日新).[5]

Another skill that a critical thinker should develop is to be aware that personal desires and the opinions of others can influence thinking (Paul & Elder, 2006; PART, 2012). When Confucius is asked by one of his students how to deal with his own desire and peer pressure that might influence a person's analysis, he suggests five things that a *junzi* (君子), the ideal person, should be able to do. "A *junzi* in authority is beneficent without great expenditure; he lays tasks on the people without their repining; he pursues what he desires without being covetous; he maintains a dignified ease without being proud; and he is majestic without being fierce" (*Analects* 20.2: 君子惠而不费, 劳而不怨, 欲而不贪, 泰而不骄, 威而不猛). Confucius also suggests how to deal with others' views: "when walking in a group of three, my teachers are always present. I draw out what is good in them so as to emulate it myself, and what is not good in them so as to alter it in myself" (*Analects* 7.22: 三人行, 必有我师焉; 择其善者而从之, 其不善者而改之). In another example, he said, "Meet the virtuous and think how to be their match. Meet those not virtuous and use it for self-evaluation" (*Analects* 4.17: 见贤思齐焉, 见不贤而内自省也). Thus, a *junzi* can learn through reflecting on interpersonal relationships and other people's good qualities and weaknesses.

In modern Western scholarship, a critical thinker should be a person who is self-aware and self-reflective. He or she should be an active and empathetic listener (Paul & Elder, 2006; PART, 2012). Confucian principles are consistent with these concepts; a good student should always be self-reflective, be brave to correct mistakes and learn from them, and be empathetic in daily interpersonal interaction. For instance, Zengzi, a disciple of Confucius, states: "Each day I reflect on myself upon three points. In transacting business for others, whether I have been faithful or not? In intercourse with friends, whether I have been sincere or not? And whether I have mastered and practiced the instructions of my teacher or not? (*Analects* 1.3: 吾日三省吾身。为人谋而不忠乎？与朋友交而不信乎？传不习乎？). Confucius also states: "Having made a mistake and not correcting it, is another mistake itself" (*Analects* 15.29: 过而不改，是谓过矣). In other words, learning from one's own mistakes that are found during self-reflection is a very important way to become a *junzi*. In addition, Confucius proclaims: "A person who can bring new warmth to the old while understanding the new is worthy to take as a teacher" (*Analects* 2.11: 温故而知新，可以为师矣). Confucius considers learning to include processing old ideas. Similarly, an important characteristic of a critical thinker is being able to understand new knowledge by reviewing the old (Kim, 2003; Lam, 2016; Scheffer & Rubenfeld, 2000).

Furthermore, a critical thinker should be able to consider information from multiple sources, even from those that are difficult (PART, 2012; Paul & Elder, 2006). This is consistent with one of the requirements of being a *junzi*, that is, to broaden his or her horizon and learn knowledge from a wide range of sources. Specifically, Confucius comments in the *Book of Rites*: "To acquire extensive information and remember retentively, while (at the same time) he is modest; to do earnestly what is good, and not become weary in so doing—these are the characteristics of him whom we call the ideal man" (*Book of Rites* [*Li Ji*] 1. 61: 博闻强识而让，敦善行而不怠，谓之君子).[6] Furthermore, Confucius states, "Listen extensively to what people say and cast away doubts, repeat those that you do not doubt with caution and you will make fewer mistakes. Observe extensively how people do things and cast away those you feel uneasy, put the rest into practice with caution and you will have few regrets" (*Analects* 2.18: 多闻阙疑，慎言其余，则寡尤；多见阙殆，慎行其余，则寡悔). That is, a good learner can synthesize what is heard and seen in an open-minded, fair, and autonomous way, then integrate them into oneself as wisdom, meanwhile being cautious when explaining and applying the wisdom to practice (Kim, 2003; Zhao, 2013).

The ability to recognize faulty thinking, pseudoscience, fraud and quackery, and other elements of manufactured reality that reflect dominant discourse and not necessarily truth is another important critical thinking skill. Regarding the dominant discourse, Confucius argues that an ideal learner should listen to viewpoints from different populations, distinguish truth from false information, and not easily rest on authority alone. "A *junzi* is harmonious and open-minded. He can accept different opinions, but not blindly agree" (*Analects* 13.23: 君子和而不同). Mencius, the most representative Confucianist after Confucius, affirms this argument: "Believing everything in books is worse than having no books at all" (*Works of Mencius* 14.3: 尽信书，则不如无书).[7] As these two quotes demonstrate, learners should think independently and critically. An exemplary learner should not only memorize what is written in books, but also question the existing knowledge and make one's own decisions.

Last, but not least, a critical thinker should be good at conducting analysis, drawing accurate conclusions, and articulating thoughts. Confucius states: "Studying without thinking is a vain effort. Thinking without studying is a dangerous effort" (*Analects* 2.15: 学而不思则罔，思而不学则殆). Studying—here meaning seeing, hearing, remembering, and imitating the wisdom of others—must be accompanied by thinking, and thinking should be accompanied by studying. Studying here is not comprehensive Confucian learning. Confucius divides the comprehensive learning process into five phases: "The extensive study of what is good, accurate inquiry about it, careful reflection on it, the clear evaluation of it, and the earnest practice of it" (*Zhongyong* 19: 博学之，审问之，慎思之，明辨之，笃行之).[8] This learning process as a whole is congruent with Bloom's taxonomy of educational objectives, highly related to the skills of critical thinking (Anderson & Krathwohl, 2001). "Extensive study" is the lowest level of thinking, knowledge, and comprehension. The higher-order thinking skills include "accurate inquiry" and "careful reflection" (analysis and synthesis), then "clear evaluation," followed by "the earnest practice" (application), and finally creation. These Confucian thoughts encourage people to learn by thinking analytically and critically (Lam, 2016; Zhao, 2013).

Ultimately, the purpose of Confucian education is to foster a student to become a *junzi*, the exemplary person depicted in Confucian classics.

One of the five most basic virtues of a *junzi* is *zhi* (wisdom, 智). Confucius explains the thinking of a *junzi* in detail: "For a *junzi*, there are nine things he needs to take notice of: In seeing, he must seek understanding. In hearing, he must listen with clarity. His demeanor must be cordial. His countenance must be of respectfulness. Be conscientious when he speaks. Be serious in his tasks. Seek advice when in doubt. Anger causes difficulty in thinking. Think of what is righteous at the sight of profit" (*Analects* 16.10: 君子有九思: 视思明, 听思聪, 色思温, 貌思恭, 言思忠, 事思敬, 疑思问, 忿思难, 见得思义). A *junzi* should always be 1) open to new knowledge and good at making connections between old and new information; 2) self-aware, self-reflective, and empathetic; 3) able to conduct analysis and recognize truth from false information; 4) able to consider information from multiple sources; 5) dare to doubt authority and draw accurate conclusions; and 6) good at doing evaluations to correct mistakes. Accordingly, an ideal person in Confucianism is essentially a critical thinker who can "identify its [the objective's] strengths and weaknesses and recast it in improved form" (Paul & Elder, 2005, p. 22).

Finally, it is worth mentioning that Confucius articulates *chi* in depth, which counters the argument that in a Confucian context, students avoid challenging or critiquing authority (Flowerdew, 1998). Confucius states that "those who're always willing to learn would be near to wisdom; those who strive to achieve would be near to humanity; while those who always bear the word 'shame' in mind would be near to bravery. Those who know these three things above would not be bothered in wondering why all should spare no effort in perfecting our morality" (*Zhongyong* 20: 知耻近乎勇, 好学近乎知, 力行近乎仁, 知斯三者, 则知所以修身). The bravery here is the courage to correct one's mistakes, indicating that men who know shame and have courage to self-correct are worthy of praise. Thus, the meaning of shame and that of courage equate. Shame is not a passive state, but a self-reflective action in which one can reflect on his or her conduct and values. This is the reason that shame connects to courage in Confucianism, because the goal is to bring positive change into one's life. On the one hand, for a teacher to have mistakes pointed out by students in public can be identified as shame; on the other hand, being able to admit mistakes and correct them is a great quality that is appreciated in Confucianism. Shame certainly exists as part of Confucianism, but so does personal courage, which is an element of critical thinking as well (Kim, 2003; Lam, 2016).

In summary, conceptions of critical thinking in Confucianism and Western scholarship share many commonalities. The importance of critical thinking is advocated and emphasized in Confucian traditions. The perceived incompatibility between Confucianism and critical thinking is based on an incomplete and oversimplified understanding of Confucianism in educational practices, which is one of the factors inhibiting students' growth as critical thinkers.

Cultivating Critical Thinking through Confucian Conceptual Lenses

The term "critical thinking" was introduced to China in the late 1980s. Recently, improving students' critical thinking skills has become one of the primary tasks of education in China (He, 2012). It is formally emphasized through official policies. According to the latest outline of College Entrance Examinations (*Gao Kao*) issued by the Ministry of Education, one of the major components of all examinations across subjects is critical thinking skills. Students' ability to analyze, suggest, define problems, reason, test hypotheses, interpret, explain, solve problems, and innovate is assessed. Based on how they place in the assessment, students are selected for college admission (Ministry of Education of China, 2014). Consequently, how to foster students' growth as critical thinkers has become a matter of importance for Chinese educators across the educational spectrum.

Few empirical studies have directly focused on the application of Confucian principles to improve critical thinking skills. Only two studies have explored the potential relationship between Confucian principles and critical thinking. One study reported the results of a one-year longitudinal study in Hong Kong that examined a teaching intervention designed to enhance students' development of critical thinking (Fung, 2014). The most interesting finding was that Chinese traditional values play an important role in students' perceptions of ground rules, potentially influencing their critical thinking development as measured in debate-type discussions. Confucian values, such as *li* (propriety, 礼) and *chi* (shame or "face disgrace," 耻), likely influence Chinese students' understanding of ground rules. In another study, there was a positive correlation found between the establishment of these rules and students' demonstration of critical thinking abilities (Fung, 2014; Fung & Howe, 2012). These two studies shed light on the value of Confucian beliefs in fostering students' critical thinking.

There is an urgent necessity to explore how to properly apply the Confucian view of critical thinking to benefit students' development in both East Asian and Western countries. Although the theme of fostering critical thinking is deeply embedded in Confucian traditions, this aspect of Confucianism has been largely neglected in Confucian countries. Instead of denying Confucianism, more emphasis should be placed on properly integrating more of the essence of Confucian heritage into the curriculum. In this way, when taking the cultural context and the deeply rooted Confucian tradition into account, critical thinking can be inspired by better understanding Confucianism. To achieve this goal, more guidance and effective intervention for students, teachers, and parents are required to integrate Confucianism into educational practices.

In China, the sages of ancient times have played positive roles in individual cultivation for more than 2,500 years. Lifestyles and ways of thinking are consciously and unconsciously influenced by Confucian traditions. However, students may not fully comprehend Confucian concepts and internalize these concepts as values. Simply including some Confucian texts as part of curriculum objectives is not appropriately promoting Confucianism. Even students recognize that the Confucianism they are taught is one-sided and not the full picture—an incomplete philosophy. They seldom challenge the teacher because they want to save face for both parties (Lam, 2016). On the teacher's side, test-oriented education and concern for their own authority makes teachers ignore or give up delivering the invaluable ideas in Confucianism that can benefit all students and society (Guo, 2013).

On the other hand, critical thinking cannot be separated from basic skills. Higher-order thinking activities are based on mastering fundamental knowledge (Anderson & Krathwohl, 2001). Having excellent basic knowledge and skills is an advantage of Chinese students (Guo, 2013; O'Sullivan & Guo, 2010). It is extremely important to let students realize their advantage with regard to facilitating development of critical thinking skills. For primary and secondary school teachers, combining more activities that let students make use of their knowledge to solve real-world problems is a key to fostering habits of critical thinking (Fung, 2014). For instance, students are familiar with Confucius's crisis-coping strategies as a part of the curriculum. The teacher can ask students to complete a group project, including the process of introducing a real-world crisis (e.g., international terrorism), collecting background information, analyzing the causes, proposing strategies, and evaluating the feasibility of the plan. During this project, students could make connections between knowledge from different disciplines (including history, politics, geography, science, and mathematics) and explore possibilities to apply the knowledge instead of just preparing for a test. They can also acquire interpersonal skills through peer evaluation of group members postactivity. Different forms of activities can also make the classroom a much more interactive and intellectually dynamic environment.

Some parents have realized the educational benefits of Confucianism on students' comprehensive development. For example, sending preschool children to tutoring classes to read Confucian classics is now a boom among parents in China. But the reading-only process is not effective in developing children's critical thinking if it only requires children to remember knowledge without a solid understanding of Confucian virtues. Children should be encouraged to express their own opinions, raise questions, and interpret what they have learned in their own ways, such as through storytelling, role-playing, and drawing pictures. That is, even without tutoring, parents can still support children in learning how to think analytically and critically as long as the children are provided with opportunities to experience a process that includes information seeking, questioning, articulating, evaluating, and decision making.

The Confucian view of critical thinking should also have implications for Western countries. Western education systems—for example, American education—could benefit from Confucian thought about the significance of self-reflection. Even in a society less influenced by Confucianism, developing students' critical thinking skills is one of the most significant tasks facing educators (Facione, 1989). However, in American education, a tendency of putting too much emphasis on critique leads to less attention to other important dimensions of critical thinking (Durkin, 2008), for instance, self-reflection, which is an essential aspect of Confucian learning (Zhao, 2013).

People in Western countries, including Americans, tend to think that the most central aspect of critical thinking is questioning and challenging existing knowledge and social habits (Durkin, 2008; Scriven, 1985). Questioning and challenging are emphasized over the processes of analyzing, evaluating, problem solving, and so on (Vyncke, 2012). Confucianism offers insights that could result in improvements in critical thinking methods in Western schools. Americans may put more emphasis on critiquing and criticizing different objectives but neglect reflection, internal observation, and evaluation of one's own opinion (Durkin, 2008). Self-reflection is one of the six dimensions of critical thinking (PART, 2012). The importance of thinking self-reflectively in the development of critical thinking should be promoted more in American educational practice.

Furthermore, although American students generally are more active in questioning and challenging authority, their basic knowledge foundation is not as good as that of their East Asian counterparts in terms of academic achievement (Durkin, 2008; Hofstede & Hofstede, 2005; OECD, 2016). The underperformance of American students may be attributable to schools' lacking accountability (Carnoy, Elmore, & Siskin, 2003). To narrow the achievement gap between American students and students in East Asian countries, one of the major educational reform movements in recent decades is standards-based accountability. Current school accountability reforms combine public accountability and student testing (Carnoy, Elmore, & Siskin, 2003; Hanushek & Raymond, 2005), for example, the Common Core State Standards (Common Core Standards, 2013) and the high school Regents Exams in New York State (Dee et al., 2011). In K–12 education, most states have made enormous efforts to establish rigorous academic standards to ensure that high school graduates are college- or career-ready and to hold students and schools accountable for meeting those standards. Unfortunately, the effect of the reforms on narrowing the achievement gap and improving school accountability is not significant (Dee et al., 2011; Hanushek & Raymond, 2005).

It is not possible to develop higher-level critical thinking without fundamental skills and basic knowledge, which, ironically, students in Confucian countries excel at obtaining. It is time for the stakeholders of American education to self-evaluate. Confucian practices encourage students to spend more time reflecting on themselves, observing internally, and seeking their own learning strategies, which may have a noticeable positive effect on improving students' critical thinking skills. It is quite possible that American teachers could also benefit from Confucian attributes.

To conclude, Confucian philosophy is a cultivation system that can ideally serve the primary goal of schooling: fostering students' critical thinking skills. The virtues of an ideal Confucian learner are highly consistent with the characteristics of the critical thinker as defined in Western literature. Therefore, a noticeable positive effect of improving students' critical thinking should result from appropriate promotion and proper application of Confucian concepts. To improve students' critical thinking skills, more effort to integrate Confucian values into educational practice is needed in China. Students could be cultivated to think more critically without isolation from their cultural background. Relevant Confucian concepts, for instance, emphasis on self-reflection, could also have valuable implications for educational reforms in the United States.

Notes

1. Depending on contexts, this Chinese term can be interpreted as a sense of shame, moral sensibility, conscience, dishonor/disgrace, humiliation, and so on. Representative terms for shame are well laid out in the earliest Confucian classics, such as the *Analects*, *Mencius*, and *Li Ji*. *Chi* is a generic concept of shame and is the most commonly used.

2. Confucius originally used the word *junzi* (君子) in the *Image* (Xiangzhuan, 象传), which is his explanatory book on the *Yijing* (易经).

3. The five concepts of *ren*, *yi*, *li*, *zhi*, and *xin* (仁、义、礼、智、信) were first summarized as the Five Constant Virtues by Dong Zhongshu (董仲舒) in *Ju Xian Liang Dui Ce* (举贤良对策).

4. Translation of quotes from the *Analects* are adapted from Robert Eno (Trans.), *The Analects of Confucius: An Online Teaching Translation*, p. 111, retrieved from http://www.indiana.edu/~p374/Analects_of_Confucius (Eno-2012). pdf and http://www.chinese-wiki.com/Analects_of_Confucius

5. The original quote is cited from *Da Xue* (大学, *Great Learning*), one of the four Confucian books. Translation of the quote is adapted from http://www.en84.com/cihui/201510/00016688.html

6. The original quote is cited from *Li Ji* (礼记, *Book of Rites*), one of the five Confucian classics. Translation of the quote is adapted from http://www.studychineseculture.com/book.asp?id=444

7. The original quote is cited from the *Mengzi* (孟子, *Works of Mencius*), one of the four Confucian books. Translation of the quote is adapted from http://ctext.org/liji/qu-li-i

8. The original quote is cited from *Zhongyong* (中庸, *Centrality and Commonality*), one of the four Confucian books. Translation of the quote is adapted from http://www.cnculture.net/ebook/jing/sishu/Zhongyong_En.html

References

Anderson, L. W., & Krathwohl, D. R. (2001). *A taxonomy for learning, teaching, and assessing: A revision of Bloom's taxonomy of educational objectives* (Abridged ed.). Boston: Addison-Wesley Longman.

Atkinson, D. (1997). A critical approach to critical thinking in TESOL. *TESOL Quarterly, 31*, 9–37.

Biggs, J. (1998). Learning from the Confucian heritage: So size doesn't matter? *International Journal of Educational Research, 29*(8), 723–738.

Carnoy, M., Elmore, R., & Siskin, L. (Eds.). (2003). *The new accountability: High schools and high-stakes testing*. New York: Routledge.

Chaffee, J. (2014). *Thinking critically*. Boston: Cengage Learning.

Common Core Standards. (2013). K–8 publishers' criteria for the Common Core State Standards for Mathematics. Retrieved from http://www.corestandards.org/assets/Math_Publishers_Criteria_K-8_Summer %202012_FINAL.pdf

Confucius, Mencius, et al. (2009). *The Four Books and the Five Classics*. Beijing: Zhonghua Book House.

Dee, T. S., Jacob, B. A., Rockoff, J. E., & McCrary, J. (2011). Rules and discretion in the evaluation of students and schools: The case of the New York Regents Examinations. Retrieved from https://cepa.stanford.edu/content/rules-and-discretion-evaluation-students-and-schools-case-new-york-regents-examinations

Dewey, J. (1933). *How we think: A restatement of the relation of reflective thinking to the education process*. Washington, DC: D.C. Heath and Company.

Durkin, K. (2008). The adaptation of East Asian master's students to Western norms of critical thinking and argumentation in the UK. *Intercultural Education, 19*(1), 15–27.

Egege, S., & Kutlieh, K. (2004). Critical thinking: Teaching foreign notions to foreign students. *International Education Journal, 4*(4), 75–85.

Elliott, J., & Tsai, C. T. (2008). What might Confucius have to say about action research? *Educational Action Research, 16*(4), 569–578.

Ennis, R. H. (1996). *Critical thinking*. Upper Saddle River: Prentice-Hall.

Ennis, R. H., & Millman, J. (1985). *Cornell critical thinking tests Level X and Level Z manual* (3rd ed.). Pacific Grove: Midwest Publications.

Eno, R. (Trans.). (2015). *The Analects of Confucius: An online teaching translation*. Retrieved from http://www.indiana.edu/~p374/Analects_of_Confucius_(Eno-2012).pdf

Facione, P. A. (1989). Critical thinking: A statement of expert consensus for purposes of educational assessment and instruction: Research findings and recommendations. ERIC Document Reproduction Service [for] US Department of Education, Office of Educational Research and Improvement.

Fisher, A. (Ed.). (2011). *Critical thinking: An introduction*. Cambridge: Cambridge University Press.

Flowerdew, L. (1998). A cultural perspective on group work. *ELT Journal 52*(4), 323–329.

Fox, H. (1994). *Listening to the world*. Urbana: National Council of Teachers of English.

Fung, D. (2014). Promoting critical thinking through effective group work: A teaching intervention for Hong Kong primary school students. *International Journal of Educational Research, 66*, 45–62.

Fung, D., & Howe, C. (2012). Liberal studies in Hong Kong: A new perspective on critical thinking through group work. *Thinking Skills and Creativity, 7*(2), 101–111.

Guo, M. (2013). Developing critical thinking in English class: Culture-based knowledge and skills. *Theory and Practice in Language Studies, 3*(3), 503–507.

Hanushek, E. A., & Raymond, M. E. (2005). Does school accountability lead to improved student performance? *Journal of Policy Analysis and Management, 24*(2), 297–327.

He, G. (2012). Cultivation mechanism of critical thinking skills based on language learning tasks. In *Second International Conference on Future Computers in Education: Lecture Notes in Information Technology* (Vols. 23–24, pp. 102–107). Changchun, China.

Hofstede, G., & Hofstede, J. (2005). *Cultures and organization: Software of the minds* (2nd ed.). New York: McGraw-Hill.

House, R. J., Hanges, P. J., Javidan, M., Dorfman, P. W., & Gupta, V. (2004). *Culture, leadership, and organizations: The GLOBE study of 62 societies*. Thousand Oaks: Sage.

Kim, H. K. (2003). Critical thinking, learning and Confucius: A positive assessment. *Journal of Philosophy of Education, 37*(1), 71–87.

Kracke, E. A. (1957). Region, family, and individual in the Chinese examination system. In J. K. Fairbank (Ed.), *Chinese thought and institutions* (pp. 111–112). Chicago: University of Chicago Press.

Lam, C. M. (2016). Does Confucianism hinder critical thinking in education? In *Sociological and philosophical perspectives on education in the Asia-Pacific region* (pp. 179–192). Singapore: Springer.

Ministry of Education of the People's Republic of China. (2014). The outline of college entrance examination 2014. Retrieved from http://gaokao.eol.cn/gkdg/

O'Sullivan, M. W., & Guo, L. (2011). Critical thinking and Chinese international students: An East-West dialogue. *Journal of Contemporary Issues in Education, 5*(2), 53–73.

Organisation for Economic Co-operation and Development (OECD). (2016). PISA 2015 Results: Volume 1: Excellence and Equity in Education. Retrieved from http://www.keepeek.com/Digital-Asset-Management/oecd/education/pisa-2015-results-volume-i_9789264266490-en#.WIWPe7YrIdU

Paton, M. (2005). Is critical analysis foreign to Chinese students? In E. Manalo & G. Wong-Toi (Eds.), *Communication skills in university education: The international dimension* (pp. 1–11). Auckland: Pearson Education New Zealand.

Paton, M. (2011). Asian students, critical thinking and English as an academic lingua franca. *Analytic Teaching and Philosophical Praxis, 32*(1), 27–39.

Paul, R., Binker, A. J. A., Martin, D., & Adamson, K. (1989). *Critical thinking handbook: High school*. Tomales: Foundation for Critical Thinking.

Paul, R., & Elder, L. (2005). *The thinker's guide to the nature and functions of critical and creative thinking*. Dillon Beach: Foundation for Critical Thinking.

Paul, R., & Elder, L. (2006). *Critical thinking: Learn the tools the best thinkers use*. Upper Saddle River: Prentice-Hall.

Practice and Research Together (PART) (2012). Taking the path less travelled: Critical thinking for child welfare practitioners. Retrieved from http://www.partcanada.org/critical-thinking—eip

Scheffer, B. K., & Rubenfeld, M. G. (2000). A consensus statement on critical thinking in nursing. *Journal of Nursing Education, 39*(8), 352–359.

Scriven, M. (1985). Critical for survival. *National Forum, 55*, 9–12.

Vyncke, M. (2012). The concept and practice of critical thinking in academic writing: An investigation of international students' perceptions and writing experiences (Doctoral dissertation). Retrieved from British Council.

Willingham, D. T. (2008). Critical thinking: Why is it so hard to teach? *Arts Education Policy Review, 109*(4), 21–32.

Yang, C. K. (1961). *Religion in Chinese society: A study of contemporary social functions of religion and some of their historical factors*. Berkeley: University of California Press.

Yuan, H., Kunaviktikul, W., Klunklin, A., & Williams, B. A. (2008). Improvement of nursing students' critical thinking skills through problem-based learning in the People's Republic of China: A quasi-experimental study. *Nursing and Health Sciences, 10*(1), 70–76.

Zhang, H., & Lambert, V. (2008). Critical thinking dispositions and learning styles of baccalaureate nursing students from China. *Nursing and Health Sciences, 10*(3), 175–181.

Zhao, J. (2013). Confucius as a critical educator: Towards educational thought of Confucius. *Frontiers of Education in China, 8*(1), 9–27.

Zhu, J. (2015, June 9). Critical thinking, an ability Chinese students need. *China Daily*. Retrieved from http:// www.chinadaily.com.cn/opinion/2015-06/09/content_20945294.htm

Part 3

Confucianism and the Social and Moral Functions of Education

9

From Self-Cultivation to Social Transformation

*The Confucian Embodied Pathway
and Educational Implications*

JING LIN

Major Confucian classics, especially the *Great Learning*, point to the pathway for one to acquire wisdom and ability and to be part of the social force transforming our world for peace and justice. The pathway is an embodied one. In Zajonc's (2006) words, an "epistemology of love" (p. 1742) is to be engaged. Confucianism focuses on the cultivation of virtues, which is about resonance with the Heart of Heaven and the will of people (Tu, 2008). This resonance requires sensitivity, energy, and an innate understanding of the underlying force that propels the universe. This chapter argues that there is much to be rediscovered in Confucianism that aims to help learners achieve tranquility of mind and to cultivate the "Great Expansive Qi" (*hao ran zhi qi* 浩然之气), which has the function of filling one with aspiration and developing the capacity vital for self-fulfillment and for doing good in the world. Arts, music, calligraphy, and chanting of Confucian classics are some educational methods to achieve the goals of acquiring energy, but the most important practice lies in the cultivation of virtues along with contemplative practices. This chapter elaborates on these ideas and notes that, historically, sages such as Confucius, Mencius, and Wang Yangming all employed contemplative practices such as meditation, which gave them great insight. The practices were mostly forgotten, which led to the loss of an effective approach for people to embody Confucian learning and teaching.

The Confucian Cosmology of Heaven-Human Oneness

Confucian thoughts, as extrapolated in Confucius's *Analects*, and in the other Confucian classics posit a world of connectivity, as the individual, world, and cosmos are one. Humans are in a reciprocal relationship to others, as the self and the cosmos are seen as intrinsically integrated. The element that creates all existence is the primordial *qi* (混元气), and this primordial *qi* links all forms, animate or inanimate, sentient or insentient, and it is forever in the process of condensing into physical matter, shaping its growth, and when energy sustaining the matter is expended, matter returns to the formless existence of *qi* again (成住坏空).

The *Book of Changes* denotes a universe originating from *qi*, and it states:

> *Wuji* is the realm of the primordial *qi*, which generates *taiji*, and *taiji* is formed of *yin* and *yang qi*, which then generates four different states of *qi*, old *yang* and young *yang*, and old *yin* and young *yin*, which eventually generates eight elements of existence, followed by events and the myriad things as we see in the cosmos (无极生太极, 太极生两仪, 两仪生四象, 四象生八卦, 八卦定吉凶). (*Book of Changes, The Great Commentary*, the first, chapter 11).

In a word, all existence is enwrapped in *qi*, although it manifests in different forms and forces. They can be material, physical forces or informational, bio-informational, and spiritual forces.

More specifically, *qi* can be seen in everything. Zeng Zhenyu (1997), a scholar studying the Chinese philosophy of *qi*, summarizes the concept, which includes *yin qi* and *yang qi*; the four seasons' *qi*; the five elements' *qi*, which are wood, fire, earth, metal, and water; and *qi* in nature, such as those that bring wind, thunder, rain, and lightening. In traditional Chinese medicine classics, such as the *Inner Sutra of the Huang Emperor* (黄帝内经), *qi* flows in our blood and organs, and *qi* forms our spirit, which gives us consciousness and the ability to think and feel. *Qi* is also related to one's moral virtues: Those who are not virtuous can lose their *qi* and disturb the balance of *qi* in the body, which results in illness. Hence, Heaven and humans both emerge from the original, primordial *qi*, and all existence is connected by this primordial *qi* that manifests in many forms. That is why Taoist and Confucian philosophy insist on Heaven-Human Oneness (天人合一).

Zeng (1997) explained that Heaven-Human Oneness has these elements:

- Heaven and humans both originate from the same sources; they are similar, hence, the same principles penetrate them.
- Heaven and humans are of the same structure; they form reciprocal relationships and mutually influence each other.
- They interpenetrate each other and are immersed in each other; hence, nothing in the universe happens by chance.

Major philosophical and medicinal works in China support this notion. In the *Internal Sutra of the Huang Emperor*, elements such as directions, seasons, our body organs, our emotions, and our health are all interrelated. For example, the direction east corresponds with spring, with liver in the human body, with the emotion anger, and with the virtue of 仁 or loving-kindness.

In the classic *Chun Qiu Fan Lu: Wang Dao* (春秋繁露: 王道),[1] by Dong Zhongshu, a leader's acts affect not only human society but also natural phenomena. In the *Book of History* (史记), by Si Maqian, there is a volume called the Heaven Palace Book (天宫书), which details how human behaviors affect the sun, moon, and stars in other constellations. A major change in the sun can cause war on earth, and war on earth can lead to violent reactions in the sun.

In the Taoist classic *Zhou Yi Can Tong Qi* (周易参同契), the human body, energy, and spirit correspond and relate intricately and inextricably with the movement of the moon and the sun. Mencius said that "All That Exists is within me" (万物皆被于我) (*Mencius*, Jin Xin I) (孟子: 尽心上).[2]

Further, the universe is a moral and spiritual force. In the *Book of Changes*, the cosmos is always changing, with the *yin* and *yang* forces intersecting with and transforming each other. But there are underlying virtues that guide the forces, that is, virtues such as *ren* or loving-kindness can bring fortune to a family. The Kun Hexagram (坤卦) has these interpretations: Those families that accumulate good virtues will have good fortunes, and those that do not accumulate good virtues will have disasters (积善之家必有余庆, 积不善之家, 必有余殃). The *Doctrine of the Mean* states that "those who have great virtue will be blessed with status, fortune, fame, and longevity. These people are also given great missions to represent the Will of Heaven and to fulfill their life's purpose" (大德必得其位, 必得其祿, 必得其名, 必得其壽 . . . 大德必受命) (*Doctrine of the Mean*, 16).³

In sum, Tu (2008) argues that Confucius talked about virtues as cosmic laws that are manifested in the human world. People living a moral life following the virtue of love fulfill their cosmic missions. By being a loving person, one bridges Heaven and Human.

In short, Chinese cosmology believes that the primordial *qi* is the fundamental energy that forms the physical, spiritual, and informational energy for all existence. It is similar to Plato's idea of Forms: *Qi* can manifest in physical existence when it is condensed into matter, and the physical matter will return to its Form when the qi energy has dissipated. Life is about unfolding and enfolding, and this is a perpetual process. Virtues generate and sustain the force for all existence. The *yang* force rises and strives; the *yin* force descends and sustains. As a person aspiring to become a *junzi* (君子), or an enlightened person, as the *Book of Changes* says, one needs to strive to strengthen oneself and to be as virtuous as the earth that sustains all worldly existence (天行健, 君子以自強不息. 地勢坤, 君子以厚德載物) (*Book of Changes*, Xiang Zhuan).

Cultivating and Embodying Virtues

Confucian philosophy is therefore a cultivation system. One does not locate Heaven or humans as separated or distant from each other but as integral and manifested in one another. Virtues are heavenly principles that need to be followed in every aspect of one's life. As Guan Zhong (管仲) says in his essay "Neiye" (*nei ye* 內業 or Inner Work):

> The primordial *qi* gives birth to the crops on earth and the stars in the sky, and those who harbor the primordial *qi* will become sages. This *qi* can only be acquired through the heart and maintained through virtues, and with *qi* one grows virtues and wisdom is bred, and this will benefit all existence in the universe (凡物之精, 比則為生下生五穀, 上為列星. 流於天地之間, 謂之鬼神, 藏於胸中, 謂之聖人; 是故此氣, 杲乎如登於天, 杳乎如入於淵, 淖乎如在於海, 卒乎如在於己. 是故此氣也, 不可止

以力, 而可安以德. 不可呼以聲, 而可迎以音. 敬守勿失, 是謂成德. 德成而智出, 萬物畢得). (*Guanzi*, 49)

Hence, the five virtues in Confucian teaching need to be seen as forming an action guide for the cultivation of virtues that undergird the accumulation of *qi* energy. *Ren* (仁) is love or loving-kindness in action, *yi* (义) is selfless help to others, *li* (礼) is treating others with respect, *zhi* (智) is the act of seeking of wisdom, and *xin* (信) is practice by faith and sincerity (Lin & Wang, 2010; Peng, 2007). When we practice these virtues well, we benefit ourselves and the world by generating positive energy that circulates from the self to others and that returns to the self. It is a positive reciprocal relationship.

To embody these virtues is to fulfill one's true nature and mission in life. Character building based on virtues is critical for Confucian learning. In daily life, this touches on how one thinks, speaks, and acts and how one interacts with people, plays music, and performs arts. In premodern China, doctors traditionally believed that illnesses come from emotional disturbances, summed up as the emotions of excessive excitement, anger, sadness, worry, fear, and insecurity (喜怒悲伤忧恐惊). A virtuous person maintains a healthy mind and a tranquil heart, which generates the harmonious *qi* that spawns and nurtures all lives (*Doctrine of the Mean*, 1).[4] A kind and loving person can let go of excessive desires and be in a positive relationship with other people. He or she can have tranquility in his or her mind and heart that generates and preserves energy. Hence, Confucius said in the *Analects*, those who have *ren* (仁) or loving-kindness achieve tranquility (仁者静), and those who live by *ren* live a long life (仁者寿) (*Analects*, Yong Ye Pian 6–23).[5] The *Great Learning* says: Virtues nurture the body (德润身) (*Great Learning*, 3).[6] Finally, the *Doctrine of the Mean* says: People of great virtues will be rewarded with long life (大德必得其寿) (*Doctrine of the Means*, 16).[7]

The Pathway to Accumulating the Great Expansive *Qi*

Mencius said: "I am good in cultivating my own vital and Great Expansive *qi*" (我善养吾浩然之气). When asked what *qi* is, he said:

> It is hard to put into language. As *qi*, it is expansive and powerful, and nurturing it and not wasting it, it fills up the whole universe. As *qi*, it follows the rules of the Tao and

violating the rules the *qi* will be gone. The *qi* is accumulated from one's selfless help to others, and it cannot be gained through using force or by attacking others. In action, if one is not humble in the heart, the *qi* is also gone. I often said that people do not know the real meaning of serving other people; they treat it as an external act (rather than as inner cultivation of *qi*) (曰: "难言也. 其为气也, 至大至刚, 以直养而无害, 则塞于天地之间. 其为气也, 配义与道; 无是, 馁也. 是集义所生者, 非义袭而取之也. 行有不慊于心, 则馁矣. 我故曰, 告子未尝知义, 以其外之也"). (*Mencius*, Gong Sun Chou 2A-2)[8]

This statement implies that only when one has the great expansive *qi* can one join the spirit of the world. As *qi* is the organic energy that links all existence, and we as a species have *qi*, elevating our *qi* will enable us to be in touch with the greater scope of life.

Qi is obtained by virtues that lead to growth in wisdom. If one sees the *Analects* in this way, Confucius is telling people how to cultivate *qi* and virtues. *Qi* flows naturally and accumulates when one is in a tranquil state. Hence, in the *Analects*, Confucius is said to be fond of music and arts and sports—Confucius himself was a seeker. He went to Laozi, who was a master in energy cultivation, able to fly like a dragon to the sky, as Confucius said metaphorically or maybe literally in *Zhuang Zi* (庄子). So when Confucius's students asked him what the Tao is, he said, "My Tao is to integrate my life with the One" (吾道一以贯之) (*Analects*, Li Ren), which I interpret as the cultivation of the primordial *qi* energy that embeds all existence and lives. Tao is not an abstract term. It is the energy field and force that breeds and nurtures all existence. In pursuing the Tao, Confucius did not talk much about the specific methods of cultivation in the *Analects*, but other classics, such as the *Great Learning*, talk about "illumination," a state of being when energy has transformed the body and spirit. More specifically, the *Great Learning* starts with this sentence: "The way of the Great Learning lies in illuminating bright virtues." In my interpretation of the phrase "illuminating bright virtues," this may be a physical description of a person in a state of enlightenment. A person who can illuminate virtues connotes a person of high energy similar to auras in the pictures of religious figures. The enlightened beings emit an aura that results from having high energy and high spiritual attainment. This brightness is connected to virtues. When one attains the Tao, one embraces others as one's family, and one is unconditionally loving and kind to others—these are the ways to the Great Learning, or to the Tao. With Great Learning, one brings peace and harmony to the world (大学之道在明明德, 在亲民, 在止于至善) (*Great Learning*, 1).

The *Great Learning* discusses a process of Confucian inner cultivation: 格物至知, 知止而后有定, 定而后能静, 静而后能安, 安而后能虑, 虑而后能得 (*Great Learning*, 1).[9] Literally, *ge wu* 格物 means studying the world, *zhi zhi* 至知 means arriving at understanding, *zhi zhi* 知止 means knowing when and how to stop, *you ding* 有定 means finding one's grounding, *neng jing* 能静 means being able to achieve tranquility, *neng an* 能安 means being able to attain peace, *neng lv* 能虑 means being able to worry for the world, and *neng de* 能得 means being able to achieve goals. In the *Great Learning*, this process leads one to bring peace to the family, community, country, and even the cosmos.

In terms of the methods embedded in the process, my interpretation is as follows:

- *Ge wu* 格物 is a body-based learning. It is not just book learning or intellectual endeavor. In *Zhuangzi*, there is a story about Confucius consulting Laozi on the cultivation of the Tao. As we know, Taoism is a system that stresses the cultivation of *qi* through myriad meditation methods. This emphasis on cultivation of energy was also in Confucius's teaching, but it tends to be hidden among various texts such as the *Doctrine of the Mean*. *Ge wu zhi zhi* 格物至知 means one studies matters of the world and gains knowledge about the working of the universe; this study is through inner work such as meditation as well as learning from others and books.

- *Zhi zhi* 知止, or being able to stop, means stopping the meandering of thoughts and the ability to prevent the mind from wild racing; it means reining in one's endless desires; it means returning the *qi* to oneself, as letting one's mind race expends energy recklessly. This is a process that many people who meditate go through.

- *Neng ding* 能定 means one is in command of one's thoughts and emotions; one is not disturbed by the outer world of chaos and one can solidly ground oneself in mind and deeds here and now.

- *Neng jing* 能静 means one can sense the world in subtle and powerful ways; one can hear what is not audible and observe what is not visible. One is open to a higher level of knowing, understanding the cause and effect of things and events.

- *Neng an* 能安 means one knows one's origin and future; one is in peace with the world; and the body, mind, and spirit are integrated.

- *Neng lv* 能虑 means one can deeply understand the rules that govern the world; one gains wisdom and knows a higher-meaning purpose behind things and events.

- *Neng de* 能得 means one is at the gate of Great Learning, knowing how the Tao operates and how one can emulate the Tao (物有本末, 事有终始, 知所先后, 则近道矣).

The Confucian ideal person, *junzi*, is said to be a sage inside in her internal cultivation and a leader in the world (内圣外王). This state can be acquired through the preceding rigorous cultivation process. This cultivation leads to a change of one's character and to the acquisition of transformative abilities:

> With embodied learning, one gains real understanding that makes one want to learn sincerely and set one's heart right; with this, one acts morally and brings harmony to the family, country, and the world (物格而后知至, 知至而后意诚, 意诚而后心正, 心正而后身修, 身修而后家齐, 家齐而后国治, 国治而后天下平). (*Great Learning*, 5)[10]

In these stages, virtue cultivation and one's inner efforts are critical: One needs to "set the heart right and be sincere in intention" (正心诚意). Technique and virtue cultivation take place together.

The cultivation process has an inherent emotional aspect, as the ability to bring harmony to the family, community, country, and world necessarily involves emotional and moral intelligence (Lin, 2006). One's emotional attachment to the larger natural world also involves ecological intelligence (Lin, 2006). Hence, I believe that the compassion inherent in our nature (恻隐之心), as described by Mencius (*Mencius*, Gao Zi I), comes from a deep connection in energy and spirit throughout all existence, with integrated intelligence built into us (Lin, 2006). Aspiration for peace of the world is a state that would result ideally from Confucian cultivation: It comes from the deep sense of bondage one feels with all of humankind, as well as with other life forms and existences. I believe the cultivation of the primordial *qi* that gives us a deep connection with all that exists also intensifies our conviction to virtue; we connect with the "collective unselfconscious" of the Tao. Virtues come from body cultivation, and body cultivation can lead us to the Tao (Culham, 2013). One's body is part of the universe, and the universe is undergirded by virtue. Hence the *Great Learning* says:

> From kings to commoners, all should see cultivation as their fundamental mission and this is for setting their heart right (自天子以至于庶人，一是皆以修身为本. 此谓修身在正其心). (*Great Learning*, 6)[11]

In Confucian cultivation, one is many and many is one, as the world is inextricably interconnected. As *qi* permeates all existence, Heaven and humans are confluent: "A virtuous family can help a country become virtuous; a conciliatory family can help a country become conciliatory, and a person's greed and violence can cause chaos and unrest in a country" (一家仁，一国兴仁；一家让，一国兴让；一人贪戾，一国作乱) (*Great Learning*, 10).[12] Therefore, those who have achieved a high level of cultivation can do what Zhuangzi said: "They share spirit with All That Exists" (与天地精神相往来) (*Zhuangzi*, Tian Xia).[13] Ultimately, in Zhang Zai's words, a Confucian and Taoist student hopes "to establish heart for Heaven and Earth, to establish destiny for the People, to continue on the lost teaching of the sages, and to bring peace to thousands of future generations" (为天地立心，为生民立命，为往圣继绝学，为万世开太平) (Zhang Zi Quan Shu, vol. 14).

Educational Implications

Education today needs to chart a clear pathway for students to develop themselves individually and socially. And this is a process that not only incorporates learning and formation of habits, but also invokes inner change through virtue cultivation, which elevates one's energy to reach a higher level of awareness and a much broader heart-mind. Once this is achieved, the student becomes a transformative force to improve the world. The embodied approach in Confucianism needs to be rediscovered.

Currently in our educational practice, we focus too much on the mind, based on the belief that we are rational, analytical beings. We focus greatly on imparting knowledge and skills, neglecting the importance of the heart and the soul. Considering the Chinese philosophy of *qi*, we also grossly neglect the body as an inherent part of who we are, that is, we are physical, moral, emotional, bio-energetic, and spiritual beings. As we have discussed, *qi* is the energy that propels the universe as well as our bodies. Through cultivation of *qi* and virtues, we become closer to the great Tao, and we can achieve a more profound learning of life and the cosmos.

In the *Analects*, Confucius said, "We should aspire to learn the Tao, establish ourselves based on virtues, live with loving-kindness, and become good in arts and skills" (志於道, 据於德, 依於仁, 游於艺) (*Analects*, Xu Er 7-6).¹⁴ Confucian scholar Han Yu said, "The role of a teacher is to pass on the Tao, teach expertise, knowledge, and answer students' questions" (师者, 传道, 授业, 解惑也) (Han Yu, *Shi Shuo*). I believe the Tao mentioned by Confucius and Han Yu pinpoint the importance of cultivation of energy, as Tao is known not only as principles of the cosmos but also as the energy field that creates all life-forms. We have, however, largely forgotten what it means to cultivate the Tao and transmission of the Tao by teachers. We perform banking education, and we seldom urge our students to ask fundamental questions and to wonder about the mystery of the universe and our life.

To accomplish what the *Great Learning* indicates, we should bring meditation back to the process of learning. There are thousands of methods for contemplative inquiry, which can also include calligraphy, arts, poetry, and learning Confucian and Taoist classics. These methods can be adopted by students to calm their minds and to feel the movement of *qi*. We can help students align their energy and open their spiritual minds so that they can sense and connect with the force that creates all existence. In this process, compassion for others may be enhanced, cognitive development is brought to a higher level, and understanding of the meaning of life is much deepened, as research has demonstrated (Grace, 2011; Miller, 2014). The Chinese Taoist cultivation traditions contain thousands of methods that can be adopted to supplement Confucian-oriented education. Breathing techniques and mindfulness practices can be adopted from Buddhist and other traditions as well. Movement meditation such as yoga and tai chi are effective ways to calm the mind and increase one's energy.

Chinese philosophy as represented in Confucius's teaching is an embodied philosophy, in sum. It is to be lived and put into action. Hence, in Confucian learning, one puts into action the content of *ren* (仁) by being loving and kind; *yi* (义), by serving the family and the community; *li* (礼), by being respectful to all people; *zhi* (智), by seeking wisdom; and *xin* (信), by being sincere and trustworthy. There is no separation of inner and outer worlds, physical and psychological from the spiritual, as these are all integrated from a *qi* perspective. Reflecting on education today, we should emphasize the learning of loving-kindness and the development of integrated intelligence (Lin, 2006). The school curriculum needs to be a guide for children to learn to expand their focus of care and compassion from the self to the family, from the family to the community, then to the world and the cosmos. Chinese culture needs to be rendered "alive" or embodied again. Meditation encompasses an "epistemology of love" (Zajonc, 2006), which has the potential to open our *qi* energy system to be in connection with other beings. Meditation can enhance our experience of "interbeing" (Bai, 2009), allowing us to be kinder, more forgiving, more trustworthy, and so on. Contemplative pedagogy such as meditation can lead to a new understanding and implementation of Confucian education.

Meditation and other contemplative practices are obviously suggested in the *Great Learning*, but the specific methods ancient people adopted are no longer clear to modern society. What is still emphasized in Confucian education includes arts, calligraphy, poetry, and studying of Classics. These pedagogies have the potential to calm the mind, still the heart, and enhance the spiritual sensitivity of students (Lin, Culham, & Oxford, 2016). But more are needed if we are to elevate individual *qi* to connect with the *qi* of the world and the cosmos. *Qi*-based knowing and *qi*-based education can draw much from Taoist philosophy (Culham & Lin, 2016).

Engagement with other living beings requires what Bai (2013, 2009) calls "animism" or "reanimating the universe." We need to open our sensory abilities and deepen our connection with other people and beings, including all that exists in nature. As we have said, the cultivation of *qi* through meditation has been largely lost in Confucianism, yet it is well maintained in Taoism and Buddhism. So to understand the Chinese culture of Human-Heaven Oneness, we need to go beyond Confucianism. Buddhism denounces the killing of animals and other species, so compassion for animals and for all beings is key in Buddhist cultivation. Taoism upholds nature as sacred and stresses building a peaceful connection with nature, and this is achieved through the experiential learning of the energy at work in the universe (Sun & Lin, 2011).

Qi is a deeply embedded idea in Chinese culture, including the Chinese language. The purpose of education is to transform the disposition of the students, which means modifying their *qi* energy. Many Chinese words connote this: We are to change our *qi* quality (变化气质); we need to increase our aspirational *qi* (增长志气), to increase our courageous *qi* (勇气大增), to change our *qi* temperament (改变脾气), and to become peaceful in mind and harmonious in *qi* (心平气和). That education is about cultivation of a new being is also shown in other Chinese words: 教育—education is to nurture and foster; 教养—education contains the element of upbringing; 教化—education leads to metamorphoses or transformation. The traditions that we have come from require that teachers have the energy to nurture and transform students in an experiential and energy-elevation level, which requires that teachers themselves are first and foremost cultivators of *qi* and virtues.

Rediscovering the Confucian embodied pathway points to the need for inner work and experiential learning. Students need to gain an understanding. Using the Chinese words again, 领悟 means to gain an inner understanding, 感悟 means to have understanding from direct feeling, 体悟 means revelations through firsthand body cultivation, and 渐悟, 顿悟, 彻悟 means gradual, sudden, and complete understanding or revelation. These processes indicate the need for inner cultivation to open students to new and higher levels of awareness. The tipping point, or quantum leap, for a higher awareness requires an elevation in energy and virtue cultivation. It reminds us that we need to embody what we learn. An exam-oriented education does not help with inner reflection and deep introspection. A place for students to explore their inner selves must be reserved in the curriculum.

In today's world, we are connected by information technology and transportations of all kinds; however, the inner bondage, based on our basic nature as energy beings, and as a species of the cosmos, necessitates cultivation from within, and this sense of oneness requires a sense of interbeing that fosters love, civility, compassion, and wisdom.

In conclusion, education nowadays fails to give students a solid grounding in morality and the ways by which to cultivate the associated cosmic primordial *qi* that propels all lives. Confucianism understood holistically opens a way to integrate the personal with social, the outer with the inner, and the personal learning of knowledge with socially transformational action. However, many contemplative and transformative cultivation methods have been lost, and the spiritual energy cultivation based on virtue learning needs to be rediscovered. Hence, our topic has great significance and relevance for education today.

Notes

1. http://ctext.org/chun-qiu-fan-lu/wang-dao
2. http://ctext.org/mengzi/jin-xin-i
3. http://www.acmuller.net/con-dao/docofmean.html
4. http://www.acmuller.net/con-dao/docofmean.html
5. http://www.acmuller.net/con-dao/analects.html#div-7
6. http://www.acmuller.net/con-dao/greatlearning.html
7. http://www.acmuller.net/con-dao/docofmean.html
8. http://www.acmuller.net/con-dao/mencius.html#div-4
9. http://www.acmuller.net/con-dao/greatlearning.html
10. http://www.acmuller.net/con-dao/greatlearning.html
11. http://www.acmuller.net/con-dao/greatlearning.html
12. http://www.acmuller.net/con-dao/greatlearning.html
13. http://ctext.org/zhuangzi/tian-xia
14. http://www.acmuller.net/con-dao/analects.html#div-8

References

Bai, H. (2009). Re-animating the universe: Environmental education and philosophical animism. In M. McKenzie, H. Bai, P. Hart, & B. Jickling (Eds.), *Fields of green: Restoring culture, environment, education* (pp. 135–151). Cresskill: Hampton Press.

Bai, H. (2013). Peace with the Earth: Animism and contemplative ways. *Cultural Studies of Science Education* (CSSE), 2(8), DOI 10.1007/s11422-013-9501-z. (M. P. Mueller & D. A. Greenwood [Eds.], Special Issue of CSSE on ecological mindfulness and cross-hybrid learning.)

Culham, T. (2013). *Ethics education of business leaders*. Charlotte: Information Age.

Culham, T., & Lin, J. (2016). Exploring the unity of science and spirit: A Daoist perspective. In J. Lin et al. (Eds.), *Constructing a spiritual research paradigm for social sciences and education*. Charlotte: Information Age.

Grace, F. (2011). Learning as a path, not a goal: Contemplative pedagogy—its principles and practices. *Teaching Theology and Religion, 14*(2), 99–124.

Lin, J. (2006). *Love, peace and wisdom in education: Re-envisioning education in the 21st century*. Lanham: Rowman & Littlefield Education.

Lin, J., Culham, T., & Oxford, R. (Forthcoming). Constructing a spiritual research paradigm from a Confucian perspective. In J. Lin et al. (Eds.), *Constructing a spiritual research paradigm for social sciences and education*. Charlotte: Information Age.

Lin, J., & Wang, Y. (2010). Confucius's teaching of virtues and peace education. In E. J. Brantmeier, J. Lin, & J. Miller, J. (Eds.), *Religion, spirituality and peace education* (pp. 3–17). Charlotte: Information Age.

Miller, J. P. (2014). *The contemplative practitioner: Meditation in education and the workplace* (2nd ed.). Toronto: University of Toronto Press.

Peng, H. (2007). *A Conversation between Confucius and Dewey on individual and community: A hope for human unity* (Doctoral dissertation). University of Tennessee. Retrieved from http://trace.tennessee.edu/utk_graddiss/263

Sun, X. Y., & Lin, J. (2011). Chinese landscape painting and Taoism: Reflection on environmental education. In J. Lin & R. Oxford (Eds.), *Transformative eco-education for human and planetary survival*. Charlotte: Information Age.

Tu, W. (2008). Toward a "dialogical civilization": The Confucian *Analects* as an exemplification. Keynote speech at Symposium on Contemporary Significance of Confucianism: Implications for Harmonious Society, Sustainable Development and World Peace, at Library of Congress and University of Maryland, January 24–25.

Zajonc, A. (2006). Love and knowledge: Recovering the heart of learning through contemplation. *Teachers College Record, 108*(9), 1742–1759.

Zeng, Z. (1997). Principles of Dong Zhongshu's philosophy of *qi*. *Confucius Research [孔子研究], 2*, 74–83.

10

Confucian Selfhood and the Idea of Multicultural Education

CHENYU WANG

While the literature on multicultural education continues to grow (e.g., Arasaratnam, 2013; Banks, 1993, 2008; Nieto, 2002), little research has been done on the relationship between multicultural education and Confucianism. Perhaps people simply assume that Confucianism, as a philosophical tradition in the East, is not pertinent to discussions about multicultural education, which attempts to respond to cultural and racial tensions emerging in the West. However, as scholars (de Bary, 2000; Tu, 1996, 1999) have pointed out, while the Enlightenment legacy is already a common heritage of the global community, its intellectual scope should be broadened and its moral basis deepened so that it can continue to serve as a guiding principle for human flourishing. In this endeavor, Enlightenment thinking could be enriched by the thought of Confucius, a philosopher and an educator who exerted profound influences on issues related to education in civilizations in the East.

In this chapter, I bring ideas of Confucianism into a discussion of multiculturalism and multicultural education in the global age. Largely informed by the disciplinary orientation of anthropology, I first clarify some conceptual issues about education and self-making. I then briefly discuss the central goals of multiculturalism and multicultural education in existing scholarship. An analysis follows of the Confucian notion of self and its relation to a Confucian view of education. Finally, I discuss ways in which a Confucian self can refine the current multicultural education framework, while multiculturalism gives new ground for Confucian thought to evolve. Through this, I argue that the Confucian notion of self is compatible with a diverse and multicultural society, and it provides an approach to enriching current multicultural education. This chapter contributes to scholarship on East-West dialogues and their practical implications for contemporary society.

Education and Self-Making: Some Conceptual Issues

I begin with a discussion about the notion of self vis-à-vis education. While there is much debate as to the meaning of self and divergence in views of self depending on one's disciplinary frame, in this chapter, selfhood is understood from a psychoanalytic perspective (Hoffman, 1999). Here the self is a culturally patterned way of relating to others; to the material, natural, and spiritual worlds; and to time and space, including notions of agency, mind, person, being, and spirit. Simply put, the self is a way of being and acting endowed with reflexivity and agency (Sokefeld, 1999). This definition is capacious enough for different conceptualizations of selfhood across cultural contexts. It also allows for constructive discussions about the role of education in making the self.

It is worth mentioning that the concept of the self is not to be understood interchangeably with that of the individual. The difference between these two concepts is beyond the scope of this chapter. However, suffice to say, on the one hand, individuals exist across cultures—they are biological entities, forming groups where cultures exist—yet, on the other hand, it is the pattern of the self that shapes each culture. The self is a "potential site of flexible adaptation to culture rather than a cultural identity that offers no points of discontinuity with culture" (Hoffman, 1999; Spindler and Spindler, 1997). The character of a culture in turn shapes the self. In other words, self and culture intersubjectively coexist with one another.

Relatedly, culture is not reduced to particular national, racial, religious, or sexual categories. Ample anthropological literature has stressed the fluid and postmodern nature of culture in the contemporary age (e.g., Appadurai, 1996; Hoffman, 1999; Latour, 2005; Sökefeld, 1999) and the danger of such essentialization in theoretical discussions about and practical engagements with the concept of "culture" (Bashkow, 2004; Paris, 2012).

Following this tradition, anthropologists of education have pointed out the critical link between education—undertaken in formal and informal ways—and self-making. That is, education centers on the formation of culturally valued personhood in a given context (Cave, 2004; Holland et al., 1996; Levinson et al., 2000; Tobin et al., 1989, 2009). Education is a "calculated effort" (Spindler & Spindler, 1997) on the self of an individual, and its purpose is to enculturate an individual.

Multicultural Education and a Multicultural Self

Having established the relationships between culture, the self, the individual, and education, I now turn to a discussion about the goals and approaches of multicultural education in existing literatures, particularly to the model of self embedded in the mainstream multicultural education model.

The historical roots of multicultural education lie in the civil rights movement. Many scholars trace the history of multicultural education back to the social action of African Americans and other people of color who challenged discriminatory practices in public institutions during the civil rights struggles of the 1960s (e.g., Banks, 1993; Davidman & Davidman, 1997). Thus, multicultural education strives for an equal, just, and democratic polity where deep-seated conflicts between races, ethnicities, classes, and genders can be resolved. It attempts to reorient schooling practices from exclusivity and alienation to inclusivity and empowerment. Banks (1989, 1993, 2008) identifies five dimensions of schooling for multiculturalism, including content integration, knowledge construction, prejudice reduction, equity pedagogy, and empowering school culture. These dimensions must not exist in isolation; rather, they should complement each other for the creation of a holistically multicultural schooling environment.

With this conceptualization, multicultural education is applicable across disciplines. It is capable of recognizing racial and cultural differences, social norms, and perspectives while espousing social, political, and economic identities (e.g., Banks, 2008; Lalas, 2007; Nieto, 2005). Relatedly, starting in the 1990s, scholars have highlighted the importance of social justice in a multicultural framework and introduced the term "social justice pedagogy." Drawing from critical theorists such as Paolo Freire, Henry Giroux, and Michael Apple, scholars emphasize knowledge reconstructions in multiple epistemologies through the lens of the marginalized, such as the black, the queer, the feminist, the indigenous, and the disabled (Chapman & Hobbel, 2010; Ladson-Billings, 2014). Embedded within diverse literatures is an ideal multicultural self: It is aware of power differences and structural oppressions and is willing to challenge unfounded hierarchies, such as those of race, gender, sexuality, and religion.

A Confucian Understanding of Self

Having briefly discussed the current multicultural education framework, I now turn to a discussion of ways in which Confucius defines the self. With the understanding that the self is different from the individual, it is easy to understand how the self plays a pivotal role in Confucian philosophy. Shun (2004) states that "if we construe the notion of self in such a way that is always presupposed in the use of reflective pronouns to talk about oneself, it seems uncontroversial that Confucian thinkers do work with such a notion" (pp. 183–184, as cited in Jiang, 2006).

The conceptual difficulty of seeing the self in the Confucian tradition lies in the way it conceptualizes the self as a relation. In this section, I analyze the Confucian self with the aid of classical Confucian texts. Unlike the Western Enlightenment tradition, in which the self is unquestionably related to both the body and the sociocultural location of the individual (Taylor, 1999), a Confucian understanding of the self does not presuppose the existence of an autonomous, independent individual. The Confucian self is a relation, a process, and a goal. The self is the center of human relationships, an expanding process through learning, as well as the realization of the Heaven-endowed humanity.

Self as a Relation

First, a Confucian self is relational in nature. It exists in a concentric circle of relationships that encompass both the community and the world at large (Tu, 1994, p. 183). It is a relation. The inherent holism recognizes the importance of human relationships and the roles individuals play in these relationships.

The relational self is best seen in Confucian understandings of basic roles that individuals must fulfill. Confucius identifies five kinds of relationships as critical to human beings: parent-child, ruler-subject, husband-wife, sibling-sibling, and friend-friend. This is the Confucian concept of "Five Relationships" (*wu lun*, 五伦). Of these relationships, parent-child is the foundation: In Analects, the theme of filiality (xiao, 孝, also translated as filial piety) appears as the foundational value in Confucian social and ethical thought. Confucius stipulates that the individual does not have much meaning without the five relationships that make up the self. Who I am is concerned with "how the self is identified and what makes one's self different from others' selves" (Jiang, 2006, p. 544). In other words, a Confucian selfhood situates in "a center of relationships, a communal quality which was never conceived of as an isolated or isolable entity" (Tu, 1985, p. 53).

More importantly, the Confucian self links individuals to society in an organic manner (Ghai, 1998). Individuals are embedded in the webs of relations where the selves reside. Because the webs of relations are interconnected, individuals bear multiple responsibilities. Fulfilling these responsibilities, in turn, strengthen the human-relatedness among individuals. Unlike in Western societies, where individuals usually have fixed anchor points to define themselves, Confucian individuals define themselves referentially, thus linking to others in an fluid and organic way.

Self as an Expanding Process

The interdependent network of selfhood also positions the self in a world of the new, the unknown, and the unexpected. As such, the Confucian individual is never an isolated or isolable being. To cope with these differences, the self engages in a lifelong process of learning (Tu, 1985, p. 113). Learning is critical to the existence of a living Confucian self. Confucius himself states this explicitly: "In a group of three people, there is always someone I can learn from. Choose to follow the strengths of others, use their shortcomings to reflect upon ourselves" (Analects, 7:21, author's translation). Hence, learning is central to the everyday experiences of the Confucian.

In this sense, Confucius proposes a different conceptualization of learning. That is, the self learns for "the sake of the self" (xue er wei ji, 学而为己), which goes beyond a mechanical acquisition of facts. Learning is a process of spiritual and moral cultivation, where the self learns to adapt and integrate into an ever-expanding circle of human relatedness. This process is, itself, social, because it happens in a network of relations in which the self resides.

The social nature of learning then gives learning a humanist twist. According to Confucius, learning for the sake of the self is the best way to manifest common humanity (as cited in Tu, 1985, p. 76). This is because learning cultivates one's potential to be an observer, an appreciator, and a participant in the complex web of human relations. The self and learning become symbiotic: No true Confucian self exists without learning, while no true learning happens without adjustments of the self.

"Learning for the sake of the self" also highlights the significance of self-cultivation in Confucian teaching. In Confucian texts, the meaning of learning is translated as two characters, *xue* (学) and *xi* (习). *Xue* means study, while *xi* means practice. As such, learning encompasses two interrelated activities: studying and practicing. This process is self-cultivation, because the self is always practicing the new skills in the process of learning.

Self as the Realization of Heaven-Endowed Humanity

Although the Confucian self is always dynamic, the goal is to realize a Confucian ideal. This is the *junzi* (君子), a sage who embodies the ultimate virtues of Confucian thinking. Confucius himself stresses the nobleness of the *junzi* throughout his teachings, and he always endeavors to help his disciples to seek and realize virtues. The inner structure of a composite Confucian selfhood is one that starts with the origin (a relation), engages in reflection (learning and self-cultivation), and achieves the target (a *junzi*, or a Sage) (Cheng, 2004, p. 126).

A Confucian *junzi* is a true human being. Constant self-cultivation trains the self to be responsive to the world and culture at large. One is an observer, who constantly tries to tour and understand the world; an appreciator, who understands the world with no utilitarian motivations; and one who engages in the cosmic process as a participant (Tu, 2011). A *junzi* is the embodiment of common humanity: an inclusive sense of community based on the communal critical self-consciousness of reflexive minds (Tu, 1999) and the ability to take one's own feelings as a guide to the course of human-relatedness (*Analects*, 6:28). He is a man of propriety, wisdom, faithfulness, righteousness, and humanity. He is also compassionate and curious (*Haoxue*, 好学, love of learning).

The sage and Heaven are hence symbiotic. In Confucianism, divine forces, Heaven (*tian*, 天), are embodied through a sage's heart and deeds. These forces do not take the form of a god or a deity; rather, they are co-created through self-refinement and constant learning. Everyone could follow the state of sagehood regardless of one's social and cultural origins, because the relational self does not stipulate a starting point for its growth.

In summary, a Confucian selfhood is active, dynamic, and ever-expanding. Through the relations, a Confucian self bonds with the others. It is reflexive through interactions with the new and the different. Ultimately, the self is a living embodiment of the Heaven-endowed virtues, the state of sagehood. The self is never the private possession of a single individual, but a shareable experience that underlies all of humanity.

The Confucian Self and Multicultural Education

Reorienting the self as an active and dynamic process provides the means to analyze ways it contributes to multiculturalism and multicultural education. It is a capacious concept that allows for new conceptualizations to tackle tension between races, genders, ethnicities, and religions and sexual orientations in the multicultural project. A Confucian multicultural education provides new ways to think about realizing multicultural education.

A Confucian Multicultural Project: Theoretical Relevance

Living and learning. One widely accepted contribution of Confucius to the field of education lies in his attempts to redefine the meaning of learning. Unlike the Western model of education, which focuses on knowledge acquisition, standardization, and competition, a Confucian model of learning focuses on self-reflection and cultivation. The direct translation of the Chinese term for education (教育, *jiaoyu*) indicates that it encompasses both teaching (教, *jiao*) and cultivation (育, *yu*). To teach means to impart knowledge; to cultivate means to develop virtues through thinking and reflecting (Zhao, 2013). The saying "He who learns but does not think is lost. He who thinks but does not learn is in a great danger" (*Analects*, 2:15) best expresses this idea. Education therefore is an ongoing, ceaseless activity that exists beyond classrooms. To live is to learn, and to learn is to live.

Reorienting the multicultural self to a multiplicity of selves. With the centrality of others in the formation of a Confucian self, multiculturalism underlies the Confucian ideal. This is because of the ultimate task that the self shoulders, that is, the task of expanding itself to embody Heaven as a *junzi*. Confucians are constantly exploring the critical distance between themselves and the Other. In the course of such explorations, they reflect on their own actions and thoughts and are eager to learn from interactions with the Other through self-reflection.

In this regard, the multicultural self is no longer singular. That is, there is no one single set of criteria for evaluating the "multiculturalness" of an individual. Unlike existing literature that gives a single definition of the multicultural self (see Hoffman, 1996; Paris, 2012; Zhao, 2003), the Confucian self recognizes the postmodern nature of social realities and makes rooms for multiple understandings about multiculturalism. Recognizing each individual's unique cultural location—culture not in the sense of race, gender, or ethnicity but in the sense of the network that the selves bring together—the Confucian recognizes the many dimensions of individual differences and is willing to understand the origins of such differences. Put it terms of the Western philosophical discourse, recognizing the intersectionality of the multiple dimensions that make up an individual is de rigueur in the Confucian tradition. Never is an individual confined to his or her original racial, social, or gender locations: The innate multiculturalness of the self is recognized.

In this new model of multiculturalism, the new and different is organically linked to the individual. As the Confucian goal of self-cultivation is to become a participant or even a co-creator in the cosmic process (Tu, 2011), self-cultivation necessitates the Other's participation. "Wishing to establish oneself, one establishes others; wishing to enlarge oneself, one enlarges others" (*Analects*, 6:30). Confucius advocates a symbiotic relationship between self and Other. This relationship is also reciprocal: The self should not do to others what it does not want to have done to itself (*Analects*, 15:23). This Confucian golden tenet requires one's ability to understand the Other in terms of respecting differences (Tu, 1999).

The multiplicity of multicultural selves can then be understood in the Confucian tradition. Just as everyone is capable of following the virtues of the *junzi* and ultimately achieving the status of sagehood without losing his or her individuality, the Confucian self does not stipulate a single way to achieve multiculturalism. Confucian thought can be understood as a particular model of multiculturalism.

Moving beyond equality for harmony. A profusion of multicultural selves brings with it a renewed goal of multicultural education. With deep-seated tension between distinct social groups, advocates have always strived for an equal and just society where individuals can peacefully coexist. However, the social landscape of America remains steeped in inequality, injustice, and group fragmentation. Bearing the task of remedying social problems, the relational self has much to contribute.

In the contemporary globalized world, where technology facilitates virtual and physical connections, society ironically is still divided by spiritual and moral separation. With unequal distribution of material goods and modern modes of production, such separation gives rise to privilege, power differentiation, and ultimately oppression. Discrimination based on race, gender, sexuality, and ethnicity is the product of this separation. Therefore, the pivotal task for multicultural education is to reestablish spiritual and moral connection among individuals.

In this regard, the relational self discerned in Confucian teachings moves equality a step further, because the Confucian ultimate, the Great Harmony (*da tong*, 大同, literally translated as "big sameness"), encompasses equality and diversity in an organic way. Confucius explains this status through the expression "harmony but not sameness" (*he er bu tong*, 和而不同). In stressing "not sameness" in harmony, Confucius reorients equality from a mechanical to an organic status. Simply becoming the same (*tong*, 同) requires mere replication of what one already has; on the contrary, harmony (*he*, 和) is a state where individuals exist and coexist. To be in harmony is to produce something new—the connections between individuals. These connections add to the self and forge mutually advanced relationships. Confucius reminds his disciples that the *junzi* is someone who "acts in harmony with others but does not ape them" (*Analects*, 13:23). The relational self renders individuals open and nonaggressive because the individual recognizes that discrimination first and foremost deprives the self of precious opportunities to expand and grow. Indeed, diversity is vital for human survival, and harmony is capable of sustaining differences.

In this regard, Confucian equality does not encourage an "I am me and you are you" mentality. It moves a step beyond and connects the "me and you" into a "we." That is, the underlying ethics of harmony is not only to live and let live; it also mandates individuals to live together in mutual recognition, respect, learning, and flourishing. The Confucian relational self provides an answer to multicultural education's challenge of how to move individuals from being "tolerant" to "appreciative" of differences. Harmony encompasses equality and diversity at the same time.

Self-Cultivation and Multicultural Education: Practical Implications

Education as innately multicultural. In its current framework, multicultural education attempts to revolve deep-seated tensions between racial, gender, and ethnic groups in primarily two ways. First, it recognizes the value of alternative ways of knowing as defined by racial, gender, or ethnic boundaries and attempts to recenter such knowledge amid a technocratic, neoliberal culture (Banks, 2008). Pushing against standardization and homogenization in mainstream schooling practices, multicultural education aims at bringing minority voices into education. However, just as scholars (Banks, 1993; Hoffman, 1996; Ladson-Billings, 2014) have reminded multicultural educators and scholars, multicultural education is *not* a single school subject. "Teaching about" multicultural education defeats its purpose: Just as history should be multiculturally oriented, science and technology are multicultural as well. This requires a reintegration of the technical and rational with the moral and spiritual. Educators should recognize that values—be they multicultural or not—are always embedded in curricula, and there are reasons behind every sentence, activity, and assignment. This requires teachers to embody the multiculturalist framework themselves and resist thinking about "culture" as a concept that is relevant or irrelevant to education.

In this sense, the Confucian mode of thinking has much to contribute to the multicultural project. With its holistic approach to learning and knowledge, a Confucian self recognizes the embeddedness of culture in pedagogical practices across disciplines. Drawing from a Confucian understanding of the self, educators reestablish the interconnectedness of different knowledge domains. That is, physics, biology, art, music, and literature should be understood as cultural entities: Formulas in physics and biology, painting strokes, and musical scores are as cultural and as literary as Shakespeare's sonnets and hip-hop performances. This is not to say that students should not know facts, definitions, and formulas by heart; rather, this requires educators to go beyond the technical and foster the recognition that all school subjects are both technical and cultural. Take "accounting" as an example: It should be understood as a way of systematically processing economic entities' financial information *and* a particular kind of epistemology that places exchange value at the heart of the knowledge system. In this way, multicultural education permeates all school subjects because students learn to appreciate the cultural logic behind different subjects. Working out a math problem involves a move into the world of others, an activity that enlarges the self. Hence, following Confucian teaching helps educators and students alike to recenter humanist values in schooling practices.

Similarly, teaching in this orientation also allows room for enacting the value of equality in an organic manner. As stated before, the hybrid, fluid, and postmodern nature of culture requires educators to tackle the intersectionality about how race, gender, ethnicity, and sexual orientation impact one's social and cultural position. The holistic, humanist emphasis in Confucianism moves a step further by *not* compartmentalizing the various interconnected domains of the self in the first place. An individual is recognized as a person with various identification "markers" that hold the person together. Following the Confucian understanding of the self as a relation not to be disintegrated into different dimensions avoids the reification of "culture" in a superficial way (see Hoffman, 1996; Ladson-Billings, 2014; Paris, 2012). It *sustains* the characteristics of a particular group without confining these characteristics as the only way of defining them. For example, it recognizes the roots of Chinese culture in the Chinese American community while also allowing for the creative reinvention of Chinese Americanness and Chineseness in a postmodern age. In the same way that the discipline of anthropology in the 21st century has painstakingly demonstrated how culture does not belong to one particular group, and human beings are creative and resilient enough to adapt themselves and their cultural expressions to material and spiritual environments, multicultural educators should come to the same recognition.

Self-reflexivity and role modeling. To implement multiculturalism in this way requires educators to develop a high level of self-reflexivity. This is because it is only through a deep understanding of how they themselves are cultured beings in multiple dimensions that they can impart multiculturalism in classrooms. Being mindful, or living in a status of "consciousness that incorporates self-awareness and attention with a core characteristic of being open, receptive, and non-judgmental" (e.g., Brown & Ryan, 2003), helps educators to recognize interconnectedness across different subjects, pedagogical activities, as well as schools and the surrounding communities. Educators are to be constantly aware of the present moment and pay attention to the context in which they reside.

As the context is an organic entity composed of a web of relationships, it inevitably includes the Other. To put it another way, the context is the intrinsically flexible and accommodating area concerned with the things in people's lives they categorize as different. Anthropologist Bashkow (2004) calls it "the zone of the foreign" (p. 450). Educators need to pay attention to this foreign zone, expanding to allow themselves to make sense of intercultural experiences using preconceived notions of the Other. They should develop an enhanced awareness of the self and context and interrogate their own assumptions that are inherently culturally embedded. Going through such interrogations, or, in Confucian terminology, self-reflection, educators can explore the critical space between the self and the Other and learn to accept and appreciate differences. It requires being empathetic to other human beings, to reconstruct others' worlds using their own knowledge.

Doing so renders educators as the embodiment of multiculturalness themselves. This is also why Confucius places such high standards himself and always tries to embody sagehood. A Confucian multicultural education would place a premium on educators. They are the role models for their students.

Educators would then encourage reflexive activities across disciplines. This allows students to spontaneously re-create knowledge within their cultural frameworks. In the same way that educators interpret the culturally embedded nature of school subjects, curriculum, and activities, they should guide students to think about these issues as well. Moreover, a critical task in multicultural education is to guide students to reconstruct, and even restore, the cultural systems they have learned in class. In this way, students' innate cultural knowledge—knowledge based on the social position they occupy in the network of selves—are integrated into the curriculum. An African American student could recognize the alienating nature of technical knowledge, while a "mainstream" white, middle-class student could realize how his or her understanding of the world is limited. Following their teachers as role models, students are to realize that they, as individuals, are innately multicultural beings.

Civic-mindedness and community services. Practice is central to a Confucian education. The self is never complete without putting what it has learned into real-world contexts. This gives rise to the possibility of a civic-minded individual (Tu, 1985, p. 57) who is concerned about conflicts, tensions, and alienations and eager to resolve these issues. The interconnectedness between human beings demands that a Confucian individual see the public and private spheres as a whole. Hence, multicultural education should accommodate the innate civic-mindedness in a Confucian mode of thinking and create opportunities for students and educators alike to think about and design practical projects.

One critical yet often ill-conceived form of practice is community service. Despite its popularity in teacher training, university, and K–12 schools, scholars have argued that service-learning functions as an identity marker for privileged youth (Cororaton & Handler, 2013; Heron, 2007; Holdsworth & Quinn, 2011; Snee, 2014) and creates status distinctions in local communities (Eliasoph, 2014; Larsen, 2016). This is because participants usually—albeit unfortunately—impose their own frames of reference in interactions with community members. Even when they "listen to the needs of the local community" (a frequently cited golden rule of being empathetic), they inevitably separate "us" and "them," treating the "local community" as a fixed entity, existing "there," "waiting to be served" by well-intentioned youth. In other words, participants do not recognize the interconnectedness among selves. Practicing service as autonomous beings leads to unsatisfying and deconstructive interactions with the community.

To this problem, the Confucian mode of thinking also has much to contribute. First, before sending students out to communities, schools should prepare them to understand the interconnectedness between the school and the community, the public and the private, and the local, the national, and the global. Doing so would require educators to integrate concepts such as poverty, power, race, and gender in a *culturally* informed way. This might include leading students through classical and contemporary anthropological works and guiding them to apply these works in real-life situations. In this process, students understand how individuals are embedded in the network of selves.

Another useful pedagogy in preparation for community service is to have students go into the local community and observe daily routines *before* taking any action. In the terms of educational anthropologists, this forces students to be enculturated (Spindler & Spindler, 1997) into the world of "others." This is also a process of enlarging students' selves. Through careful listening and observing of routines, students can understand the differences and the similarities between the community and themselves. They can also peek into the power dynamics in the community.

Moreover, observations are never isolated from reflections. Students should document what they see on the ground and analyze this using knowledge they have learned in class as well as their own frames of reference. In this way, they can discern the cultural in the community and in themselves. This is "self-cultivation" in the Confucian mode of thinking. Innately intersubjective and connecting the local with the selves, students are then able to conceptualize their "service" in the community from a reciprocal perspective.

The gap between the "helper" and the "helped" is hence narrowed, and even bridged. Putting students into contact with community members constitutes a pivotal step, where the symbiosis between the self and the world (Tu, 1994) is realized. Through interaction with community members, students can see how "others" see themselves. They can acknowledge status distinctions in themselves and in the community, develop ethical intelligence, and complete community service projects with care and ethics. This process is a multicultural experience with transformative potential.

A Confucian Multicultural Framework

In this Confucian multicultural framework, critical multiculturalists (Freire, 2000; Giroux, 2013; Nieto, 2005) might point out the embedded conservative or even reactionary potential. That is, placing power at the center, critical scholars and activists advocate for social movements and collective action to alleviate social problems. Indeed, in an age where human beings are obsessed with materiality and themselves, focusing on power relationships is pivotal in ameliorating racism, sexism, homophobia, xenophobia, and the like. Giving room for disadvantaged groups to voice their experiences and express their demands is critical to realizing diversity and social justice. This is precisely the first step in the Confucian multiculturalist framework, where the self listens to and honors others' voices. The Confucian relational self contributes to collective action by moving beyond the discourses of "resistance" and "empowerment": It can encompass these voices without reifying and essentializing the "us" or the "them." It also avoids privileging ideas such as revolution and resistance, constructs originating in the Enlightenment (Hoffman, 1999; Sangren, 1995). A live-and-let-live mentality only goes as far as achieving the façade of equality; a Confucian relational self moves beyond this mentality.

However, this is not to say that the Confucian relational self does not have anything to learn from the Enlightenment project or that such a relational self provides a final answer to the diversity puzzle. Because

Confucius lived in a warring period of chaos in which various feudal states of the Zhou dynasty waged war for the power to rule, Confucian teachings attempt to help people find a way—an ethical way—that could bring back the old days when the country was a stable, civil, unified, and virtuous community (Reid, 2000). For Confucius, then, the result of "social change" is an internal reorganization of a puzzle's different pieces that make up the whole. In other words, the Confucian mode of thought sees the goal of change to be not to change. Yet as multiculturalism demands to integrate the originally excluded and marginalized, it gives new meaning to "social change" in Confucian thought. Using the puzzle metaphor, the originally excluded and marginalized could enlarge the whole, adding an entirely new dimension to the puzzle. Equality and diversity enlarge harmony. In this regard, putting the multicultural demands in a Confucian framework gives harmony a postmodern twist: It adds fluidity to the concept of harmony, a dynamic entity guided by virtues that emerged in the globalized age.

Hence, at its core, a philosophical dialogue between Confucian thought and multiculturalism gives both schools renewed energy in the search for human rights, peace, liberal citizenship, and social justice (de Bary, 2003; Lin & Wang, 2010; Nuyen, 2002; Wang, 2004, 2010). In terms of the multicultural project, Confucian thought leads to a viable pluralism, an "acknowledgement of significant differences and the recognition that difference can be the basis of *productive* relationships of mutual understanding, reciprocity, and respect" (Bashkow, 2004, emphasis added). Such a dialogue adds a nuanced ground to the projects of diversity, equality, and harmony, on the basis of which racial, social, ethical, and religious tensions can be diminished. Confucianism and multiculturalism both hold great relevance to common human flourishing.

Multiculturalism and the Great Harmony

I would like to conclude with two quotes on diversity, one from Dr. Martin Luther King Jr., the other from Tu Wei-ming, a prominent philosopher and Confucian scholar. In a speech on racial relations given by King (1962) during his visit to Cornell College, he states,

> I am absolutely convinced that there are hundreds and thousands, nay, millions of white people of good will in the South,

> but most of them are silent today because of fear—fear of political, social and economic reprisal. . . . One of the tragedies of our whole struggle is that the South is still trying to live in *monologue*, rather than *dialogue*, and I am convinced that men hate each other because they fear each other. They fear each other because that don't know each other and they don't know each other because they don't communicate with each other, and they don't communicate with each other because they are separated from each other. (King, 1962)

In calling for dialogues between blacks and whites, Dr. Martin Luther King Jr. argues for communication on deep levels. He believes that deep communication could enact courage, hope, and authentic leadership to the struggle for freedom. Such dialogue is easier to achieve with the recognition of a relational self that honors the multiplicity of the human condition.

Relatedly, in a dialogue with Ikeda on the issue of diversity in a global age, Tu Wei-ming responds to Ikeda's remarks on difference:

> . . . although I fully agree with the necessity and desirability of overcoming obsession with difference, I suggest that we do not downplay difference prematurely as we move deliberately and cautiously toward the common goal of social happiness and peace. The danger of abstract universalism, like that of closed particularity, is that it cannot match the human need for both experienced concreteness and transformational sociality. (Tu & Ikeda, 2011, p. 41)

Tu's point about "closed particularity" is precisely what King warns people to stay away from. Human beings trapped in closed particularity tend to speak in monologues and talk past others, missing critical opportunities to realize concrete freedom. That is, to "deal with" diversity in a global age does not necessitate conformity, uniformity, or universality; it is the equality and diversity embedded in harmony that multiculturalism should be striving for. A Confucian relational self is one possible approach to forge organic and meaningful relationships between "us" and "them," transcending the limited and limiting boundaries human beings constructed for their sense of security.

In summary, if multiculturalism seeks to promote an equal and just world and to realize freedom, where individuals can explore and appreciate critical differences between the self and the Other (Geertz, 2000), a Confucian relational self holds great relevance. It bears critical relevance for the realization of equality, social justice, and harmony in the United States and the world at large.

References

Anderson-Levitt, K. (2003). A world culture of schooling? In K. Anderson-Levitt (Ed.), *Local meanings, global schooling: Anthropology and world culture theory* (pp. 1–26). New York: Palgrave Macmillan.

Appadurai, A. (1996). *Modernity at large: Cultural dimensions of globalization.* Minneapolis: University of Minnesota Press.

Arasaratnam, L. A. (2013). A review of articles on multiculturalism in 35 years of IJIR. *International Journal of Intercultural Relations, 37,* 676–685.

Banks, J. A. (1993). Multicultural education: Historical development, dimensions, and practice. *Review of Research in Education, 19,* 3–49.

Banks, J. A. (2008). Diversity, group identity, and citizenship education in a global age. *Educational Researcher, 37*(3), 129–139.

Bashkow, I. (2004). A neo-Boasian conception of cultural boundaries. *American Anthropologist, 106*(3), 443–458.

Briggs, J. L. (1991). Mazes of meaning: The exploration of individuality in culture and of culture through individual constructs. In L. B. Boyer & R. Boyer (Eds.), *The psychoanalytic study of society* (Vol. 16, pp. 111–153). New York: Analytic Press.

Briggs, J. L. (2010). Emotions have many faces: Inuit lessons. In R. A. LeVine (Ed.), *Psychological anthropology: A reader on self and culture* (pp. 60–67). Malden: Wiley-Blackwell.

Brown, K. W., & Ryan, R. M. (2003). The benefits of being present: Mindfulness and its role in psychological well-being. *Journal of Personality and Social Psychology, 84,* 822–848.

Cave, P. (2004). "Bakatsudo": The educational role of Japanese school clubs. *Journal of Japanese Studies, 30*(2), 383–415.

Chapman, T. K., & Hobbel, N. (2010). *Social justice pedagogy across the curriculum: The practice of freedom.* New York: Rowman & Littlefield.

Cheng, C. (2004). A theory of Confucian selfhood: Self-cultivation and free-will in Confucian philosophy. In K. Shun & D. B. Wong (Eds.), *Confucian ethics: A comparative study of self, autonomy, and community* (pp. 124–147). Cambridge: Cambridge University Press.

Cororaton, C., & Handler, R. (2013). Dreaming in green: Service learning, global engagement and the liberal arts at a North American university. *Learning and Teaching*, 6(2), 72–93.

Davidman, L., & Davidman, P. (1997). *Teaching with a multicultural perspective: A practical guide*. New York: Longman.

de Bary, W. T. (2000) *Asian values and human rights: A Confucian communitarian perspective*. Cambridge: Harvard University Press.

Eliasoph, N. (2009). *Making volunteers: Civic life after welfare's end*. Princeton: Princeton University Press.

Freire, P. (2000). *Pedagogy of the oppressed* (M. B. Ramos, Trans., 30th anniversary ed.). New York: Continuum.

Geertz, C. (2000). The uses of diversity. In *Available light: Anthropological reflections on philosophical topics* (pp. 68–88). Princeton: Princeton University Press.

Ghai, Y. (1998). Human rights and Asian values. In W. T. de Bary (Ed.), *Asian values and human rights: A Confucian communitarian perspective*. Cambridge: Harvard University Press.

Giroux, H. A. (2013). *Youth in revolt: Reclaiming a democratic future*. Boulder: Paradigm.

Heron, B. (2007). Negotiating subject positions, constituting selves. In *Desire for development: Whiteness, gender, and the helping imperative* (pp. 91–122). Waterloo: Wilfrid Laurier University Press.

Hoffman, D. (1996). Culture and self in multicultural education: Reflections on discourse, text, and practice. *American Educational Research Journal*, 33(3), 545–569.

Hoffman, D. (1998). A therapeutic moment? Identity, self, and culture in the anthropology of education. *Anthropology and Education Quarterly*, 29(3), 324–346.

Hoffman, D. (1999). Turning power inside out: Reflections on resistance from the (anthropological) field. *International Journal of Qualitative Studies in Education*, 12(6), 671–687.

Holdsworth, C., & Quinn, J. (2011). The epistemological challenge of higher education student volunteering: "Reproductive" or "deconstructive" volunteering? *Antipode*, 44(2), 386–405.

Holland, D., Lachicotte, W. S., Jr., Skinner, D., & Cain, C. (1996). *Identity and agency in cultural worlds*. Cambridge: Harvard University Press.

Jiang, X. (2006). The concept of the relational self and its implications for education. *Journal of Chinese Philosophy*, 33(4), 543–555.

King, M. L., Jr. (1962). An address by the Reverend Dr. Martin Luther King, Jr. Retrieved from http://news.cornellcollege.edu/dr-martin-luther-kings-visit-to-cornell-college/

Ladson-Billings, G. (2006). It's not the culture of poverty, it's the poverty of culture: The problem with teacher education. *Anthropology and Education Quarterly*, 37(2), 104–109.

Ladson-Billings, G. (2014). Culturally relevant pedagogy 2.0: Aka the remix. *Harvard Educational Review, 84*(1), 74–84.

Lalas, J. (2007). Teaching for social justice in multicultural urban schools: Conceptualization and classroom implications. *Multicultural Education, 14*(3), 17–21.

Larsen, M. (2016). *International service learning: Engaging host communities.* New York: Routledge.

Latour, B. (2005). *Reassembling the social: An introduction to Actor-Network-Theory.* Oxford: Oxford University Press.

Levinson, B. A., Borman, K. M. Eisenhart, M., Foster, M., & Fox, A. (2000). *Schooling the symbolic animal: Social and cultural dimensions of education.* New York: Rowman & Littlefield.

Lin, J., & Wang, Y. (2010). Confucius's teaching of virtues and peace education. In J. Lin, J. Miller, & E. J. Brantmeier (Eds.), *Religion, spirituality and peace education* (pp. 3–17). Charlotte: Information Age.

Littlejohn, R. L. (2011). *Confucianism: An introduction.* New York: I. B. Tauris.

Nieto, S. (2002). *Language, culture, and teaching: Critical perspectives for a new century.* Mahwah: Lawrence Erlbaum Associates.

Nieto, S. (2005). Social justice in hard times: Celebrating the vision of Dr. Martin Luther King, Jr. *Multicultural Perspectives, 7*(1), 3–7.

Nuyen, A. T. (2002). Confucianism and the idea of citizenship. *Asian Philosophy, 12*(2), 127–139.

Paris, D. (2012). Culturally sustaining pedagogy: A needed change in stance, terminology, and practice. *Educational Researcher, 41*(3), 93–97. doi: 10.3102/0013189x1244124.

Reid, T. R. (2000). *Confucius lives next door: What living in the East teaches us about living in the West.* New York: Vintage.

Sangren, P. S. (1995). Power against ideology: A critique of Foucaultian usage. *Cultural Anthropology, 10*(1), 3–40.

Shun, K. (2004). Conception of the person in early Confucian thought. In K. Shun & D. B. Wong (Eds.), *Confucian ethics: A comparative study of self, autonomy, and community* (pp. 183–202). Cambridge: Cambridge University Press.

Snee, H. (2014). *A cosmopolitan journey? Difference, distinction, and identity work in gap year travel.* Farnham: Ashgate.

Sokefeld, M. (1999). Debating self, identity, and culture in anthropology. *Current Anthropology, 40*(4), 417–448.

Spindler, G., & Spindler, L. (1997). *Education and cultural process: Anthropological approaches.* Long Grove: Waveland Press.

Taylor, C. (1999). Conditions of an unforced consensus on human rights. In J. R. Bauer & D. Bell (Eds.), *The East Asian challenge for human rights.* New York: Cambridge University Press.

Tobin, J. J., Wu, D. Y. H., & Davidson, D. H. (1989). *Preschool in three cultures: Japan, China, and the United States.* New Haven: Yale University Press.

Tobin, J. J., Yeh, H., & Karasawa, M. (2009). *Preschool in three cultures revisited: China, Japan, and the United States.* Chicago: University of Chicago Press.

Tu, W. (1985). *Confucian thought: Selfhood as creative transformation.* Albany: State University of New York Press.

Tu, W. (1994). Embodying the universe: A note on Confucian self-realization. In R. T. Ames, W. Dissanayake, & T. P. Kasulis (Eds.), *Self as person in Asian theory and practice* (pp. 177–186). Albany: State University of New York Press.

Tu, W. (1996). Beyond the enlightenment mentality: A Confucian perspective on ethics, migration, and global stewardship. *International Migration Review,* 30(1), 58–75.

Tu, W. (1999). A Confucian perspective on the core values of the global community. *The Review of Korean Studies,* (2), 55–70.

Tu, W. (2001). The context of dialogue: Globalization and diversity. In G. Picco (Ed.), *Crossing the divide: Dialogue among civilizations* (pp. 49–96). South Orange: School of Diplomacy and International Relations, Seton Hall University.

Tu, W. (2011). Confucianism and liberal education for a global era: Lectures with Tu Weiming. Retrieved from http://berkleycenter.georgetown.edu/events/confucianism-and-liberal-education-for-a-global-era

Tu, W., & Ikeda, D. (2011). *New horizons in the Eastern humanism: Buddhism, Confucianism, and the quest for global peace.* London: I. B. Tauris.

Wang, H. (2004). *The call from the stranger on a journey home: Curriculum in a third space.* New York: Peter Lang.

Weisz, J. R. (1991). Culture and the development of child psychopathology: Lessons from Thailand. In D. Cicchetti (Eds.), *Rochester symposium on developmental psychopathology,* vol. 1 (pp. 89–118). Hillsdale: Lawrence Erlbaum Associates.

Zhao, G. (2003). Identity discourse and education. *Journal of Thought,* 38(3), 73–85.

Zhao, J. (2013). Confucius as a critical educator: Towards educational thoughts of Confucius. *Frontier of Education in China,* 8(1), 9–27.

11

Confucian Philosophical Foundations for Moral Education in an Era of Advanced Technology

Vincent Shen

As globalization through advanced technology shapes our world, moral/ethical education has become more crucial than ever in the assertion of individuals' humanity. This chapter focuses on the Confucian foundation of moral/ethical education. According to Confucianism, moral/ethical education targets the development and unfolding of human nature, characterized by specificity, relatedness, and growth on which the impact of advanced technology is felt by both reinforcing human interconnection and increasing human freedom.

I discuss the primary Confucian foundation for moral life: the individual's desire for his or her well-being, as well as the well-being of others, as expressed by *ren* (humanity). The autonomous and systematic character of advanced technology results from this profound dynamism of human nature. This way of understanding the advancement of globalizing technology enables us to see how it is ultimately related to the project of the full realization of human potential.

From the primary meaning of *ren* 仁 (humaneness), we can derive basic moral norms such as the secondary meanings of *ren* as love (*airen* 愛人) and moral justice (yi 義, righteousness). And from the moral norms, individuals should constitute their moral characters as commitment and critique; and from the moral characters, they should lead a way of life of both action and reflection.

Thus, the founding process of moral/ethical life and education goes from reflection and action as ways of life, back to critique and commitment as moral characters, and then from these back to justice and love as moral norms, finally arriving at a philosophical foundation established by the Confucian concept of *ren* as the person. From this foundation, there could be a process of manifestation that goes from the person as desiring good for him- or herself and many others to moral justice and love as moral norms, then to critique and commitment as moral character, then to reflection and action as ways of life. Moral education should pay attention to the processes of both foundation and manifestation.

Meaning and Function of Moral Education in a Time of Advanced Technology

Today, the need for a philosophical foundation of moral/ethical life and education has taken on new urgency because of the process of globalization led by advanced technology. Globalization not only pushes all countries beyond their borders and engages them in networks of intensive informational, political and economic interaction, and mutual dependency, but, more profoundly, it also consciously or subconsciously accepts this universalization as the destiny of the postmodern world. I define globalization is defined as "a historical process of border-crossing, in which human desire, human interconnectedness and universalizability are to be realized on this planet as a whole, and to be concretized in the present as global free market, trans-national political order and cultural glocalism" (Shen, 2004, p. 111).

Science and technology have been the universalizing powers leading the process of globalization, not only socially as the focus of economic and political decisions worldwide, but also philosophically as the consciously or unconsciously accepted destiny of contemporary world history. Heidegger (1958, p. 88) is right, especially in this scientific and technological era, when he reads *Geschichte* (history) as *Geschick* (destiny)[1] and says that metaphysics, as the essence of technology, is the necessary destiny of the West and the condition of its domination over the whole world.

With the universal extension of technological civilization, it has become evident that not only Western but also non-Western countries have begun to be determined by this common destiny. In occupying themselves with the development of science and technology, they are now carried along by the whirlwind of occidentalization, which, unfortunately, sometimes is seen as a form of domination by the West. Deeper reflection shows that, in fact, it is the process of rationalization of the world's history, accelerated by rapid technological development.

One of the leading elements of globalization is the advanced technology that is creating a dynamically expanding network for the rapid transmission of information via the Internet, iPhone, iPad, and so forth. The aim of this advanced technology is increased connectivity to establish relationships, communicate, and share information to increase our understanding the environment. On the other hand, advanced technology also increases one's autonomy and self-reflection—for example, when one travels by driving comfortably in a well-equipped automobile or listens to music of all kinds with headphones in virtual isolation. Indeed, globalizing technology has a profound effect on one's everyday life and cultural development.

In this rapid and universal shaping of the world by science and technology, moral life and education have the essential task of assuring humankind of its own humanity and its capacity to be the master or, better, the good user and friendly companion of science and technology. The term "education" is understood here not merely in its strict sense as an institutionalized process of teaching and learning, but more in its broad sense as the formation of persons, either by themselves or with the help of others, toward the full realization of their human nature. As the *Doctrine of the Mean* says, "What Heaven imparts to man is called human nature. To follow human nature is called *dao*. Cultivating *dao* is called education" (Chan, 1963, p. 98). Also, here the term "education" is similar to the notion of *Bildung* in the Hegelian sense of a process toward the "universal," though I prefer the term "universalizable" because I don't believe that in the context of human life limited by time and space there is anything purely "universal." At most there are values and truths that are more "universalizable" than others.

Moral education is crucial for the human being in order to reassert his/her humanity in this rapid universalizing shaping of the world by advanced technology. Moral/ethical praxis must be based in human nature as well as in the metaphysical structure of reality, as is observed by the *Doctrine of the Mean*. Therefore, human moral education has its philosophical foundation in both Heaven and human nature. This chapter focuses on the impact of advanced technology on moral/ethical praxis and gives a novel interpretation to the Confucian philosophical foundation for moral education, which, in facing the challenge of advanced technology, is in need of new and creative interpretation.

The terms "ethical" and "moral" are different yet related in meaning. Although they sometimes have the same usage,[2] their specific meanings are distinguished in both Western and Chinese philosophy. For example, German philosophers since Kant have often made a distinction between *Ethik* and *Moral*. For Hegel, "moral" is more concerned with subjective intentions, while "ethics" concerns the *Sittlichkeit* or the objective spirit as manifested in the family, civil society, and the state (Hegel, 2001, p. 138). For Confucianism, the term *daode* 道德 is distinguished from, though still related to, *lunli* 倫理. For example, in *the Great Learning*, *daode* refers to the steps to "making the will sincere," "rectifying the mind" and "cultivating one's self," while *lunli* refers to further steps for "regulating the family," "bringing order to the state," and "pacifying all under heaven" (Chan, 1963, p. 86). On the whole, ethics consists in practicing the norms according to which one interacts with many others in a specific community. On the other hand, morality concerns the cultivation of the self with regard to subjective intention, effort, and fulfillment of one's humanity. It is the process by which a person raises him- or herself to higher universalizable ideal values. Both morality and ethics aim at the development and unfolding of human nature. According to Confucianism, human nature has the following characteristics.

Human specificity. Human nature has its own specificity in terms of rationality and morality. Mencius tends to specify the human being in terms of morality and believes that the moral consciousness of human beings differentiates them from animals. However, Xunzi seems to emphasize the human intellectual capacity to discern right from wrong or even the ability to argue. Although they may differ among themselves in underlining either the rational or the moral, both agree that human beings have something specific that differentiates them from all other beings.

Human relatedness. The human being is related to other beings, even to the whole universe, despite his or her specificity. Confucius posits *ren* 仁 as human interconnection and responsiveness among all human beings. Some Neo-Confucians even see human self-realization as related to all things in Heaven and earth. Wang Yangming's notion of *yiti ziren* (一體之仁, humaneness forming one body with all things) is the best idealist presentation of this universal relativity.

Human development. Human nature has a dynamic ability to develop its own potentiality and, in fact, possesses an immense capacity to do so.

This dynamism may take two directions: either to develop the human being's specificity and/or to develop his or her relatedness with other beings. For example, Mencius thinks that every human being has four good beginning (four sprouts) within his or her own nature and says, "Since all men have these four beginnings in themselves, let them know to give them all their development and completion, and the issue will be like that of fire which has begun to burn, or that of a spring which has begun to find vent" (Legge, 1970, pp. 203–204).

We can say that morality concerns the realization of values and norms that promote the specificity of human nature, while ethics concerns the extension of human relatedness with other persons, society, and nature. The contrast between these two aspects constitutes what I call the "structure" and "dynamism" of human nature (Shen, 1980, pp. 4–36).[3] This leads us to ask: What is the moral and ethical situation of the modern person under the impact of the rapid technological development in which human nature develops?

Impact of Advanced Technology on Moral/Ethical Life

The advancement of technology has brought about an overall change in social structure, that is, how humans interact with one another. This in turn affects their ethical relationship, hence, the context of their ethical life. Ethical life is affected by globalizing technology through changes in ethical relations. Because of the impact of rapid technological advancement, the moral-ethical context of the postmodern has the following prominent characteristics.

Regarding Human Interrelation

Advanced technology has reinforced the interconnections and multiplied the interactions between human persons and also between human and non-human beings, thus rendering the ethical relation more complicated. Technological objects constitute diverse systems that mediate between persons, nature, and society and increase interaction and its intensity. Through the mediation of technology, human control over nature becomes more efficient, and with this come various forms of exploitation and manipulation. Nature is no longer considered the concrete substance of external reality, but rather as consisting of materials that can be combined and transformed in new ways. Indeed, nature provides a field for human creativity and its realizations. However, the overexploitation and abuse of nature has given rise to urgent environmental problems, even to the extent of depriving us of the biological space in which we live. Because this exploitation has resulted from humanity's exercise of free will, a new domain of ethics, namely environmental ethics, has been created.

Also, the advance of globalizing technology has facilitated transportation and communication, meaning that people now interact more frequently and intensively with other people. More people have more contact in a shorter duration. This makes what originally were personal and affective relationships impersonal and institutional. Relationships of contract, competition and—even worse—domination and violence have replaced personal and affective relations. Professional ethics outweighs person-to-person and family ethics. In everyday life, we encounter what I call "strangers of acquaintance."

Moreover, human beings interact increasingly with inhuman technological objects that mediate their interaction with nature and other people. Humanity now lives among signs and machines; its life-world has become a world of *techne* rather than one of *phusis*, a world of organization rather than one of organism. Technology is synonymous with rationality. The essence of the human being is now defined in terms of rationality, which in turn is reduced to what Max Weber calls "instrumental rationality" (*Zweckrationalität*). In comparison with the overwhelming instrumental rationality, value rationality (*Wertrationalität*) becomes pale and weak. Human reason, reduced to instrumental rationality, is defined in terms of its efficacy as an instrument to obtain calculable ends. Other people are also reduced to the status of instrument, losing their own human dignity as an end in itself. Critical reflection is impoverished: Deprived of its deeper meaning as self-understanding and self-awareness, reflection is now reduced to mere scientific theorization. Human action, deprived of its deeper meaning as moral praxis, is now reduced to mere technical application of scientific theories.

The technologically built connection between human beings, nature, and technical systems now constitutes a new context for ethical life. An analogy could be made here between philosophy of language and ethical action: The more complex and rigorous the syntactical structure of a proposition, the more precise its semantic meaning becomes. Similarly, in moral philosophy, the more complicated and rigorous ethical relations become under the impact of technological advancement, the more precise the moral/ethical action taken must be in that context. This situation requires of the human being a higher moral creativity and more psychological flexibility. However, what actually happens, in fact, is that, lacking the required creativity and flexibility, people's attitudes tend toward moral indifference or ethical apathy.

Regarding Freedom and Responsibility

On the other hand, the development of advanced technology has given human beings greater freedom, increasing their autonomy in action and therefore their moral responsibility. This constitutes a contrasting situation for moral/ethical life. While the advancement of technology is knitting the world into diverse networks of relations, it increases by the same token an individual's freedom and autonomy. This is because the scope for human free choice is greatly extended by technological advancement, and human responsibility is extended to the same extent. The reason for this is that it is only when an individual is fully aware of the consequences of his or her action that he or she is responsible for that action. Morally responsible action is a known and freely chosen action.

Now the development of science increases our knowledge about things, for example, about the life process and its diseases, and with the progress of technology we are equipped with more effective instruments to control areas of reality that have previously been beyond our control. Natural technology increases our knowledge of nature and how to control natural phenomena; therefore we are able to go beyond certain areas of physical determinism. Scientific knowledge and technical know-how increase human freedom and the efficiency of human action. The more we are free and effective in action, the greater our moral responsibility. Thus we can say that human freedom is increased by the advancement of technology and not at all diminished by it.

The advancement of technology also creates new moral values, because it enables us to freely and consciously initiate a process of action, to control the action, and to assess its consequences. This freedom renders technology morally relevant. For example, the professional actions of a medical doctor, an engineer, a businessman, and so on, when doing good things supported by their knowledge and technique, become moral actions. Human free will can transform scientific/technological norms of action into norms of moral action. For example, a medical doctor, in caring for people's health, may transform his or her medical knowledge and technique to norms of action for saving a patient's life. In this way, human moral decisions can always transform new scientific and technical discoveries into new moral values.

Confucian Foundation: The Human Person as the Center of Moral Education

The contrast between freedom and relatedness brought to light by advanced technology leads us to a new understanding of human nature. In rethinking the Kantian question "What is man?" in the era of globalization, we should avoid the one-sidedness of defining man either only by his autonomous self, as many modern Western philosophers since Descartes have done; or merely by human relatedness with other beings, as many Chinese philosophers do. Instead, we should take into account both his or her autonomous self and relatedness, which are different and complementary, in considering human nature.

Human relatedness and human freedom differ in their unity and unite in their difference. For me, this inspires the philosophical insight that a person is constituted, in his or her innermost dynamics, of an original direction toward goodness, what the *Zhongyong* calls the *zhong* 中, or what Mencius calls the *xin* 心, or even "original heart" (*benxin* 本心). Now, in response to the positive vision of human desire by Dai Zen 戴震 (1724–1777), a Neo-Confucian in the Qing dynasty, together with my reading of Lacan's (1901–1981) saying "Desire is the language of the other" (Lacan, 1966, pp. 524, 838), I would call this original heart (*benxin*) the "desiring desire" if seen from the perspective of its "direction toward x." I should say that the desiring desire is always motivated by the desirable, taking it as its beginning outlet and thereby manifesting itself. This can then be concretized into a specific object and becomes the desired desire with the desired object. We may discern philosophically the good as desirable and its object as desired, even if in the real act of desire they are most of the time confused. In fact, what is intended is always the good as desirable; then what is perceived as the desired is always a specific object of our desire. Desiring desire and its desirable good are different from the desire for an object attained, called "desired desire," which produces thereupon happiness, anger, sorrow, joyfulness, like, dislike, lust, and so on. Because desiring desire fuels energy to go, even unconsciously, beyond one's self-enclosure, to reach the good of something or some person, it is not selfish in its original form. It is only in the effort to obtain the desired object or in the act of enjoying it that the desired desire could become self-enclosed again and thus becomes selfish. Therefore, the first moment or the original state of mind, the *benxin* or the desiring desire of a person for good, is unselfish, and when it is directed, in its second moment, toward the desirable in its beginning outlet, it still considers the desirable as good; only in its third moment, when it fixes on an object or objects, can it become a selfish desire.

Now the human *benxin* or desiring desire can move toward the good of other things or people, and in moving to the realization of this good intention, one is aware of it in one's heart/mind and therefore knows the goodness of one's self. It is in this regard that we can agree with Kant that only good will can be called good. Nevertheless, good will, apparently pure as it is, is also related to the goodness of others, and it is through willing the good of others that we are aware of our good will. Thus, we can say that the original state of a person, the *benxin* or desiring desire, is moved on the one hand by the good of related others (relatedness), which shows one's original generosity, altruism, and love, and, on the other hand, by the good of self that aims at self-realization, freedom, and ultimately autonomy. That's why I say that in its original state as desiring desire, and in its beginning orientation to the desirable, it is always a dynamism toward the good and the realization of the good. Only when one labors for a particular object and enjoys the possession of the object in question can one be fixed or caught in the *jouissance* (enjoyment) of the self and therefore become selfish.

In light of the positive impact of advanced technology on the human being's moral/ethical life, we can see the person as constituted and moved by both the desire of good for others (relatedness) and the desire of the good for the self (self-realization). Such an understanding preserves the person's wholesome and innermost dynamism and avoids the one-sidedness of other philosophies: for example, Kant's autonomous free will as a postulate of moral action or the Modern New Confucian Mou Zongsan's moral subjectivity as infinite free heart/mind (*zhiyou wuxian xin* 自由無限心)—all these philosophers see the person only from the aspect of self-realization, freedom, or ultimately autonomy. On the other hand, classical Confucianism stresses the aspect of relatedness of the individual with nature, society, and Heaven.

To avoid one-sidedness, we should understand the "person" as constituted of and moved by his or her desire for both self-realization and relatedness. These two constituents of the person interplay in a dialectical manner toward the full realization of humanity. The human being must realize a meaningful life through the rhythmic movement of two interplaying moments: the desire for self-realization, freedom, and autonomy; and the desire to connect and relate for the good of others.

To realize one's desire for self-realization, one must distance oneself from (*epoché* in the phenomenological sense) all external and heterogeneous constraints coming from those things other than one's own will: nature, society, even transcendent beings. One must disengage oneself from all external constraints and act according to one's own free will. It is obvious that a person's free will cannot set up norms of action against his or her own self-realization; on the contrary, each person tends to act in a way that enhances his or her self-realization to the highest degree. In this sense, we can accept the autonomous self as posited by Kant and Modern New Confucianism neither as a mere condition of possibility or formal postulate nor as an infinitely free subject denying any transcendent divinity. The self is autonomous in the sense that a person tends toward the full realization of his or her own potentiality and fulfillment of the meaning of existence in his or her unique way.

As I see it, the self of is always a self-in-the-making. Even in its imagined autonomy, the realizing self-in-the-making is always relative to other beings, human and non-human: A person is relatively free and relationally autonomous. A person, even in search of his or her autonomy, still belongs to the same realm of existence to which all other beings belong, as best shown by Confucianism.

Indeed, Confucius emphasizes the connection and balance between "learning for others" (*weiji zhi xue* 為己之學) and "learning for oneself" (*weiren zhi xue* 為人之學) in saying, "In the old days people learned for the self, nowadays they learn for others" (Zhu Xi, 1983, p. 155, my translation). He never in any way says anything that is biased against learning for one's self, because he sees *ren* as the ultimate foundation of both self and others, both related and self-realizing. *Ren* is the related self-awareness or the self-aware relatedness of the person. To learn to be human is to learn to live in this related self-awareness or the self-aware relatedness.

The relatedness with self-awareness in the person is thus the foundation of moral/ethical life. The impact of advanced technology on this is as follows. On the positive side, the advancement of technology has promoted human freedom and extended the networks of relatedness.

On the negative side, it also gives rise to the abuse of free will through blind acceptance of and passive determination by technical systems. In this context, if human beings want to be the master and not the slave of technology, they must restore the concept of personhood as the center of moral/ethical life. The problem is not how technology undermines the autonomy and relatedness of the person, but rather how we view the advancement of technology, which should be seen as moved by the desire of the person to promote autonomy and extend relatedness with other beings.

First, we could see the self-organizing technological system as a symbol of the kind of autonomy humankind wants to realize through moral, social, and historical actions. Seen from this perspective, advanced technology may prepare the ground for realizing moral autonomy. With the help of advanced technology, people could liberate themselves from external determinism, avoid dependence on pure contingency, and establish a well-known and controllable world that is subject to the demands of the person and assists in the person's realization.

Second, we should see the networks built by advanced technology as symbolizing the interconnection between man, nature, and society and articulating this in an eloquent manner. The inherent complexity of technological systems, in differentiating into ever more detailed subsystems while grouping ever more subsystems into higher and bigger systems, eventually could be seen as preparing a rational field for the realization of the relatedness of persons both among themselves and to other beings.

In short, the restoration of the person as the focus of moral/ethical life in technological global society means setting up the person's self-realization and relatedness as prior to, and productive of, the autonomy and relatedness of technological systems.

From Philosophical Foundations to Ways of Life

It is crucial for a moral person, in his or her ethical life, to internalize essential moral norms and form stable moral characters, keeping in mind that these have to be derived from the inner dynamism of human nature. The function of moral norms is to make explicit the manner in which a person needs to conduct his or her action in concrete situations to develop relatedness with other beings and realize autonomy.

Moral norms function, therefore, as a kind of mediation through which a person can extend his or her existential interconnection with other persons and beings and affirm his or her autonomy at least partially in concrete situations.

From each person's interrelatedness with other beings, we can see the principle of love at work. This norm was summarized by what Confucius referred to as "to love men" (*ai ren* 愛人) (Chan, 1963, p. 40), or what Mencius observed as "The man of humanity loves others" (*renzhe airen* 仁者愛人) (Chan, 1963, p. 77). Love could be said to be a tender concern for the goodness of others in a way that reveals and purifies one's existential relatedness with other beings. Through love, the realization of the goodness of the loved one and/or that of other people could contribute to the goodness of the self.

From the norm of love we can set up the norm of respect for life, which is quite evident in all civilizations. This norm is expressed, in a negative way, as the prohibition against hurting or killing any person or even any sentient being; and in a positive way, it is expressed as the moral demand to save another life when it is threatened and to improve that life.

From each person's desire for self-realization, it is possible to derive the moral norm of justice. The concept of justice has been defined by thinkers and scholars in numerous ways. Confucius focuses on righteousness, the moral justice represented by respecting and properly dealing with each individual's innermost desire and therefore that person's right to self-realization. A Confucian should always be concerned with righteousness. This respect could be ultimately based on human love for the good of many others, that of *ren*, which means both humaneness and love for others. Thus, from the relatedness and responsiveness to others, we can determine the respect for others as righteousness.

Thus, with this original generosity toward the other's good and sense of respect, there comes a situation of reciprocity in which the original/moral sense of justice becomes fairness, both in the allocation and exchange of wealth, power, and other social goods. For me, what John Rawls calls "justice as fairness" (Rawls, 1985) is to be understood in the sense of "distributive justice," which is in fact secondary in comparison to moral justice: Distributive justice is morally significant only when it contributes to the self-realization of the person in question. Normally, it is when the human's right to self-realization is not respected that there is no justice in the distribution of power and resources. The same is true of justice in exchange, which demands that commercial exchange should be in equal values. When distributive justice and justice in exchange are not respected, or even are abused by violence, there will be retributive justice. This means that retributive justice is derived from distributive justice and justice in exchange, because often an offense against these forms of justice brings about retribution. In their turn, distributive justice and justice in exchange are derived from moral justice, because they are based on the respect for each person's right to self-realization and the demand to treat each person properly, both of which are necessary to maintain and implement distributive justice and justice in exchange.

Thus, moral justice as a moral norm is essentially concerned with the right of each person to realize him- or herself as a self-realizing person. From the norm of moral justice, we may derive other relevant norms, such as respect for human rights, which could be made concrete in a bill of human rights, the contents of which might vary from one country to another.

In the process of moral/ethical praxis, the internalization of these norms should contribute to the formation of basic moral characters. For me, in this time of globalization, the contemporary world needs individuals with the moral characters of commitment and critical reflection. On the one hand, love demands a moral character of commitment. This does not mean a blind engagement in actions without knowing the cause. Rather, commitment is self-conscious participation in the active realization of people's common goodness and togetherness. A Confucian is always committed to the common good, starting with the family and extending to the community, to the state, or even to all under heaven.

On the other hand, justice demands a moral character of critical reflection or critique. Confucius always invites his students to think critically. For example, he praises Zi Gong on his critical questioning and advancing of critical comments:

> Zi Gong said, "What do you think of a man who is poor and yet does not flatter, and the rich man who is not proud?" Confucius replied, "They will do. But they are not as good as a poor man who is happy and the rich man who loves the rules of propriety." Zi Gong said, "*The Book of Odes* says, 'As a thing is cut and filed, as a thing is carved and polished.'

Does that not mean what you have just said?" Confucius said, "Ah! Ci. Now I can begin to talk about the odes with you. When I have told you what has gone before, you know what is to follow" (Chan, 1963, pp. 21–22)

Thus self-cultivation and learning advance by critical reflections. From today's point of view, "critique" means a self-distancing reflection on the part of each person to attain a just or proper degree of freedom and autonomy proportionate to his or her self-realization in this increasingly complicated and rapidly changing society.

In summary, commitment plays the role of social cohesion to reinforce one's ontological interconnection with other beings, while critique plays the role of distancing oneself from others to make justice possible and proper. Critique and commitment are thus two moments of the same dynamic movement toward the fuller realization of each person's subjectivity and intersubjectivity.

To realize the critique that targets justice and the commitment that manifests love, a person must live a life of both action and reflection. These are crucial to the practice of moral/ethical life today. Critique demands reflection, not in terms of theorizing or referring to any theory of natural or social sciences to explain or predict a phenomenon, but rather as a mental distancing to circumscribe the situation of justice and to criticize it in referring to ideal values. Commitment demands action, not merely what Habermas calls the "application of scientific theories to manipulate natural or social phenomena" (Habermas, 1974, pp. 1–40, 253–282).[4] Confucius not only pays attention to what people say, but he also observes how they act when he says, "Now I listen to what they say, and watch what they do" (Leys, 2014, p. 13). Here action is emphasized because indeed it is a creative intervention in the flux of events produced by the relatedness of the world.

Conclusion

Socrates's words "an unexamined life is unworthy of living" urge us to contemplate the foundation of life through a critical examination of the meaning of life. This is normally a job for philosophers, and both Western and Chinese thinkers have undertaken it. However, while

Chinese philosophers—for example, Confucians—agree that the meaning of life needs to be examined, they do not agree with Socrates that any life can be unworthy of living. For a Confucian, any life is worth living, examined or not, because one must live first to examine life and to live it meaningfully.

For Confucians, to live and to give birth to life both have a cosmological foundation. The *Great Appendix* of the *Book of Changes* even goes so far as to say "The greatest characteristic of Heaven and Earth is to *give birth to life*" (Chan, 1963, p. 268 with my correction in italics). In the *Zhongyong*, the act of giving birth has an unfathomable relation with sincerity the ultimate reality, as it says, "The Way of Heaven and earth may be completely described in one sentence: They are without any doubleness and so they produce things in an unfathomable way" (Chan, 1963, p. 109). Therefore, the production of things, or better, giving birth or even life itself, is the most important value. From this foundation of life, one may proceed to examine the meaning of life. However, if one loses one's life, one has no more chance to examine it.

Nevertheless, Confucian philosophers, like their Western colleagues, are looking for the meaning of life. The *Daxue* (*Great Leaning*) says the Way of great learning, or that of the meaning of life, is "to manifest the clear character, to *renew people's life*, and abide in the highest good" (Chan, 1963, p. 86, my correction in italics). The philosopher Zhang Zai (1020–1077) of the Northern Song dynasty says the meaning of life is "[t]o stand in the impartial heart of Heaven and earth, to establish a paradigm of life for common people, to inherit the highest wisdom of past sages, and to build peace and prosperity for ten thousands generations" (Zhang Zai, 2010, p. 376, my translation). All these Confucian sayings have indeed inspired Chinese people in their moral education and ethical praxis.

In the process of globalization led by rapid technological advancement, moral/ethical life is crucial for the development of humanity. The purpose of moral/ethical life today is to reassert the individual's humanity and to render human beings capable of being the master or, better, the good user and friendly companion, of globalizing technology. The person as desiring good for him- or herself and for related others is constituted by the contrast of self-realization and relatedness. This is the foundation of all moral/ethical life and education. Seen from this perspective, the autonomous and systematic character of advanced technology results from this profound dynamism of human nature. This way of understanding the advancement of globalizing technology enables us to see how it is ultimately related to the project of full realization of all human potential.

In the formation of personality through moral/ethical education, we must establish a model of the person capable of action and reflection: reflection with a view to obtaining justice through critical evaluation, and action with a view to fulfilling love through commitment. The logic of contrast between action and reflection, commitment and critique, love and justice, leads finally to the fullest realization of human subjectivity and intersubjectivity. These crucial moments of moral/ethical life have their philosophical foundation in human nature, namely the autonomous and related person desiring goodness for him- or herself and for others. The whole Confucian ethical system can thus be represented as follows:

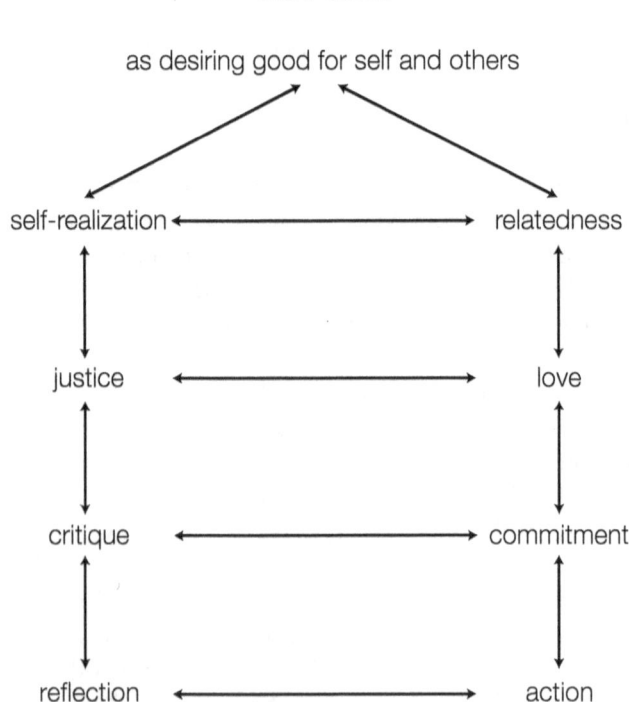

Figure 11.1 Founding and Manifesting Processes of Moral/Ethical Life

As seen in this diagram, the founding process of moral/ethical life goes from reflection, to critique, to justice, to self-realization of the person as desiring good for him- or herself and for others; and from action to commitment, to love, to relatedness, and again to the person as desiring good for self and for others. Then we have another process: the manifesting process of moral education, which goes from the person as desiring good for him- or herself and for others to self-realization, to moral justice, to critique, to reflection, and from the person as desiring good for him- or herself and for others to relatedness, to love, to commitment, to action. The two moments of each stage (reflection and action, critique and commitment, justice and love, self-realization and relatedness) are in structural and dynamic contrast. Thus the dialectics of contrast permeates the whole process of the formation of an integral person. Moral/ethical education in a time of globalization should take into consideration both the founding and manifesting processes of moral life. Thus, in forming the person of action and reflection capable of realizing justice and love through critique and commitment, and thereby attaining the fulfillment of his or her self-realization and relational personality, such a moral/ethical education hopefully will be able to realize humanity in a world of globalization.

Notes

1. See, for example, Heidegger (1958, p. 88). However, I hesitate to agree with Heidegger, who limits it only to the West, and says that metaphysics, as the essence of technology, is the necessary destiny of the West and the condition of its domination over the whole world. In fact, this phenomenon is spreading all over the world with the process of globalization.

2. For example, Cicero said in *De fato* that he used the Latin adjective *moralis* to translate the Greek word *ethikos*.

3. "Contrast" means for us the interplay between identity and difference, distanciation and co-belongingness, rupture and continuity, which constitutes the structure and dynamism of an object under investigation. It is our manner of replacing Hegelian dialectics with a creative positivity. See Shen (1980, pp. 4–36).

4. Concerning the critique of reflection as theorization and action as technical application of scientific theories, see Habermas (1974, pp. 1–40, 253–282).

References

Barbour, I. G. (Ed). (1973). *Western man and environmental ethics.* London: Addison-Wesley.

Chan, W. T. (1963). *A source book in Chinese philosophy.* Princeton: Princeton University Press.

Gadamer, H.-G. (1976). *Wahrheit und methode* (Truth and method) (G. Barden and J. Cumming, English trans.). London: Sheed & Ward.

Habermas, J. (1974). *Theory and practice* (J. Viertel, Trans.). London: Heinemann.

Heidegger, M. (1958). *Essais et conferences* (A. Preau, French trans.). Paris: Gallimard.

Hegel, G. W. F. (2001). *Philosophy of right* (S. W. Dyde, Trans.). Kitchener: Batoche Books.

Lacan, J. (1966). *Écrits.* Paris: Seuil.

Legge, J. (Trans.). (1970). *The Works of Mencius.* New York: Dover.

Leys, S. (Trans.). (2014). *Confucius: The Analects.* New York: W.W. Norton & Company.

Rawls, J. (1985). "Justice as fairness: Political not metaphysical." *Philosophy and Public Affairs, 14*(3), 223–251.

Shen, V. (1980). *Action et créativité, une étude sur les contrastes génétiques et structurels entre l'action Blondelienne et la créativité Whiteheadienne.* Louvain-la-Neuve: Université Catholique de Louvain.

Shen, V. (2004). "A book review of Michael Hardt and Antonio Negri's *Empire*." *Universitas: Monthly Review of Philosophy and Culture,* (361), 109–112.

Stanley, M. (1978). *The technological conscience: Survival and dignity in an age of expertise.* Chicago: University of Chicago Press.

Weber, M. (1978). *Wirtschaft und gesellschaft* (Economy and society) (G. Roth & C. Wittich, Eds.). Berkeley: University of California Press.

Zhu Xi. (1983). *Sishu Zhangju Jizhu* 四書章句集註 (Collected commentary on chapters and sentences of the *Four Books*). Beijing: Zhonghua Shuju.

Zhang Zai. (2010). *Zhang Zai Ji* 張載集 (Collected works of Zhang Zai). Beijing: Zhonghua Shuju.

12

Rethinking Confucian Values in a Global Age

Huey-Li Li

The aging of modernity has unmasked various interrelated ecological risks confronting Western cultural, economic, political, and military hegemony. In response to the vexations of modernity, there have been varied intellectual movements to rejuvenate non-Western cultural and religious traditions. Notably, White (1973) argues that contemporary ecological problems are rooted in the Christian doctrine of human dominion over nature. In line with White, Jung (1972), Callicott (1987), and Deutsch (1986) further claim that Confucianism is a favorable alternative to Christianity. In the meantime, Berger (1988) points out that Confucianism appeared to be a functional analogue of the Protestant ethic and might have facilitated the rapid economic development in East Asia. The pursuit of industrialization and economic growth inadvertently led to ecological destruction. In fact, China has surpassed the United States as the largest carbon dioxide emitter (Institute for Energy Research, 2015).

Academic discourse on Confucianism to a large extent appears to be compartmentalized and polarized. More specifically, there has been a tendency to romanticize ecologically congenial Confucian values, that is, an organic worldview and reverence for nature, without attending to how Confucianism might have facilitated rapid economic development at the cost of ecological decline. As a result, the apparent contradiction in the function of Confucianism—embracing the unity of humans and nature while sanctioning ecological destruction—is overlooked.

To engender a more inclusive understanding of Confucian values in the global age, this chapter presents a critical inquiry into the intricate and complicated conceptual connections among Confucianism, economic development, and ecological decline. Specifically, the chapter unravels the inherent ambiguities surrounding the Confucian conception of the unity of nature and humans. Drawing insight from Confucianism, the chapter aims to sketch an ecologically congenial pedagogy that is grounded in an ethical recognition of the interconnection between cosmic order and human morality in the global age.

The Unity of Humans and Nature Revisited

Berkson (1968) points out that human ethics in the West is deeply rooted in the belief that the cosmos (God or nature) supports the human ethical ideals of mainstream Western tradition. Since the Enlightenment era, the appeal to nature has led to the reconstruction of social, political, and economic institutions. As ecological crisis has become a recurring issue in the Industrial Age, it is not surprising that contemporary environmental philosophers also call for a reexamination of the modern conception of nature. Echoing White's (1973) critique of the Christian doctrine of human dominion over nature, Aldo Leopold's (1949) land ethics, and Arne Naess's (1986) deep ecology are especially known for underscoring intrinsic values of nature in the theorizing of environmental ethics. More specifically, Aldo Leopold (1949) argues that "we have a well-articulated human-to-human ethic; what we need is a comparable human-to-land ethic" (p. 203). Here Leopold refers to "land" as an ecosystem that includes soil, water, plants, and animals. In critiquing the human exploitation of nature, Leopold considers that it is important to "change the role of Homo sapiens from conqueror of the land-community to plain members and citizens of it" (p. 204). In the same vein, Naess claims that a genuine ethical concern for environmental issues must go beyond a pursuit of human interests. In his own words, "[a] new ethic, embracing plants and animals as well as people, is required for human societies to live in harmony with the natural world on which they depend for survival and well-being" (p. 12).

As the Confucian conception of the unity of humans and nature appears to be in line with non-anthropocentric environmental ethics, it is not surprising that scholars in Asia and beyond have continued to explore how the renewal of Confucian values would shed new light on reconstructing ecologically congenial cultural practices (Agyrou, 2005; Tucker & Berthrong, 1998). However, it should be noted that Confucianism has not been able to reshape ecologically destructive "industrialization" in the so-called Confucian nations in East Asia. Clearly it is problematic to attribute the global ecological decline to Euro-American cultural hegemony without recognizing colonized people's agency in their encounter with hegemonic forces (Bhabha, 1994; Dirlik, 1997). As colonization results in cultural hybridization rather than wholesale cultural imperialism, it is essential to inquire into the conceptual roots of global ecological decline at both global and local levels. To this end, in what follows I reexamine the intricate relationships among economic development, ecological decline, and the Confucian conception of the unity of humans and nature, which has been widely regarded as the long-lasting foundation of Confucian ethics (Pfister, 1995).

In view of the long, complex, and evolving history of Confucianism, an attempt to inquire into its relationship with contemporary ecological devastation in East Asian countries is a formidable task (Makeham, 2003; Tu, Hejtmanek, & Wachman, 1992).[1] Because the *Analects* is a canonical text of Confucianism, Confucius's conception of *t'ien* as recorded in the *Analects* offers an important clue for an understanding of the unity of humans and nature (*t'ien-ren ho-yi*). The Chinese character *t'ien* conveys a wide range of meanings—from the sky, firmament, day, the heavens, to the immanent natural environment. In the *Analects*, Confucius does not articulate and define the concept of *t'ien* clearly. Robert Eno (1990) notes that only 17 of 500 chapters in the *Analects* have references to *t'ien*. A lack of elaboration on *t'ien* should not be attributed to the philosophical insignificance of *t'ien* in Confucian ethics. Rather, we need to be aware of Confucius's disinclination to make metaphysical speculation. He exhorts his students to "respect spiritual beings but keep distance" (6.20). He also admonishes his students, "Until you are able to serve man, how can you serve spiritual beings? Until you know about life, how can you know about death?" (11.11).[2] In his rare discussion on *t'ien*, Confucius inherits the traditional immanent and naturalistic characterization of *t'ien*. To illustrate, the teaching of Confucius stresses the cultivation of human morality. When his students complain that his unwillingness to talk about *t'ien* would deprive them of the opportunity to learn about human ethics, he states: "What does *t'ien* ever say? Yet there are the four seasons going around and there are the hundred things coming into being. What does *t'ien* ever say?" (17.19). Implicitly, Confucius suggests that regularity and constancy of the immanent natural order correspond with the ethical norms that human beings ought to observe. Instead of preaching a set of moral codes, Confucius urges his students to become aware of how human moral behaviors reflect the immanent natural order.

Moreover, Confucius considers that ideal political leadership represents a counterpart to the immanent cosmic order. Specifically, there is no equivalent Christian conception of God as a creator in Confucianism. Instead, Confucius affirms the effort of the paradigmatic "sage-kings," such as Yao, Shun, Wen, Wu, and the Duke Chou, in establishing a civilized social order that reflects the virtue of *t'ien*. Confucius acclaims, "Great indeed was Yao as a ruler! How lofty! It is *t'ien* that is great and it was Yao who modeled himself upon it" (8.19). It is clear that political leadership is supposed to assume a profound ethico-religious significance within the Confucian tradition.

On the other hand, Confucius seems to suggest that human virtue derives from *t'ien*, and *t'ien* can safeguard his mission of transmitting an ideal cultural tradition. When Confucius was under siege in K'uang, he also stated, "With King Wen perished, is not culture invested here in me? If *t'ien* intends culture to be destroyed, those who come after me will not be able to have any part of it. If *t'ien* does not intend this culture to be destroyed, then what can the men of K'uang do to me?" (9.5). Here Confucius seems to suggest that *t'ien* has deterministic influence on human actions. He also associates *t'ien* with *ming*, which is commonly rendered "destiny" or "fate." The popular conception of *t'ien ming* (the command of *t'ien*) is assumed to determine the legitimacy of the ruler's continuance in office as well as an individual's longevity, social status, and wealth. For instance, Confucius's disciple Tzu-Hsia said, "Life and death are a matter of *ming*; wealth and honor depend on *t'ien*" (3.8).

The Confucian conception of *t'ien* appears to be ambiguous. It is not clear whether *t'ien* refers to the immanent natural order or a transcendent ethical deity. Such an ambiguous conceptual orientation reflects a holistic metaphysical tradition in China. In his survey of pre-Chin philosophical literature, Tang (1962) points out that "the term 'ming' represents the interrelationship or mutual relatedness of Heaven and man" (p. 196). In other words, *t'ien ming* does not predetermine the moral and social order. Instead, human beings must perceive themselves as agents in constructing an ideal social order that would reflect the virtue of *t'ien*. By inheriting such a metaphysical tradition, Confucius does not consider *t'ien* to be the ultimate source and standard of meaning and values. More specifically, Confucius argues that moral cultivation is about holding three things in awe: the *t'ien ming*, the great person, and the words of the sage (16.8). Because a moral offense against *t'ien* is a transgression of one's own moral commitment, Confucius believes that no attempt should be made to deceive *t'ien*. He states, "In pretending that I had retainers when I had none, who would we be deceiving? Would we be deceiving *t'ien*?" (9.23) Evidently the moral authority of *t'ien ming* does not surpass human moral endeavors in the framework of Confucian ethics. Above all, *t'ien* does not reveal a specific set of ethical codes, such as the Ten Commandments. Nor can one redeem one's unethical behavior by worshipping *t'ien*. For instance, Confucius warns that "when you have offended against *t'ien*, there is nowhere you can turn to in your prayers" (3.13). From this standpoint, neither *t'ien* nor *ming* can be regarded as a supramundane ethical deity or as a causal principle that exists above or outside human beings. Rather, the Confucian concept of *t'ien* denotes the organic unity between humanity and nature. Thus, Chung-Ying Cheng (1989) remarks that Chinese metaphysics cannot be viewed as a pure cosmological inquiry because it is closely interrelated to individual ontology. He characterizes such an inquiry as both an onto-cosmological and a cosmo-ontological inquiry. Within this framework, nature is neither a sacred creation of God nor a profane object. Consequently, there is no clear and definite distinction between the transcendent and the immanent. In Tu's (1989) words, "the Confucian perception that human beings are earthbound yet strive to transcend themselves to join with Heaven clearly indicates that Confucians see humanity as not only an anthropological concept but also as an anthropocosmic idea" (p. 102).

From the standpoint of G. W. F. Hegel (1827), the Chinese conception of *t'ien* is not an independent realm. Rather, *t'ien* and "earth" are interrelated. F. W. J. Schelling also claims that Confucianism is "the absolute secularization of the religious principle" (quoted in Roetz, 1993, p. 19). Max Weber (1951) considers the this-worldly orientation of Confucianism as in opposition to the Protestant commitment to "rational mastery of the world." Following Weber's argument, Parsons (1956) further argues that the "Confucian ethic failed to move the world precisely because its worldliness denied it a place to stand outside the world. The Protestant ethic, on the other hand, had such a place to stand, its transcendental God and its conception of salvation" (pp. 548–549). To

Weber and Parsons, the transcendental basis of the Puritan ethic leads to the pursuit of "modernization," whereas the Confucian sanctification of tradition inevitably inhibits industrial and scientific "progress" in China.

As Hegel, Schelling, Weber (1951), and Parsons fail to grasp the nonantithetical relationship between nature and humans, they also fail to understand that the core of Confucian ethics lies upon a moral effort to transform the world from within. More specifically, there is no definite distinction between the "natural" world and the "social" world in the framework of Confucian ethics. In fact, neither the "natural" world nor the "social" world is viewed as static. Rather, they are in a constant process of transformation. It follows that any artificiality in the pursuit of social perfectibility does not come into, conflict with what would be considered "nature" in Confucian society. In fact, Confucians have made a deliberate effort to affirm and emblazon the sage-king Yi's technological achievement in redirecting the rivers that caused floods.

Furthermore, the perfectibility of human nature, an embodiment of t'ien's virtue, has been central to Confucian doctrine. Tu (1989) notes, "The Confucian's optimistic attitude is predicated on the ontological assertion that if human nature is conferred by Heaven, the realization of our human nature is tantamount to the fulfillment of a Heavenly-ordained mission" (p. 99). In particular, the realization of human nature must take place in concretely interpersonal and social contexts rather than in a social vacuum. Tu points out that "a defining characteristic of Confucian religiousness is its emphasis on the fiduciary community as an irreducible reality in ultimate self-transformation" (pp. 96–97). In other words, self-transformation is a communal act, and an individual's self-cultivation is to contribute to the establishment of an ideal social order, which is by no means predetermined. The fiduciary community must function as a cohesive polity as it strives for societal perfectibility.

Anthony Giddens (1990) notes that the emergence of the modern nation-state has been intertwined with capitalism, industrialism, and military power because the modern nation-state plays an important role regarding the mobilization of social and economic resources. The Confucian ideal of a cohesive polity might have been conducive to the establishment of the modern nation-state in consolidating collective effort for the pursuit of industrialization in the face of Western imperialism in East Asia. Specifically, political leadership is parallel to the ethical principle of t'ien. To a certain degree, Confucianism renders crucial support for government's leadership in the process of social transformation, including industrialization.

As discussed earlier, the Confucian conception of unity between humans and nature stresses a dialectic interaction between the two. It does not inhibit human intervention on nature, which after all does not represent a static and immutable order. At the same time, the unity of humans and nature can foster a consolidated support for the process of social transformation, including industrialization, technological development, and economic growth. The pursuit of a cohesive polity in turn can mobilize a massive coalition for governmental actions for growth-oriented economic development without taking precautions against ecological decline (Kassiola & Guo, 2010). Thus, an organic worldview is not a panacea for resolving all ecological problems.

Nevertheless, the Confucian conception of the unity of nature and humans denotes that the perceived "intrinsic" and "extrinsic" values are interrelated. J. B. Callicott (1989) argues, "There can be no value apart from an evaluator" . . . all value is as it were in the eye of the beholder. The value that is attributed to the ecosystem, therefore, is humanly dependent or at least dependent upon some variety of morally and aesthetically sensitive consciousness" (p. 27). After all, human beings are an integral part of nature. Human actions, thus, should not be excluded from the constitution of the intrinsic values of nature, such as "integrity," "diversity," "stability," and "beauty," as suggested by Leopold (1949) and Naess (1986). Above all, it is human beings who construct scientific disciplines, such as ecology, to articulate the "objective" values of nature. Furthermore, the intrinsic values of nature, grounded in objectivity, do not necessarily lead us to reach consensus about certain moral actions. For instance, we might think that "diversity" and "stability" as intrinsic and objective values of nature are self-revealing; however, it is human beings who must make a deliberate effort to protect an endangered species or commit ourselves to nonintervention in the face of the "natural" extinction of endangered species. In particular, there are potential and actual conflicts between the perceived intrinsic and objective values of natural objects and nature as a whole. To show moral respect for the diversity of life-forms in the biosphere, Naess suggests that it is important to decrease the human population to permit the flourishing of both human and nonhuman lives. At the same time, Naess's theory of biospherical egalitarianism stresses the inviolable right of the individual members of the biosphere. Accordingly, the richness and diversity of life-forms should not outweigh an individual organism's right to live and blossom. Naess's support of population control apparently contradicts his own theory of biospherical egalitarianism. Because the perceived "objective" values of nature do not automatically prescribe certain legitimate moral actions, human moral consciousness must be involved in clarifying and resolving value conflicts. Thus, the involvement of human consciousness in the configuration of the "intrinsic" values of nature indeed represents a constant effort to expand the boundary of ethical community, especially in the global age. Drawing from Confucian insight in the ever-extensive ethical community, the next section of the chapter explores the possibility of developing an ecologically congenial pedagogy in the global age.

Toward an Ecologically Congenial Pedagogy in the Global Age

To a large extent, we are living in the global village envisioned by Marshall McLuhan (1989). However, localities do not evaporate in the process of globalization. Popular slogans such as "think globally, act locally," "local struggles with global support," and "local problems with global solutions" illustrate the intricate relations between the local and the global. Thus, Timothy Luke (1996) calls our attention to the existence of a "glocal" space where the global intersects with the local. The dialectical interplay between the global and the local is especially evident in worldwide environmental movements. On the one hand, because the impact of today's ecological problems, especially climate change, cannot be enclosed within a particular region or nation, phrases such as "one earth, one family" have permeated the mass media. On the other hand, we continue to see tensions between developed and developing countries, a not-in-my-back-yard mentality, and environmental racism. Consequently, there has been a renewed interest in cosmopolitanism.

Martha Nussbaum (1996) applies the "very old ideal of the cosmopolitan" to "the person whose allegiance is to the worldwide community of human beings" (p. 4). Such an allegiance to the entire human is in line with ancient Greek and Confucian cosmopolitan traditions. While ancient cosmopolitanism seems to represent a transcendent ethical ideal, modern cosmopolitanism appears to emerge out of practical necessity. After all, no one can be immune from climate change in an increasingly globalized society. Global problems indeed call for global solutions. By embracing common humanity across cultural boundaries, cosmopolitanism signifies international efforts that seek global solutions to global problems. At the same time, neither ancient nor contemporary proponents of cosmopolitanism necessarily advocate relinquishing one's affinity with one's locality (a fiduciary community). Specifically, one must recognize that one is always surrounded by "a series of concentric circles," namely the self, the immediate family, the extended family, the local community, the nation, and the world (Nussbaum, 1997). In the same vein, Walter C. Parker, Akira Ninomiya, and John Cogan (1999) advocate the notion of multidimensional citizenship "to capture the personal, social, spatial, and temporal aspects of the citizen identity that are necessary for meeting the challenges of the early twenty-first century" (p. 127). The cultivation of such multidimensional world citizenship is reminiscent of Confucian cosmopolitanism that situates self-cultivation in the concentric contexts of family, community, nation-state, and the universe. In the *Analects*, Zixia, Confucius's disciple, remarks, "I have heard the saying: Life and death are matters of fate; Wealth and honor depend upon Heaven. Cultivated people are reverently attentive and do nothing amiss; they are respectful and practice the rites, regarding all within the four seas as brothers. How could cultivated people ever worry about having no brothers?" (12.5). While neither Confucius nor his disciples articulated the belief that "all within the four seas are regarded as brothers," Confucian cosmopolitanism appears to be "more than a view about how we should relate to other human beings; it concerns our relationship with 'all under Heaven' (that is, the world). It calls on us not to be citizens of the world, but to see ourselves as one with it" (Ivanhoe, 2014, p. 42). Tu (2000) also notes, "The Confucian tradition offers profound insights on the relationship between humanity and nature, and between individual and society. Its philosophy of the unity of heaven and humanity and its familial model (i.e., that all things form one unified whole and that all human beings are members of one family) confirm that it constitutes a broadly humanistic worldview" (p. 381). Within the Confucian cosmopolitan framework, the living world is an integration of both the natural and social worlds. It follows that the ecological decline cannot be separated from the ruining of the social world. Hence, self-cultivation should include recognizing and fulfilling one's responsibilities of caring for all living beings under Heaven.

Ivan Illich (1978) notes that modern educational systems in both developed and developing nations are inclined to guide individuals "away from their natural environment and pass them through a social womb in which they are formed sufficiently to fit into everyday life" (pp. 76–77). As modern education severs the organic connections between humans and nature, it perpetuates our homogenized political and economic systems. The Confucian conception of the unity of humans and nature echoes Arne Naess's (1989) advocacy of *ecophilosophy*: "a philosophical worldview or system inspired by the conditions of life in the ecospheres" (p. 38). More specifically, as Richard Borden (1986) points out, the "study of ecology leads to changes of identity and psychological perspective, and can provide the foundations for an 'ecological identity'—a reframing of a person's point of view which restructures values, reorganizes perceptions and alters the individual's self-directed, social, and environmentally directed actions" (p. 1). As a first step toward such a reframing, it is crucial to recognize how a number of different binaries (such as the global versus the local, nature versus culture, and modern universal science versus traditional knowledge system) have shaped our cultural as well as our educational practices. To this end, cosmopolitan global education must involve an effort to reclaim human agency through participatory reevaluation of local cultural values, through inquiry into place-based ecological knowledge, and through the establishment of global community. As a result, learning about one's place and local traditional culture could facilitate one's appreciation of biodiversity and cultural diversity at both local and global levels.

The Confucian recognition of the interdependence between humans and the natural environment sheds light on delineating an ecologically congenial pedagogy. Undoubtedly, the recognition of either the intrinsic or instrumental values of nature can commit us to solving or mitigating ecological decline. Beyond such a pragmatic concern, it should be noted that nonanthropocentric moral reasoning actually derives from human-centered ethical traditions. Human morality need not be confined to interhuman affairs, and our concerns for moral inclusion or exclusion can be related to a cultivation of human moral virtue. C. D. Stone (1987) states that "throughout civilization, the more 'we' have recognized that another person, family, or tribe is like us, both in the properties 'it' possesses and the common fate we share, the readier we have been to connect our common relations with moral filament" (p. 22). Nature is not an abstract, static, and fixed entity but rather a complex and interconnected web of life. Ethical concerns regarding environmental issues should be extended to any indication of brokenness and disharmony within the web of life. Thus, an ethical inquiry into ecological issues should not be dissociated from human ethics. War, class exploitation, poverty, and animal experimentation need not be regarded as peripheral to other ecological issues such as air/water pollution, oil spills, and the extinction of wilderness and wildlife. Thus, an ecologically congenial pedagogy usually encompasses a variety of issues: antimilitarism, the antinuclear movement, the abuse and misuse of reproductive technology, and the economic exploitation of the so-called Third World. An attempt to make a categorical distinction between the ethics of human affairs and the ethics of a human-nature relation is not apt and will prove to be a futile effort. Being cautious about our daily activities can be strenuous, but such mindfulness can actually make differences. After all, the accumulation of millions of people's seemingly insignificant daily activities, such as driving cars or saving energy, could have an imperceptible yet causal contribution to either the worsening or mitigation of today's ecological problems.

Furthermore, human moral consciousness is inevitably involved in constituting the perceived "intrinsic" values of natural objects and process. In line with Confucian ethics, it is important to stress human moral reflectivity in order to address interrelated environmental issues. Above all, we need to beware that resolving value conflicts cannot be an individual endeavor; rather, we need to make a collective effort to reflexively examine existing ethical norms and to explore possibilities of establishing new ethical norms within our moral community. Dale Jamieson states that "reforming our values is part of constructing new moral, political, and legal concepts, and eventually a new world order" (p. 324). The formation of cultural values and ethical norms is a communal process. Teachers and students must be committed to an egalitarian membership and consensus making in order to articulate and foster intersubjective recognition of our moral responsibilities in the fiduciary community. In other words, teachers and students must be seen as equal partners in a constitutive community where they can be coinquirers in examining knowledge claims, cultural values, and ethical norms concerning today's ecological problems.

Conclusion

Associated with China becoming a dominant economic powerhouse, the world has witnessed the spurring of renewed interests in Confucianism in China and beyond. The burgeoning of Confucius Institutes outside China especially epitomizes the Chinese government's efforts to promote Confucianism in the global age. Confucian values are compatible with modern cosmopolitan democracy and can render critical support for community-based sustainable economic development. The late Henry Rosemont (2008) noted that "classical Confucianism . . . is of great relevance today, especially as a variable alternative to the modern Western liberal tradition so deeply grounded in individuals that communities are always suspect as confining, conformist, constraining, stifling the human spirit" (p. 53). At the same time, it is critical to avoid romanticizing Confucianism. After all, the Confucian ideal of a cohesive polity appears to have been conducive to establishing the modern nation-state, which in turn plays an important role in pursuing economic growth at the cost of ecological decline.

Although the process of education often leads to the preservation of traditional cultural values, education is also perpetually future oriented. The teleological concept of progress embedded in modern schooling has been in command of our vision for future societies. Yet technological and scientific advancements appear to engender more ecological risks, and the future has become increasingly more uncertain. Faced with the uncertain or even unknowable future ensuing from climate change, it is essential to cultivate moral imagination that extends one's physical senses and cultural perceptions in order to unmask the "invisible" ecological interconnections among all living beings.

Notes

1. The following textual analysis of Confucian conception of *t'ien* was adapted from my earlier publication: Li, H. (1998). Some thoughts on Confucianism and ecofeminism. In J. Berthrong & M. E. Tucker (Eds.), *Confucianism and ecology: The interrelation of heaven, earth, and humans* (pp. 293–311). Cambridge: Harvard University Press.

2. Waley, Arthur (Trans. and annot.). (1938). *The Analects of Confucius*. New York: Vintage Books. Quotations from the *Analects* are cited by chapter and paragraph according to the traditional text.

References

Agyrou, V. (2005). *The logic of environmentalism: Anthropology, ecology and postcoloniality*. New York: Berghahn Books.
Berger, P. (1988). An East Asian development model? In P. L. Berger & H. M. Hsiao (Eds.), *In search of an East Asian development model* (pp. 3–11). New Brunswick: Transaction Books.
Berkson, I. B. (1968). *Ethics, politics, and education*. Eugene: University of Oregon Press.
Bhabha, H. K. (1994). *The location of culture*. New York: Routledge.
Borden, R. (1986). *Ecology and identity: Proceedings of the First International Ecosystems Colloquy*. Munich: Man and Space.
Callicott, J. B. (1987). Conceptual resources for environmental ethics in Asian traditions of thought: A propaedeutic. *Philosophy East and West, 37*(2), 115–130.
Callicott, J. B. (1989). *In defense of the land ethic*. Albany: State University of New York Press, 1989.
Cheng, C. Y. (1989). Chinese metaphysics as non-metaphysics: Confucian and Taoist insights into the nature of reality. In R. E. Allinson (Ed.), *Understanding the Chinese mind* (pp. 167–208). Hong Kong: Oxford University Press.
Deutsch, E. (1986). A metaphysical grounding for natural reverence: East-West. *Environmental Ethics, 8*(4), 351–370.
Dirlik, A. (1997). *The postcolonial aura: Third world criticism in the age of global capitalism*. Boulder: Westview Press.
Eno, R. (1990). *The Confucian creation of heaven: Philosophy and the defense of ritual mastery*. Albany: State University of New York Press.
Giddens, A. (1990). *The consequences of modernity*. Stanford: Stanford University Press.
Hegel, G. W. F. (1827). *Lectures on the philosophy of religion* (P. C. Hodgson, Ed.; R. F. Brown, P.C. Hodgson, & J. M. Stewart, Trans.). Berkeley: University of California Press.
Illich, I. (1978). *Toward a history of needs*. Berkeley: Heyday Books.
Institute for Energy Research. (2015). China: World's largest energy consumer and greenhouse gas emitter. Retrieved from http://instituteforenergyresearch.org
Ivanhoe, P. J. (2014). Confucian cosmopolitanism. *Journal of Religious Ethics, 42*(1), 22–44.
Jamieson, D. (1993). Ethics, public policy, and global warming. In R. Winkler & J. R. Coombs (Eds.), *Applied Ethics: A Reader* (pp. 313–328). Cambridge: Blackwell.
Jung, H. Y. (1972). The ecological crisis: A philosophic perspective, East and West. *Bucknell Review, 20*(3), 25–44.

Kassiola, J. J., & Guo, S. (Eds.) (2010). *China's environmental crisis: Domestic and global political impacts and responses.* New York: Palgrave Macmillan.

Leopold, A. (1949). *A Sand County almanac and sketches here and there.* New York: Oxford University Press.

Luke, T. (1996). Placing power/sitting space: The politics of global and local in the new world order. *Environment and Planning D: Society and Space 12*(4), 525–546.

Makeham, J. (Ed.) (2003). *New Confucianism: A critical examination.* New York: Palgrave Macmillan.

McLuhan, M. (1989). *The global village: Transformations in world life and media in the twenty-first century.* New York: Oxford University Press.

Naess, A. (1986). The deep ecological movement: Some philosophical aspects. *Philosophical Inquiry, 8,* 10–31.

Naess, A. (1989). *Ecology, community and lifestyle* (D. Rothenberg, Trans.). New York: Cambridge University Press.

Nussbaum, M. (1996). *For love of country: Debating the limits of patriotism.* Boston: Beacon.

Nussbaum, M. (1997). *Cultivating humanity.* Cambridge: Harvard University Press.

Parker, W. C., Ninomiya, A., & Cogan, J. (1999). Educating world citizens: Toward multinational curriculum development. *American Educational Research Journal, 36*(2), 117–145.

Parsons, T. (1956). *The structure of social action.* New York: Free Press.

Pfister, L. (1995). The different faces of contemporary religious Confucianism: An account of the diverse approaches of some major twentieth century Chinese Confucian scholars. *Journal of Chinese Philosophy, 22*(1), 5–80.

Roetz, H. (1993). *Confucian ethics of the axial age.* Albany: State University of New York Press.

Rosemont, H., Jr. (2008). Civil society, governments, and Confucianism: A commentary. In D. Bell (Ed.), *Confucian Political Ethics* (pp. 46–58). Princeton: Princeton University Press.

Stone, C. D. (1987). *Earth and other ethics: The case for moral pluralism.* New York: Harper and Row.

Tang, J. (1962). The t'ien ming (heavenly ordinance) in pre-Ch'in China. *Philosophy East and West, 11*(4), 195–218.

Tu, W. M. (1989). *Centrality and commonality: An essay on Confucian religiousness.* Albany: State University of New York Press.

Tu, W. M. (2000). Confucianism and modernity: Insights from an interview with Tu Wei-Ming. *China Review, 7*(2), 381.

Tu, W. M., Hejtmanek, M. G., & Wachman, A. (Eds.). (1992). *Confucian world observed: A contemporary discussion of Confucian humanism in East Asia.* Honolulu: The East-West Center.

Tucker, M. E., & Berthrong, J. (Eds.) (1998). *Confucianism and ecology: The interrelation of heaven, earth, and humans.* Cambridge: Harvard University Press.
Weber, M. (1951). *The religion of China* (H. Gerth, Trans.). New York: The Free Press.
White, L., Jr. (1973). The historical roots of our ecological crisis. In I. G. Barbour (Ed.), *Western man and environmental ethics* (pp. 18–30). Reading: Addison-Wesley.

List of Contributors

Fangping Cheng, Professor, School of Education, Renming University, China

Pamela Herron, Lecturer, Department of Religious Studies, University of Texas at El Paso and the Confucius Institute at New Mexico State University

Huey-Li Li, Professor, Department of Educational Foundations & Leadership, University of Akron

Jing Lin, Professor, College of Education, University of Maryland–College Park

Xiaoqing Lin, Associate Professor, Department of History, Indiana University Northwest

Yair Lior, Doctoral student, Department of Religious Studies, Boston University

Xiufeng Liu, Professor, Graduate School of Education, University at Buffalo, State University of New York

Arabella Lyon, Professor, Department of English, University at Buffalo, State University of New York

Wen Ma, Associate Professor, Department of Education, LeMoyne College

Vincent Shen, Professor, Department of Philosophy and Department of Religious Studies, University of Toronto

Bin Song, PhD candidate, Department of Religious Studies, Boston University

Chenyu Wang, Doctoral student, Curry School of Education, University of Virginia

Yang Wei, Assistant Professor, Department of History, University of Colorado

Yin Wu, Doctoral student, Graduate School of Education, University at Buffalo, State University of New York

Index

Academy of Chinese Culture, 48
accountability, 162, 165, 166
action, 203–22
American education, 80, 145, 146, 161
anthropology of education, 200
argumentation, 33–46
arts, 34, 44, 55, 62, 80, 114, 142, 169, 173–79
audience, 33–46
authority, 65–83
autonomy, 203–22

Ban Zhao, 28, 29, 31
Bao Zheng, 51
Beijing Sichahai Academy, 60
Bildung, 205
Bloom's taxonomy of educational objectives, 157, 165
Book of Changes 易经
 Great Appendix, 217
Book of History, 53, 171
bravery, 158
Buddhism, 17, 50, 54, 61, 63, 90, 91, 92, 93, 100, 102, 106, 108, 109, 114, 119, 179, 180, 202

Cai Yuanpei, 50
calligraphy, 50, 60, 113, 16, 178, 179
chi (shame or "face disgrace," 耻), 159

Chinese imperial examination, 153
Chinese language, 1, 29, 62, 180
Chinese traditional culture, 8, 48, 49, 50
College Entrance Examinations (*Gao Kao*), 159
commitment, 203–22
Common Core State Standards, 11, 33
communication, 33–46
community, 33–46
compassion, 4, 6, 8, 22, 176–80
Confucian
 academies (书院, Shuyuan), 93
 classics, 155, 157, 161
 countries, 16, 162
 Cultural Circles of East Asia, 48
 learning, 157
 values, 159, 163
Confucian educational thought, 47–63
Confucianism
 classical Confucianism, 211
 Modern New Confucianism, 212
 Neo-Confucianism, 87, 94, 103, 112
Confucius
 Education Award, 49
 Institutes, 1, 18, 29, 234
contemplative practices, 16, 179

239

contrast
  dynamic contrast, 219
Cosmology, 17
cosmopolitan, 228, 229, 230, 234
critical thinker, 152, 154, 155
critical thinking, 151–66
critique, 161, 203–22
cultivation, 169–82
culture, 65–83

Dai Zen 戴震, 210
dao, 205
daode 道德, 206
Daodejing, 20, 22, 25, 28
Daxue (Great Leaning), 217
decision making, 33–46
deliberation, 33–46
Democracy, 33–46
desire
  desired desire, 210
  desiring desire, 210
Dewey, John, 76, 77, 152
ding, 17
divination, 118, 134, 135, 137, 147
Dong Zhongshu, 5, 163, 171, 182

ecological decline, 23, 222, 223, 229, 230, 234
ecological intelligence, 176
education and teaching reforms in China, 58
educational reform, 162, 163
elementary learning, 9, 101, 132, 140–46
embodied, 66, 69j, 169, 176–80, 188
emotional and moral intelligence, 176
Emperor Yang of Sui, 51
energy, 6, 39, 169–82
enlightenment, 174, 183, 186
Ennis, 152, 165

epistemology of love, 16, 179

Feng Youlan, 48
first emperor of Qin, 51
Five Classics, 4, 99, 100, 101, 102, 104, 105, 154, 165
  Book of Changes 易经, 4
  Classic of History 史记, 4
  Classic of Poetry 诗经, 4
  Classic of Rites 礼记, 4
  Spring and Autumn Annals 春秋, 4
foundation, 203, 204, 205, 206, 210
  founding process, 204, 219
  manifestation process, 204
  philosophical foundation, 203–22
Four Books, 98, 100, 101, 102, 103, 104, 105, 114, 154
  Analects 论语, 4, 7, 19, 155, 156, 157, 158
  Doctrine of the Mean (中庸), 2, 51, 101, 172, 205
  Great Learning 大学, 4, 51, 56, 101, 142, 173, 175
  Mencius 孟子, 4, 25, 51, 101
freedom, 203–22
Fung & Howe, 160

generosity, 211, 214
global age, 183, 198, 228, 234
globalization, 203–22
Great Cultural Revolution, 5, 27, 48
ground rules, 159
Guan Zhong, 172

Habermas, J., 216, 219, 22
Han Yu, 178
He Shen, 51
heart, 54, 55, 75, 132, 169–82
Heaven-Human Oneness, 17, 171
Heidegger M., 204, 219, 22

Henry Rosemont, 13, 19, 25
heuristic learning, 140
hierarchy, 33–46
high school Regents Exams, 162
higher-order thinking, 154, 157
Howard Gardner, 57
Hu Shi, 58, 63, 102

individualistic, 19, 23, 30, 74, 94
infinite free heart/mind (zhiyou wuxian xin 自由無限心), 211
Inner Sutra of the Huang Emperor, 17
Inner Work, 172
instrumental rationality (Zweckrationalität), 208

Judeo-Christian, 20
jue 覺, 68
junzi (君子), 4, 155, 156, 157, 158
justice
    distributive justice, 214
    moral justice, 203–22
    retributive justice, 215

Kant, 206, 211, 212
King Zhouwang of Shang, 51
knowledge, 65–83

Lao Tzu, 52
Laozi, 174, 175
learning
    learning for oneself (weiren zhi xue 為人之學), 212
    learning for others (weiji zhi xue 為己之學), 212
Leibniz, 58, 63
Lessons for Women, 28
li (propriety, 礼), 159
Li Bai, 51
Liang Shuming, 48, 107
love, 203–22

loving-kindness, 171, 173, 178, 179
Lu Jiuyuan, 123
lunli 倫理, 206

Mao, L. R., 63
math, 71, 72, 73, 80
meditation, 93, 169, 175–82
Mencius 孟子, 157, 169–76
model minority, 1, 13
moral
    moral character, 203, 204, 213, 215
    moral norms, 203, 204, 213
Mozi, 54, 56
multicultural education, 183–202
multiculturalism, 183, 185, 183–202

Needham, 57, 63
Neo-Confucian orthodoxy, 154
Nishan Confucius Summer Institute, 19

organic worldview, 23, 227
original heart (benxin本心), 210

Pang Pu, 48
Paul & Elder, 152, 155, 156, 158
peace, 169, 175–77
pedagogical, 65–83
persuasion, 33–46
philosophical system, 98
poetry, 178, 179
postmodernism, 152
preschool children, 161
primordial qi, 71, 170, 172, 174, 177, 181

Qi, 169–82

Rawls, J., 22
reading-only process, 161
recognition, 33–46
reflection, 203–22

reflective thinking, 152
relatedness, 203–22
remonstration, 33–46
ren 仁, 4, 206
responsibility, 209
reverence for nature, 23
rhetoric, 36, 40, 43
righteousness, yi 義, 203
rituals, 65–83
Roger Ames, 19, 66
role-playing, 161
routinized, 75
ruling philosophy, 50

sage, 26
selfhood, 183–202
self-reflection, 156, 161–63, 189, 194, 205
Shen, G., 63
Shen, V., 22
shu, 27
Silver Rule, 27
Sittlichkeit, 206
soft power, 11, 18, 30
soul, 54, 109, 178
storytelling, 161
Su Shi, 51, 107
Sun Qifeng, 124

t'ien, 223–32
Tang Yijie, 48
Tangtaizong, 51
Tao, 173–82
Tao Yuanming, 51
Taoism, 54, 63, 175, 179, 180, 182
teaching intervention, 159, 166
technology
  advanced technology, 203–22
  Science and technology, 204
test-oriented education, 160
tranquility, 16, 173, 175
transformation, 10–14, 87–108, 169–82

tutoring classes, 161

unity of humans and nature, 222, 223, 230
unshrouded, 133, 134

value rationality (*Wertrationalität*), 208
Voltaire, 58, 63

Wang Tong, 51, 62
Wang Yangming, 120, 121, 129, 16, 206
Wang, Y., 182, 201
way of life, 203
Weber, M., 109, 22, 237
Wei Zheng, 51
wen, 111–29
wisdom, 3–13, 22–27, 51–55, 169–82
Works of Mencius (孟子), 52, 54, 155, 157
Wu Wenjun, 57
Wuhan, 63

Xing Bensi, 48
Xunzi, 54, 82, 87, 149, 15, 206

yang, 6
Ye Shengtao, 63
yin, 6
yiti ziren (一體之仁), 206

Zeng Zhenyu, 17
Zengzi, 156
Zhang Zai, 107, 217, 22
Zhang Zhidong, 50
zhi (wisdom, 智), 158
Zhongyong, 155, 210, 217
Zhou Rudeng, 124
Zhou Yi Can Tong Qi, 171
Zhu Xi (朱熹), 87–109, 212
Zhuangzi, 25, 53, 55, 175, 177
Zhuzi, 55, 108

www.ingramcontent.com/pod-product-compliance
Lightning Source LLC
Chambersburg PA
CBHW030538230426
43665CB00010B/935